D0195095

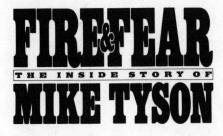

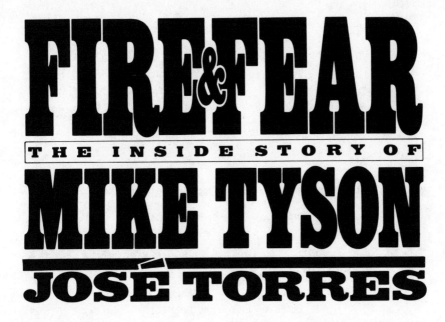

FIRE & FEAR

THE INSIDE STORY OF

MIKE TYSON

JOSÉ TORRES

WARNER BOOKS

A Warner Communications Company

An excerpt from this book originally appeared in *Playboy* magazine.

Warner Books, Inc., 666 Fifth Avenue, New York, NY 10103

A Warner Communications Company

Printed in the United States of America
First printing: July 1989
10 9 8 7 6 5 4 3 2 1
Library of Congress Cataloging-in-Publication Data

Torres, José, 1936–
    Fire and fear : the inside story of Mike Tyson / José Torres.
        p. cm.
    ISBN 0-446-51485-3
    1. Tyson, Mike, 1966–   . 2. Boxers—United States—Biography.
I. Title.
GV1132.T97T67   1989
796.8'3'092—dc20
[B]   88-40573
                                                        CIP

Book design: H. Roberts

To each and every one of my Puerto Rican compatriots who is still struggling to have a free mind and act in accordance with his best judgment. Rid yourself of the colonial mentality!

To the old
pro, who knows more
about wobbly knees than
any other fighter I know.
Merry Christmas 94'
Love Jerry

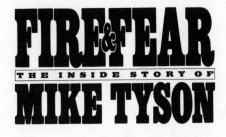

1

THIS was some press conference! The world of boxing had never experienced anything like it before. The date was March 30, 1988, just after midday, and the angels and demons were all here. As usual, the devil's crowd was well represented: young and old, girls and boys, all of them beautiful. No one could say with certainty who was with whom, since everyone's identity was shrewdly concealed. This being boxing, all were faithful to the ritual of deception and persuasion—all, that is, but the reporters, who were there to discover what in boxing is laughingly called the truth.

In a few moments the spotlight would focus on the principals for whom this extravaganza had been staged, Mike Gerard Tyson, the undisputed world heavyweight champ, and Michael Spinks, undefeated former light-heavyweight champ. As the crowd, almost two thousand strong, milled about— consuming rice and beef stew, shrimp, fruit, and coffee— television and still cameras, microphones, and tape recorders poked through the Plaza Hotel's Grand Ballroom, seeking out celebrities and names. At the same time, old boxing men with their acute sense of smell and anticipation wandered about in suspense, their noses sniffing for the odor of deceit and treachery. Not fooled by the surface glitter, they knew from experience that things could not be as they appeared. There seemed to be little prospect for a peaceful afternoon. Wafting through the elegant chamber was the faint odor of alcohol and whores, gamblers and drunks—the dirty money of Atlantic City. The mingled scent of the respectable failed to disguise deeper currents, more dangerous themes: the bitterness of the ghetto, the pride of the hustler, the dirty secrets veiled by great wealth.

Lending his authority to the occasion, as he seems to do at nearly every event of significance in New York City, was that prince of the eighties, billionaire Donald Trump. His dark suit, off-white light-blue-striped shirt, and silk necktie the color of a ripe tomato flecked with gold dots rode his frame like a uniform, while his lips turned up to form a small, amused smile. And why shouldn't the recent purchaser of the Plaza Hotel be smiling? The lavish room he was standing in was home turf. As he assumed the dais, women smiled involuntarily at his self-assured gait and good looks. He was followed by boxing promoter Don King, whose attire was similar to Trump's, except that King's tie was blue with splotches of red. Few people noticed, of course. King's trademark punched-up electric gray hair always manages to stand out. But everybody knew for certain what was to follow: King's baroque verbal gymnastics— thunder with no lightning! The man can talk.

Next in the procession was promoter-manager-impresario-publicist Butch Lewis, who wore a black tuxedo and *no* shirt. There was a black-and-white bow tie around his neck and a huge, thick gold chain glistening with diamonds resting comfortably on his bare, black chest. If there was a genuine smile on the podium, it seemed to be his. Butch had ample reason to be joyful: the short, stocky, handsome former associate of Don

King's had, by sheer obduracy and defiance, set up his fighter Michael Spinks for a share in boxing's biggest payday.

And last, but surely not least, was boxing manager Bill Cayton, a tall, thin, bespectacled man whose identity seemed bound up with that of Tyson, the fighter whom he represented. A few people who would normally give Cayton a cold shoulder or not recognize him at all now smiled at him, even embraced him—the prominence of his champion superseding integrity or contempt. Cayton, with his stony face and conservative clothes, seemed to have stepped out of an earlier era—a fugitive from some 1950s tableau.

Having equal stature as players but pretending otherwise were two beautiful black women who sat inconspicuously among the media. One was Tyson's wife, actress Robin Givens of ABC's sitcom *Head of the Class*. The other was her mother, businesswoman Ruth Roper. Cameras recorded their presence. Strangers fawned over them. Moments before, as the crowd had sought out empty seats, Brian Hamill, a professional photographer who was a friend of Tyson's, had asked the champ for his new address. "I want to send you a wedding present," he told Tyson. As Mike started to respond, Roper cut in. "They need furniture," she whispered.

As King spoke into the mircophone, explaining the epochal significance of this long-awaited confrontation, Tyson yawned and affected a bored expression. He laughed and joked with his trainer, Kevin Rooney, as Butch Lewis said a few words. He continued to act as if he were someplace else while Trump and Cayton offered their predictions on the fight's outcome. Throughout, the champ's eyes never stopped searching the room, always coming to rest on his wife. Then Spinks spoke and Tyson looked up.

"It will be a nerve-racking night for myself," Spinks started to say of his upcoming June 27, 1988, bout with Tyson. He was decked out in a flashy tuxedo that clashed with his shy, almost docile personality. "But it is inevitable," he continued. "I think most people want it."

A full six feet two inches of humility and charm, Spinks also exuded intelligence. As he laughed nervously, some in the crowd who'd never seen him before seemed ready to become members of his fan club. Aware of this, the boxer lost some of his timidity.

"I know I'm not alphabetically recognized," he said, trying to convince the crowd that the World Boxing Council (WBC), World Boxing Association (WBA), and the International Boxing Federation (IBF)—none of which recognized him as the heavyweight champ—were irrelevant. (Many in the media agreed with him, but they knew that Tyson was the champion, Spinks the challenger.) "I didn't lose my crown in the ring," Spinks reminded them, "but I'm gonna do what Michael Spinks always does. I'm gonna fight to win."

A prizefighter who had yet to lose, Spinks had first accepted then refused the chance to participate in the HBO–Dynamic Duo (Don King and Butch Lewis)–Las Vegas Hilton "Heavyweight Unification Tournament," which had been set up after former heavyweight title holder Larry Holmes retired. Appropriately, it had the blessing of the WBC, WBA, and IBF. Though Tyson had taken on all comers in the tournament, Spinks had followed his manager's advice and reneged on his original agreement. Instead of fighting IBF champion Tony Tucker for $750,000 at the Las Vegas Hilton as called for by the tournament, Spinks accepted $4 million to fight New York's six-foot-six-inch giant Gerry Cooney at the Trump Plaza in Atlantic City. Cooney, one of the few white Americans to flourish in the heavyweight ranks since Rocky Marciano ruled the roost in 1956, was, as Lewis well knew, a bigger gate attraction than most of the fighters in the HBO contest. Spinks disposed of him in six rounds.

"I wish," Spinks said at the Plaza, "that I could connect with Tyson in the first round. That way the fight can be over fast. I really won't like to be in the ring with him all night." Spinks finished to loud applause, and then Tyson went to the microphone. He was dressed in a long-sleeve black shirt with gray stripes stuffed inside a pair of expensive black trousers. He wasn't concerned with turning on the charm.

"There is not one single soul on this planet who could beat me," Tyson said, glowering. The crowd seemed to agree. He looked mean, fit, angry. What few of those in attendance realized was that this day had been agonizing for the young champion. Early that morning he had reported to ABC-TV's *Good Morning America* and waited for four hours before finally being put on the air. From there he was shuttled to the Plaza Hotel—hours in advance of the press conference—where he met a horde of photographers intent on accelerating the day's schedule. Each was pushing and shoving to get at the champ first. Following that debacle, Tyson sought some fresh air in Central Park, accompanied by Shelly Finkel, the man in charge of the Tyson-Spinks closed-circuit and pay-for-view operation.

"Over there at the park," Finkel remembered later, "a couple who couldn't speak a word of English rushed toward Tyson for autographs. It turned out that one was from Spain, the other from Italy. In a few seconds there was a long line for autographs."

"Shel, please, help me. Stop this fucking shit. . . . Oh, God!" Tyson begged Shelly.

"The poor guy just wanted to relax," said Shelly, "to have a few minutes of free time for himself."

Here at the Plaza press conference Tyson had once again been thrown to the lions, but few of those present had the stomach to antagonize him with questions. They seemed intimidated by Tyson's angry face.

Tyson and Spinks looked at each other with mutual respect as Lewis, always at arm's reach from his fighter, fixed a look of contempt on the undisputed champion. As reporters worked at getting the principals to the side so they could have something exclusive to write, Donald Trump emerged from the hubbub and hailed me good-naturedly. "My friend," he said, "what do you think is going to happen in the fight?"

"A round or two," I replied. He smiled and walked away, buoyed up no doubt by the thought that, whatever happened, the Trump Organization (which was copromoting the fight in Atlantic City), and hence Mr. Donald Trump, would once again be thrust into the limelight.

By this time I knew that I was destined to write a book about Mike Tyson. Not out of any kind of conceit but because I knew I understood him better than most writers because of our similar backgrounds. We had plenty in common. First, we had both grown up poor, he in Brownsville, New York, and I in Playa de Ponce, Puerto Rico. Here in America we both belonged to minorities. I had been a boxer and a champion and he had been a boxer and a champion. We both understood the toll that celebrity can take on your life and your family. We also understood the paranoia that comes from having to deal daily with the barracudas who infest the boxing world.

Our strongest bond, though, was that we had both been schooled by the extraordinary man and teacher Cus D'Amato. If boxing was a religion, offering salvation to so many poor kids as it did for Tyson and me, then Cus was the pope. He didn't just teach you how to bob and weave or throw the hook and the jab. Cus was also a spiritual teacher.

Cus taught his boxing pupils about life. If it were not for Cus, Mike Tyson would probably be dead or in jail today instead of reigning as the richest and youngest heavyweight champion in history.

That was the thought that kept running through my head the day of the press conference. Since he was thirteen years old, I'd watched this kid batter away at whatever demons possessed him, leaving a trail of groggy opponents in his wake. Cus had assured me he would be the youngest heavyweight champion ever. As usual, Cus was right. Mike got rich quick—maybe too quick.

Even I didn't fully appreciate how popular Mike had become until I received an offer to write his biography that was three times the amount of the biggest purse I'd earned as light-heavyweight champion of the world. That was back in

1965, but still, times and paydays hadn't just changed, they'd soared. I was going to write a book about the highest-paid athlete in the world—a very complicated man/boy from the slums who'd fought his way to the top.

After the Plaza press conference, Tyson and Spinks drove north into the countryside of New York State to begin their training at sites one hundred miles apart. Spinks glided along Route 17 west to the Concord Hotel in the Catskill Mountains, for years a favorite place to train; Tyson coasted slowly north on the New York Thruway to his boxing birthplace—the gym above the police station on Main Street in Catskill, New York.

Typically, Spinks had chosen placidity. For Mike, there was no other choice. Leaving ghetto gyms for the solitude of the mountains was not a new idea; it had been part of the game for over a century. Prizefighters of the past who trained in these areas had chopped wood as willingly as they skipped rope and used the hilly terrain to get more out of their roadwork. In the current era new training methods had been developed, but the Catskill region's unique combination of rugged hills, fresh air, and scenic grandeur was still deemed ideal for developing and honing a young fighter's skills.

Of course, in the 1980s there were so-called boxing men who were blind to the virtues of any locale. Boxing had become big business, inundated by high rollers, high-priced whores, organized thieves, and just plain depraved people—all masquerading as true boxing fans, enjoying the best seats and treatment in counterfeit-copy boxing arenas. Gambling casinos, rife with perversity, had become the major venues for the sport A. J. Liebling once called "the sweet science."

But this was not Mike Tyson's or Michael Spinks's concern as they drove to their separate destinations. On this first day, both men seemed equally determined to do well. The long season of training had begun. The contest was eleven weeks away. But both men had already traveled long distances from the ghettos where they were born.

2

O N June 30, 1966, at Cumberland Hospital in the Fort Greene section of Brooklyn, thirty-six-year-old Lorna Smith gave birth to an eight-pound-seven-ounce boy.

"He looks like a Mike!" exclaimed Jimmy Kirkpatrick at the sight of his third child with his ex-girlfriend. From that exclamation emerged the name Michael Gerard Tyson. The Tyson name dated back to a brief marriage between Lorna Smith and Percel Tyson. Lorna retained the Tyson name until her death in 1982. Shortly after Mike's birth she was living with Edward "Eddie" Gillison. Her three children all used the Tyson surname.

At that time the Tyson family lived in an apartment on Union Street and Marcy Avenue in the heart of Brooklyn's Bedford-Stuyvesant. Although the apartment was relatively spacious and there was enough money to live on, Mike's arrival forced Lorna to search for better living quarters. For the next seven years, she and her children led a nomadic existence.

She moved into several different apartments in the neighborhood, then went north to Fort Greene, Williamsburg, then doubled back to East New York, finally winding up in Brownsville. There Lorna finally found a six-room apartment on Amboy Street. The children were not thrilled. By then, Mike Tyson was seven years old, not tall but unusually strong for his age.

Brownsville was hardly the perfect place to raise a child. This section of Brooklyn, which bordered Queens, had become a classic urban slum. It was named for Charles S. Brown, who in 1865 subdivided what was then farmland into small plots for houses. In 1897 a group of politically connected realtors built cheap, inexpensive apartment buildings and encouraged Jewish immigrants, who were being dislocated from the Lower East Side by the construction of the Williamsburg Bridge and the construction of the Fulton Street elevated subway line, to move to Brownsville. The Jews were followed by a small number of Italians and Eastern Europeans. By the turn of the century, Brownsville was home to fifteen thousand sweatshop workers and their large families, a slum without sidewalks or sewers. The streets were unpaved. There was only one public bathhouse.

Between the two world wars conditions seemed to improve, at least superficially. Pitkin Avenue became the main shopping artery. On Belmont Avenue a pushcart market sprang up. By the railroad siding, vendors would sell cheap goods and leftovers from the produce market at Junius Street, to the Hispanics and blacks who were moving into the neighborhood as fast as the whites moved out.

Brownsville had its writers, Alfred Kazin and Norman Podhoretz, and was a breeding ground for kids with show business ambitions. Danny Kaye, Phil Silvers, Steve Lawrence, and Sol Hurok all hailed from Brownsville. So did boxing publicist Irving Rudd. Brownsville also bred prizefighters. The list includes men such as Al "Bummy" Davis, Bernie "Schoolboy" Friedkin, Lew Feldman, Herbie Katz, George Small, and the

Silver brothers—Pal, Joe, and Marty. These boxers put Brownsville on the pugilistic map. Most of them trained at the gym
on Georgia and Livonia avenues, which was also frequented
by another kind of Brownsville celebrity: the killers from
Murder, Inc.

Crime, poverty, and despair flourished in Brownsville fifty
years ago, and by the time Tyson began to run those streets,
things were infinitely worse. Looking back on his life in
Brownsville and Bedford-Stuyvesant, two Brooklyn slums that
are barren asteroids orbiting in the great metropolis called
New York City, the champ remembers only "awful living
conditions, poverty, and peer pressure."

Some of his earliest memories are of life at 203 Franklin
Avenue in Brooklyn and being in the hospital. "I don't remember exactly why I was there . . . probably because I had
bronchitis or something, or how old I was . . . probably three
or four. But I remember my godmother bringing me a toy gun
and a doll one day, and I broke the gun by accident right away
and I was so mad I started to cry. I cried for a long time and
I was so pissed off that I took the doll and banged it against
the floor and then pulled its head off."

Tyson told me this story ten days before his fight with
Spinks. I was his guest at a friend's penthouse condominium
at the Ocean Club in Atlantic City, where he resides every
time he fights in this part of the Garden State. He stared at
nothing in particular. The memory seemed to exhilarate him.
"That was a long time ago but I still remember that scene
very clearly," he said. "I felt an immense thrill when I ripped
the head off the doll. It was like an orgasm."

He was too young to be in school then. His only friends
were children of his mother's friends who visited the Tysons
on the weekends.

"You know something?" he said, a trace of resentment
in his voice. "I never read a book or played school when I was
a child. I didn't relate to that. I remember being close to my
sister, Denise. I only related to her, my sister."

Denise Anderson is two years older than Mike. She was born at 307 Quincy Street in Bedford-Stuyvesant. She is tall and heavy, more than three hundred pounds. She attended Kingsborough Community College for a year and the Royal School of Business for two years. She is married to Roger Anderson, and they have two children, Roger, Jr., six, and Erica, three.

One afternoon when Mike was five years old, he and Denise were passing the time, looking out their second-floor window. A few minutes before, they'd been watching cartoons in the living room and had heard what sounded like a gunshot, the kind of noise that would pull almost any young child from a television to the nearest window. "Look," Mike said gleefully to his sister, "a gun, a gun. I wanna get mine."

At the window, he saw a man leaving the bodega below, holding a revolver. The gunman had to have heard the giggling upstairs and probably looked up at the two smiling children before slipping into an old car parked a short distance away and speeding off. Young Mike hurried to his room to look for *his* gun, but the time he'd found it and began yelling, "bang, bang," his shouts were lost in the wail of police sirens. Soon there was a cluster of police cars below and a single ambulance, from which emerged two men dressed all in white. Cops kept a large crowd of onlookers from getting too close. Mike and Denise looked on, fascinated, as the white-clad men walked impetuously into the store and returned with a corpse covered with a sheet and strapped to a stretcher.

This scene was all too routine in the black-dominated section of Bedford-Stuyvesant, which made Harlem seem, by comparison, a bastion of good fellowship.

Later, when the children's mother came home from work, she saw signs posted on the walls next to the entrance of her apartment, stating that a crime had been committed at the grocery store. She hurried up the flight of stairs and discovered that Mike and Denise had seen the killer flee the scene.

"Did the killer see your faces?" she asked.

She got her answer from her children's blank stares.

"Shit!" she said, panic scrolling down her face. "He may come back to kill you, too. He surely doesn't want any witnesses to identify him."

Mike started to cry and called his sister for a conference. "From now on," he told Denise, "we have to sleep under the bed. We'll be safe there." For the next three months Mike and Denise never left home.

But their fear wasn't so overwhelming that they couldn't find some excitement. Under the bed Mike started to chip away at the wooden floor. Soon he'd tunneled through the floor into the grocery store below, which, after the murder, had been closed to the public. This was every child's fantasy and Mike and Denise's secret: a private gateway to all the candy, ice cream, soda, licorice, and other goodies they could eat. "We had a field day for a few days and nobody ever found out," Denise recalled. "And that was Mr. Mike Tyson's first criminal act."

Mike's brand of fun began to darken though. Denise recalled the time her brother came up with one of his more bizarre ideas. "We were all bored to death in the apartment and our older brother, Rodney, had fallen asleep on the sofa while watching cartoons," Denise remembered. "Meanwhile, Michael and I were looking to have some fun. It was early and the cartoons were a repeat so Michael came up with this brilliant idea." Denise could not conceal a satisfied smile as she recalled that golden moment.

" 'Let's play doctor,' Michael says, 'but we'll need a patient.' So I said, 'Doctor, would you like to perform here?' I pointed to Rodney who was dead asleep on the sofa. Michael says: 'Let's take his arm.'

" 'Okay that sounds good.'

" 'Then let's go.'

"Michael got a razor blade and a bottle of alcohol and started to cut down Rodney's arm, a really thin mark. The patient remained quiet. He didn't move an inch.

"He could barely feel it even though the cut went down the arm about seven inches. Then Michael poured alcohol all over the cut, and when that shit hit him, the patient jumped high into the roof, screaming madly, 'I'm going to kill you all! You rotten motherfuckers!' " Rodney was only eleven or twelve but weighed 280 pounds.

"So Michael and I scooted behind the refrigerator where we stayed for over fifteen hours. We knew that if we came out he was going to get us. And my mother did not interfere . . . it was a problem to be resolved by the three of us. But she served us food in there, and because we couldn't go to the bathroom, she also gave us a pail."

In the meantime, Rodney, too big to fit behind the icebox and not strong enough to move it, sat in a chair and waited for Denise and Mike to come out. Finally, he tired of waiting and stormed out of the apartment.

"Judging from my mother's behavior," Denise said, "the joke we played on Rodney was not that terrible. We didn't get punished or nothin'."

The worst punishment their mother could mete out was announcing: "No cartoons for the weekend." That was when Mike was three or four. By the time he was six and seven, he and Denise had discovered other diversions. One was flying pigeons.

"We used to fly birds together," Denise told me as we sat in Mike's old Manhattan apartment shortly after the Spinks fight. Mike still pays the rent. "Since I was older than him, I always used to go with him. I cannot imagine what made me like birds 'cause at the beginning I didn't like them. But the truth is we used to go on roofs, get on top of the bird coops, and say, 'Let's take this one' . . . late at night, you know.

"Back then it was not called stealing birds, it was called tackin' coops," said the big woman, who was as firm and vigorous as she must have been then. "They tacked our coops, and we tacked their coops. Mostly we wound up with the same amount of birds we started with. It was a five-block radius, so you'd go to somebody's coop and see your birds and say, 'That's my bird, I'll take this one back.' "

Since the coops were concentrated in abandoned buildings, Denise was forced to learn quickly about reasonable fear. "It was kind of scary after a while," she said, "and I was the scary type. I knew Mike would protect me if somebody came up to hurt us. He was always tough. But I was very careful.

"Out of the family, I was the only punk. They, Mike and Rodney, used to have to fight to help me. The only thing I hated from hanging out was that Mike would fight outside and usually he would kick the other guys' butts and then they would come looking for me 'cause they would say, 'Well, if I can't get him, I'll get the sister.' "

As a result, Denise took a few beatings. "That was the main reason why I'd stay at home," she said, laughing. "But you must know," she said, "that Mike would get them again."

Fear is often equated with respect in the ghetto. It certainly was by the Tysons. And Denise was proud of Mike's hard life in the street. "In a way," she said, "I was proud of him, yeah . . . yes, sir," she said. "If you're living in the streets of Brooklyn, either you're a goody-goody, and you always gets robbed or beat up, or you are a bad person and get that respect.

"See, Rodney was a goody-goody. No one never saw him entering or leaving the house, but they knew he lived there. Cops never came looking for him." She talked fast and with the same confidence that the champ displays in the ring. "On the other hand," she went on, "when Michael was nine, ten, he was a meany . . . a baddy. Nobody dared to say something mean to me or my mother. There were teenagers in the street, robbing and pickpocketing everybody that came by. But when my mother walked by with cash in her hands, they wouldn't dare touch her. They'd say, 'That's Mike Tyson's mother' or 'That's Mike Tyson's sister, leave her alone.' That was one of the best points of Michael being a bad kid in the street. My mother would be walking down the street with a lot of bags, and teenage kids would say, 'Mrs. Tyson, let me help you upstairs.' She would never have to worry about something missing from those bags."

Denise took a deep breath and looked at her son, Roger, who was running wild around the living room.

"That was the goodest part of it. Coming home late and the bad kids in the street would say, 'That's Mike Tyson's sister, let's walk her to the door, let's make sure she's safe.' And I was just a kid myself." I had forgotten the reasons behind such displays of courtesy by the street children; Denise reminded me.

"You know why they behaved that way? Because Michael probably kicked all their butts before, so they'd say, 'Let's be good to all his family 'cause he'll come back and kick our butts again.' José, when Mike beat you, he really beat the daylights out of you."

Inevitably, Denise and Mike had their own fiery confrontations. "I used to kick his face," Denise said triumphantly. "He was a great fighter outside of the house, but you have to realize that in order for him to be a great fighter outside, he had to get his butt whipped *inside* the house."

The free-for-all battles with her two brothers when they lived on the corner of Willoughby and Franklin avenues—"My favorite place," said Denise—are easily understood by families with more than two children.

Mike was now eight, Denise ten, and Rodney thirteen. Rodney, while big for his age, was not naturally aggressive. But among the children he was still the boss.

"Rodney is cool and calm now," Denise said, "but he was a bully back then. He felt since he was the oldest, and we had no father, he had to take over where our father left off. That was the main reason he had to be tough at home and kick our butts."

Denise leaned back and searched her mind for details of that time when violence was a form of excitement.

"As soon as my mother went shopping, Rodney would beat us up. . . . Until one day when he was really kicking our butts and we said, 'This is enough. We have to jump this man. This is the only way we can stop him.' And we jumped him —hands, shoes, broom, mops, pots, everything—and kicked his butt and other things. I was twelve when that happened."

Despite the violently played out sibling rivalries, there was much love and affection in the family. And to this day, Denise is convinced that a mysterious dynamism kept them together.

"You know," Denise told me, "now it is only the three of us. No such things as cousins, uncles, and aunts. My mother raised us . . . it was just the four of us, you know. She always told us that if we got separated and one of us got hurt, the other two would feel it. And it's true. It's like you could feel when one of the others is hurting.

"The first year Mike went away and wound up with Cus D'Amato in the country, I woke up one morning sick with chicken pox, but also depressed because I had this strong feeling that Michael was not feeling well. So I called, and you know what? He *also* had the damned chicken pox! Can you believe that? We had the same shit and we were a hundred and fifty miles apart. José, we're close . . . we are all we have."

Denise regrets that neither her mother, Rodney, nor herself ever met Cus D'Amato. "But we spoke so much over the phone," she said, "that it was as if we knew each other for a long time."

3

MIKE Gerard Tyson got off to a good start in school. He was well behaved and he had no trouble with his teacher or classmates or anyone else at P.S. 54 in Bedford-Stuyvesant. It was when the family moved to Brownsville and Mike, only eight, transferred to P.S. 178 that things started to change for the short, stocky boy.

"I used to be a good and smart student at P.S. Fifty-four," he recalled, "because I knew that formal education was good for kids and because the teachers were good and considerate and I got along with everybody."

Mike's mother, Lorna, tried to teach her youngest son the value of doing well in school. Though the two virtually parted company when he went to the reformatory at age eleven, and she died of cancer in 1982 when Mike was being reshaped by D'Amato in Catskill, Mike remembered Lorna Smith this way: "My mother was nice and intelligent. I think she went far in school. She was very eloquent and had a lot of class.

She was a tall woman, five foot seven inches, and had natural gray hair . . . gray, *wavy* hair. I felt I broke her spirit because I was bad and rebellious."

Unwittingly, his mother was the catalyst for his first troubles at the new school.

Lorna, who wore glasses, decided to examine Mike's eyes as she had done with Rodney and Denise years before. It was a simple test. She asked Mike to identify small objects around the apartment, such as the rum bottle cap under the sofa. The test was foolproof as far as Lorna was concerned, and Mike failed it, as Denise had a few years back. An optometrist confirmed her findings, and a few days later, to the delight of his classmates, Mike came to school sporting another pair of eyes, detachable ones with big rims. He became a butt of the cruel taunting that is so natural to young children.

"I began to skip classes once in a while with other kids, and later I got a kick out of playing hooky and then coming home and making up stories to my mother," Mike recalled. "I told her how good I was doing in my classes."

Mike became such a chronic truant that he had to enroll in what he called "a crazy school, one of the '600' schools." The "600" program was for troubled children, children whom the school system wanted to forget. As his life on the mean streets of Brownsville became more daring, more dangerous, his family and classmates saw less and less of him. During this time, Tyson remembered, he always wore "nice underwear," good shoes, and clean clothes, attire that from his mother's point of view was neat and fashionable. He thought he looked funny.

"But it was not so much for the way I dressed—which was probably too neat for my friends' taste—that the guys made fun of me," he said bashfully. "It was the motherfucking eyeglasses."

Tyson's anger at being the laughingstock of his second-grade class escalated when he began taking abuse on the street. He will never forget how his glasses were regularly snatched from him and thrown into moving cars. Or the time when two boys stuck them in the gasoline tank of a truck. Or when they were smashed against a wall, or when a kid his age stomped on them. "They just smacked the glasses away time after time and I just stood there and did nothing like a fucking dummy. And some just punched and pushed me around and I wouldn't do shit back to them."

The older kids started to call him "faggy boy" and "sissy" as they made fun of his glasses and his unwillingness to defend himself. "I was simply too fucking afraid to fight," he said. Mike soon tired of being the whipping boy.

"I was in the first or second grade. I fought these big guys ... they were in the fourth or fifth grade. Man, and I kicked the shit out of them. They were bigger and older than me. But I said, 'Fuck it, man, I can't keep going this way,' and I beat the daylights out of them," Mike said.

After this, Mike did not wait to be provoked. Now it was he who started things. "I didn't give a fuck who was my opponent now," he said. "I beat up friends and enemies the same way. I even had fights with guys I was afraid of because I was so short and young and I still kicked their asses." His street victories gave him more and more confidence, but no one was more surprised by his domination than Mike himself.

"After word spread throughout Brooklyn that I kicked butts for fun, everyone wanted to be my friend. I felt good and special. I was the only kid from Atlantic and Sutter who would be friends with the guys from the other side of town, the ones from Brownsville and Crown Heights, the nasty places where the really bad kids live."

"From then on," his sister, Denise, recalled, "my brother was known as Mike Tyson; no Little Mike or Big Mike or any nickname . . . Mike Tyson! Period. Name and last name. Even his teachers called him Mike Tyson."

As Mike Tyson grew in age and size, so did his acts of violence and his antisocial behavior. "We didn't have much trouble having food on the table at home every day," he said. "I ate lots of liver, chicken, a lot of pork—pork chops, pig feet, pig ears—all that stuff, and greens. Maybe that's why I hate all that shit now. As a matter of fact, I didn't feel we were poor, because I thought that everyone lived the way we did. The only problem was my life in the street. No one at home knew exactly the kind of shit I was doing in the street. They thought I was just a mischievous boy."

His brother, Rodney, remembers walking on Atlantic Avenue one afternoon. As he approached Utica Avenue near the Old Tasty Place, a huge bakery, he crossed the street so he could put his nose in the air vent to smell the fresh bread and pastry. "So, I'm looking and I see Mike in there stealing shit. I go in and he's got all these bags of donuts and stuff in his hands. I rushed in and grabbed the bags and he still had some bags in his hands. And as soon as I did that, about six factory workers came out and grabbed me while Michael got away with a couple of bags of donuts. I got arrested. . . . My mother had to come and get me out of a police station. You wanna know what happened with Mike? He went home and him and my sister ate the donuts."

When I reminded Mike of this incident, he had a belly laugh: "Yeah, it was really funny."

We were at the Ocean Club's penthouse in Atlantic City, not very far from the Trump Plaza Hotel where Mike would be fighting Michael Spinks in six days. The pressure created by the fight's proximity was palpable now, and no one felt it more than Tyson himself, his moods constantly shifting as we spoke.

"It all started," Mike recalled, "when I stole a fruit from a truck in my neighborhood." He took a breath and grinned. "An apple, an orange, I don't know. You could not believe how this fucking guy chased me for a goddamned fruit. You would think if a kid is hungry just left him take it, but this fucking Puerto Rican man was on my tail for a long time, just for a fucking fruit. After a few blocks he gave up and I was saying to myself, 'What the hell are you doing, man, chasing me for so long for a fucking fruit?' "

Stealing became a habit. Fruit and candy were fun to steal,

but after a while they became "kid stuff." He was barely nine when he stopped going to school, so he could hang out with his friends who attended junior high. His crimes became more sophisticated and more hazardous.

"From the beginning I was not afraid of the cops," Mike remembered. "I have never feared cops. What pissed me off was being caught by them. To be grabbed by these mother-fuckers was to be stupid," he said with a note of pride that could have come from any Brooklyn homeboy whose per-spective on the world doesn't go farther than the slums of New York City. At ten he'd adopted a lifestyle that was a form of intellectual and social suicide.

"I used to drink," he said, shaking his head in disbelief, "Mad Dog, 20/20, Bacardi one fifty-one, Don "Q.", Brass Mon-key, heavy stuff, *cheap* heavy stuff, gasoline. I'm talking about *straight*, fucking *straight*. I didn't get drunk, really, but I was out of my fucking mind.

"I also smoked cigarettes for a long time, cigarettes that I borrowed or robbed. But I know I was not addicted to them. People laughed when they saw me smoking, because I was so young . . . ten years old."

At eleven and a half, all that was left of his innocent youth was his age. "Then," Mike recalled, "I was already established around the tough neighborhoods of Brownsville, East New York, and Crown Heights. Even at ten, I was part of a big criminal clique all around. I knew many, many criminals already and they were my friends. We did lots of crazy shit together."

They would talk for hours about superheroes "and stuff like that," Tyson said. "About who were the big guys, and the gangsters and the tough guys in the neighborhood. We thought that the pimps, the thieves, and the drug dealers were cool. We didn't talk much then. We performed." He stretched his body and yawned, making the sound of a jungle animal.

"Shit, were we wild," he said, laughing. "We did not fuck around, man, we were a bunch of maniacs. Sometimes we got really crazy, nuts, got guns and just started shooting in the neighborhood; jumped onto our moped bikes and just go to the jam sessions in the street, you know, disco parties in the neighborhood . . . block parties. We'd ride through these parties very slow and we checked for chains and watches and money and usually there was a lookout, a black guy. If he sees something wrong happening, he'll come and then there was a crowd and we would pull the guns and start shooting at them."

Mike coughed, cleared his throat, and transported himself once again to his startling childhood.

"I had to make them mad at me first, antagonize them. I had to do something to them . . . yeah, provoke them so they could get mad and hit me. Once they attacked me, they were helpless. My friends would come up with guns and say, 'Don't move,' and we would take their stuff . . . and older people— their relatives and friends—would start running, leaving the kids alone, and then we would start shooting, Bang! Bang! Bang! Looking back, it was rough."

Once when his gang was trying to avenge itself against a big, tall kid who had fought and beaten several boys from Brownsville, Tyson got word that the tall boy was playing basketball somewhere in East New York. "I went to my friend who had the moped bike, you know, I was too young to drive it," Mike said, "and we went and picked up a couple of guns and rode to the park. We saw the tall guy playing basketball with other kids, and we just started shooting at him and everyone started to run and the guy driving the moped took off. I had to jump on the back with him. I don't know if we got anybody, but we fired to hit."

The next day a boy named Remy from Rutland Road told Rodney Tyson that Mike had shot at him and his friends. Unbeknown to Mike, the guys were members of the Puma Boys, a gang of about forty or fifty whose leaders once flew pigeons with Mike.

"I said, 'Oh, shit, these guys are all my friends and I used to fly pigeons with them and now they are going to kill me,' "

Mike told me. "The motherfuckers were ready to just wipe me out. They didn't fuck around, they killed people. I knew!"

One of the guys in the other gang, Mike remembered, had been one of his best pals just a year or two back, and they had been partners flying and stealing pigeons together. The two had shared experiences that Mike felt were too strong to forget and too valuable to dismiss casually over an incident in which no one was hurt.

"One night me and this guy were stealing pigeons and we just got caught in the act," Mike recalled. "We had no way out and these men started to beat the shit out of both of us, and somehow I felt they were going to kill us. We started to scream and they put cloth in our mouths and then they tied my hands behind my back and smacked me on the face very hard, and I was crying and having difficulty breathing and they hanged my friend by the neck from a fire escape and my friend pissed and shit on himself and I spat out the stuff I had in my mouth and started to scream at the top of my lungs, and some neighbors heard me and came around and really saved our lives."

When Rodney came home, he confronted Mike about the shooting.

"I told him the guy was lying," Mike said. "I was scared shit. You know, I lived on the border between Brownsville and Crown Heights, right next to these guys. I had to do something about this. These bastards are ready to kill me. But my brother, who was square and didn't get involved in none of that shit, he squashed it all. I don't know how the hell he did it, but he squashed it. I guess he told the guys, 'He didn't do it and he's my little brother,' or something like that. Besides, my brother used to go out with Remy's sister and I knew Rodney had put doubt in Remy's head about me being part of the fucking shooting."

A couple of nights later, however, Mike and his brother were at a dance in a nearby park when the Puma Boys, all forty or fifty of them, showed up. "My brother just ran out and mingled with the crowd and there I was surrounded by these crazy motherfuckers saying to me, 'We know you did it. You must pay for it.' I was gonna fight them but I knew I was dead. They said they were looking for the gang from my area and that they were lucky to have found me."

Then Mike saw his brother's smiling face and knew the truth. Rodney and the Puma Boys had been goofing on him.

"It was hard to figure out my brother's influence with the Puma Boys," Mike said. "He was not part of them. They were a bunch of nuts and I think Rodney never did anything illegal during my days of crime. Maybe they just liked and respected him because he was older and very nice." Or maybe because Mike Tyson was Rodney Tyson's brother.

In 1977, marijuana was the drug of choice among Tyson's peers, what "everybody did to be cool and to keep in tune with their world." Mike said he preferred feeling "nice and crazy" with rum and cheap liquor.

"I used to smoke reeferes, too," he said. "But I never went into heavy drugs, just marijuana and drinking. I loved to drink lots of that heavy shit from your country."

Tyson could name every brand of rum produced in Puerto Rico. He wanted me to understand that he had not been just a two-bit thief who took pennies from bums and women in the dark corners of his neighborhood, or that he and his friends committed stickups and muggings on the spur of the moment.

"We were clever," he bragged. "We planned things. We would even use girls to pick up guys from other neighborhoods and bring them around our area to be robbed. Not to hurt them, just to take their things and the money. We sticked up plenty of guys that way," he said, "and we would scare them with guns. But we would never shoot to kill."

Minutes before, Tyson had told me that when he and his friend had fired at the Puma Boys, they had "fired to hit." Such contradictions were not uncommon in the champion's reminiscences. The evils of the slums produce habitual defense mechanisms that are similar to those found in good prizefighters. Boxing is a sport of prevarication and deception. Tyson is better than most boxers because he lies better.

The slum code fueled his growing anger. He resented keeping quiet during those visits to his friends outside his area, when he'd be subjected to threats about his neighbors. It drove him crazy.

"I would come around there and the guys in Crown Heights would talk about my guys in Brownsville and say, 'I'm going to kill that Webb. I'm going to murder that bro' and 'Yeah, that motherfucker is dead.'

"I played off that I didn't know what they were talking about. But they were talking about the guy I was just getting high with in my neighborhood, my friend I was drinking with. I knew him and his family and these motherfuckers were contemplating in their minds that they were going to kill him. Next time they see him my friend was going to be a dead duck. 'Do you know a nigger in your area named Webb?' they would ask. And I would say, 'How he looks?'

" 'He's short, wears jewelry . . . a little guy.'

"I say, 'Yeah, I think I saw him before. Yeah, that nigger's fucking me and I'm going to rob him.' I'm telling them that, I didn't want them to think or say, 'Wow! He is on the other side,' because I'd be through. You wanna know something? I didn't know it then, but I was playing a double agent and I think the only reason I did that was because I wanted to also make money in Crown Heights, go there and rob without trouble. Shit, and these guys from Crown Heights always had guns. The guys in Brownsville had a gun here and there. But the guys in Crown Heights were more advanced . . . more experts."

Tyson conceded he learned more tricks from the young hoods from Crown Heights than from his homeboys in Brownsville. Thanks to his teachers on the other side of the border, Mike Tyson, at age eleven, became a much admired pickpocket, a skill that at least one member of his family will never forget.

"My brother, Michael Tyson," said Denise, "was the best pickpocket in the world. He could tell you, 'Check your pockets, I'm going to get your change,' and you put your hands in your pockets and it was too late, the money was gone. It was in Michael's hands. He could steal your underwear without ripping your trousers. He was simply the best pickpocket in the whole wide world."

"We liked to pickpocket," he said. "We liked to stick up people. We belonged to different gangs from different places but we didn't fight against each other; we robbed and picked pockets together."

He remembers those days when he and his friends would board a packed rush-hour bus, show a school pass, and hear the driver warn the passengers about boys like himself. "The motherfucking driver would say, 'Ladies and gentlemen, watch your money. There is too much money being robbed in these trips. Please, watch yourself.' "

But it was to no avail. The boys and Tyson would leave the bus with plenty of money to buy Puerto Pican rum. Sometimes there was even enough left for some fancy clothing. "Nothing satisfied me more than to be able to get away unscathed after the people had been warned," Mike said. "They watched their money closely but I got to it anyway. That was to outsmart them."

Tyson thought of crime as a fitting diversion, given the environment he was confronted with. And he understood that expertise and knowledge were for "the survival of the fetus," as he put it. The surreptitious flights from home increased. He paid no mind to the threats and beatings from his mother.

"I just became immune to the beatings," Mike said. "They didn't matter. I wanted to hang out with my friends because these guys would teach me certain ways to rob." He received state-of-the-art instructions about how to get inside a house and find the valuables. "I learned how to rob houses by entering through the main door with a fucking key, any key. We would find keys, any keys, and we would learn how to crack the locks with these fucking keys. Some keys would not fit, but we just kept playing with it until the motherfucker opened.

. . . I was able to open over ninety percent of the locks. Only the very complex ones could not be opened."

In one house they found antique guns. In another, they found a .38-caliber revolver, an M-1 army rifle with a bayonet, plus money and jewelry.

As his sophistication in the art of stealing increased, so did his chances of getting caught. He claims not to remember when he was first arrested. "It happened so many times that I really forgot why and where I was arrested for the first time," he said. "But it had to be for stealing. And I had to be around nine, ten."

Getting caught so incensed Mike that he began to challenge his captors. And today, Mike considers it silly for anyone to try to establish who ended up ahead of the game. "But I think," he said, still a bit proud of his accomplishments as a child gangster, "a good survey would find me way ahead . . . way, way ahead!"

Mike, Rodney, and Denise will never forget those days. "The cops would come and wake us up so my mother could come to a police station and pick up Michael," Denise remembered. "They came quite often and usually at night."

"I think I was caught about twenty-five, thirty times," Mike told me long before he won the crown. Later, he estimated that he was arrested about forty times before he was twelve years old. His sister, Denise, puts the total at *over* forty arrests before her brother was twelve.

"The first couple of times, my mother came to pick me up at night, and sometimes I was kept overnight. I also slept in the Bronx, in Spofford several times," Mike said.

Family court judges threatened youngsters with Spofford, a youth detention center in the Bronx that is New York City's boot camp for Riker's Island, the city's graduate school for criminals. Mike heard that type of intimidation in family court but soon took it for granted. "The judge yelled wolf too many times," he recalled. "So, who in hell is going to believe him?" Mike's arrests continued, and one day a judge discussed his bizarre conduct with his mother, Lorna, and his stepfather Eddie Gillison. He told them that Mike was risking his life in the streets and that he didn't know what to do with the eleven-year-old; he was too young for conventional treatment. Everyone agreed then that perhaps a night in Spofford would do the job and put some fear into him, perhaps straighten him out.

One hot Saturday night, Mike and two friends, Spike and Scarface from the Bronx, and a few others visited Times Square with bad intentions. They were having trouble finding the "right spot." Mike said he was concerned that "the entire place was covered with cops." Unafraid, but "not stupid enough to be caught," they looked for the "right moment." The location and the opportunity soon appeared.

"We were in front of a movie house on Forty-second Street," Mike recalled, "and there was this woman. I think she was a prostitute, a whore. She was showing this pack of dollars to someone, and one of my friends called her 'fucking bitch,' hit her with a radio, snatched the money from her hands—about four hundred dollars, no big deal—and took off with the loot. I played it cool and stayed put. The lady took a chocolate candy bar from her pocket and, crying and yelling, smashed it right on my face. So I took off behind my friends and followed them into an X-rated movie house and hid."

The woman chased after them, screaming at the top of her lungs, "Police, police, police!" It didn't take long for the youngsters to be rounded up. "I said, 'Man, I didn't do nothin','" Tyson remembered. " 'Man, look at me, I didn't do nothin', please look at him, it was him, my friend; not me.' Then I started to laugh."

He and his friends were handcuffed, and before they were taken away, the woman walked toward Mike, who was sitting in the police car.

"That motherfucking bitch," Mike told me, "stuck her ugly, nasty face through the window, put her ten dirty fingernails on my face and pulled down with all her might. And there I was cursing at the damned whore, blood spurting out of my whole face, and the police telling me, 'Shut the fuck up.' So, I spit on her face."

Mike was brought to family court and was ordered to spend a few days in Spofford, the first of eight or nine trips. "I was only twelve and it was nerve-racking in that place," Tyson remembered. "There were black and Hispanic kids and they were mean kids. . . . I thought I was tough myself, so what the fuck. . . . We were all crazy, mean motherfuckers." Not quite sure of what he should expect, Tyson thought it was better to just wait and see. He didn't wait long.

"These motherfuckers looked like they didn't give a fuck. They saw my sneakers and one said, 'What size you wear?' I said, 'I wear size eight or nine.' They wanted to try them on and I said okay. I really didn't think they were gonna take my sneakers. Anyhow, they said, 'Shit, man, you got big feet,' and gave them back to me. I didn't think much about it. But to tell you the truth I was scared."

On the morning of the second day, Mike jumped out of his bed in panic. He had dreamt a bad dream and the sweat poured off him. The uncertainty of the new place depressed him. But when he went to the cafeteria for breakfast, his fear vanished.

"Hey, Mike Tyson," someone called out. "Mike Tyson."

"Mike Tyson," another screamed. "Here!"

"Yo, Mike Tyson."

"Mike Tyson."

Michael Gerard Tyson looked around. "I saw this bunch of guys—friends of mine from Brooklyn—screaming all over the damned place. They were like in charge, you know—big shots. But I thought, man, I kicked these guys' ass back home and here they are bossin' around and I knew they would tell everybody I was their man, not to mess with Mike Tyson."

Tyson realized at once that Spofford represented no danger for him, especially since the one rule that every inmate always respected was the one-on-one fights.

"If you got into a fight with a guy fair and square," Mike said, "then you would get no help. I fucked up a bunch of people that way and I got my ass kicked in once. Some guy hit me in the eye. I think he was a boxer, a Puerto Rican. I remember he could fight and he hit me and I said, 'Motherfucker, I'm going to kill you.' Later, my pals said, 'Mike, if you don't get him then we have to get that motherfucker.' And I told them no because it's not the same thing. So I waited one morning when he was brushing his teeth, and when his brush was in his mouth, I hit him and he was fucked up. We became good friends after that. It's funny how some people get respect. The same thing happened with most of my friends in Brownsville. I got my respect by fucking them up."

To hurt in the name of self-respect was always justified, another of the many unwritten rules of the ghetto.

"If anyone had the idea to rape you or rob you or do something crazy," Mike said, "then you could whip his ass, or better yet they would be warned by your friends to lay off: 'Bro, that's my man.' "

"He was there for only a few days," Denise said, "before he was brought back to court. We were there, the whole family—my mother, Eddie (Gillison), Rodney, and myself—and I remember the court being packed to the hilt." Denise said her mother had mixed feelings about her son's short stay at Spofford. "My mother cried a lot thinking what Mike was going through in that filthy lockup," Denise said. "But it was the only option we had." She recalled that Mike was smiling when he was brought into the courtroom in handcuffs. "Here we are all nervous, my mother crying and all, and Michael with that stupid smile on his fresh face."

Denise never forgot the judge's words to her brother. "Young man," the judge said with the court in solemn silence, "you've spent only a couple of days in Spofford, thanks to the good heart of the court. Next time, we are going to leave you there much, much longer."

Mike looked up at the judge and like a hungry child, begged, "I wanna go back. Please, send me back now. All my friends are there. I miss them."

"The courtroom," Denise said, "went berserk laughing, and young guys started to hit palms and to make loud comments about my brother. It was crazy, Mike asking to go back to Spofford."

It was enough that his mother really started to worry about the future of her youngest son, although there was little she could do to control the twelve-year-old. He had forged his own world in the streets, seemed perfectly satisfied with it, and there was little his mother could do to change it. Still, that first trip to Spofford made a lasting impression on Mike. He had discovered that Spofford was more desirable than being on the streets of Brownsville and Crown Heights. His arrest record suddenly boomed, and anyone aware of his mental workings would have understood his "stupidity at being caught by the cops."

"I went back to Spofford about eight times after that," Mike said. "Mostly for robberies . . . I had done so many. You know, after knowing all my friends were there I was not at all afraid of it. It was like a country club and I was like a regular." Mike always seemed to be brimming with good cheer whenever he spoke about his childhood activities. "I would go to Spofford," he said, "and the staff would see me and they were just so nice. They would go to the store outside and buy me stuff and in the night bring it to my room."

Tyson's sister remembers the day they all—Lorna, Eddie, Rodney, and herself—went by subway to see Mike at Spofford and how sad they were that he was in the company of such "animals."

"We made a million subway changes," Denise remembered, "and when we finally got home tired and depressed, we hear the TV was on and we look and there was Michael watching TV like nothing had happened. 'We just left you behind bars,' I said. 'What in hell are you doing here?'

" 'I just got bored and escaped. I'm tired of that place,' he said to us. He beat us to the apartment and to this day I don't know how in hell he did it."

Mike's next stop, the Tryon Reform School in Johnstown,

New York, was a different story. "Country club" was not a description that came to mind. "It was tough at the beginning," Tyson recalled. "But then things began to change for the better. Not like before, now I just wanted to have a different lifestyle. I saw that there could be something better."

That "something better" was boxing.

Boxing or no boxing, Denise recalls hearing her mother say that Mike was one thousand times safer behind bars than in the street. "My mother told me: 'I would rather see him up there than down here,'" said Denise. "She was very scared that he was going to kill somebody or somebody was going to kill him in the street."

While Mike conducted his tour of New York's penal system, Lorna was having problems with her boyfriend. Although they had been living together for several years, Lorna and Eddie each had strong characters that brought them frequently into conflict. During these times they both disregarded the presence of the children and engaged in furious battles that would leave her bruised and bloodied. "Violence was accepted," Tyson said of his early childhood. "It was part of life. You don't want to see anyone you love get hurt, but I wasn't a stranger to that type of violence. It was acceptable."

Tyson was only seven the day that Eddie got so furious at Lorna he punched her in the mouth, knocking out a gold tooth she had been given by her father as a high school graduation gift. The shiny tooth, a status symbol of worth in the slum, flew out of her bleeding mouth, and according to Mike, his mother went crazy. Mike and Denise usually witnessed these scenes from a safe distance, taking them for granted and occasionally enjoying them.

"We were in bed this time," Mike said, "and we saw her rush to the kitchen and take a pot full of boiling water from the stove and chase Eddie throughout the apartment, trying to scald him . . . he ran out of the house screaming in pain.

And my sister and I was also crying because some of the fucking water got to us, too."

Denise remembered the same incident: "We just about poked out of the cover to see what was happening when she dashed the hot goods on him and it also caught us. He was running around screaming, but we were, too. My mother said, 'Oh, my God, I got you, too.' "

A few years later, the children realized that they were big enough to prevent their mother, or even Mike, from suffering at Eddie's hands.

"Rodney was a big thirteen, I was a big ten, and Michael, well . . . Michael was Michael. Anyhow, we decided, this is it. He's not going to hit our mother anymore. Next time they got into a fight, my mother knocked him down. I don't know how in hell she knocked him down, but she did." Denise inhaled and smiled. "Rodney used to wear platform shoes, and they were so high that if you were three feet tall, you'd look like a giant with them on. Mike grabbed one of them; I grabbed the other; Rodney had a dog, a Labrador retriever, a killer. While she knocked him down, we all hit Eddie on the head with the shoes, the dog was at him, and Rodney hit him with the bat in the ankles. Ever since he never touched Mom."

Eddie Gillison had his faults, but Denise still admired the man who had started working at age twelve, who had never missed a day's work, the man who was the only father Mike Tyson would have during his years in Brooklyn.

"You know something? When we had the transit strike and there were no buses or subways working, he would get up extra early to walk all the way downtown to work. So this way we had food on the table. He had his points. After we had jumped him to let him know that he wasn't hitting our mother anymore, he would say, 'I'm still here, you're still here, we gonna all live for the best.'

"When we didn't have food at times, he would say, 'I'm going out there and I'm gonna get some food.' And there were times, specially a couple of days before the [welfare] check arrived, there was nothing in the house but flour. But we was a family so we'd take that flour and add water and we'd make like little biscuits, star-shaped, moons, and all those things like Play-Doh. We did it together. We were a family."

On November 17, 1987, Eddie Gillison was minding his own business near his apartment in Brownsville when a police car went out of control and hit him and several other pedestrians. Eddie died instantly. He was fifty-six. Mike had by this time become one of the most famous men in the world.

Tyson's real father, Jimmy Kirkpatrick, didn't have much of a relationship with his children. Denise, unlike her younger brother, says she still cares for him.

"I have no feelings one way or the other for him," Mike told me. "If he asks for help, I would probably do it. But I don't feel any love for him."

"Michael and Rodney," said Denise, "were the men of the house, so they never got along with *him*. But he's my father and I see him as often as I can. It's not the point that he abandoned us . . . not like we never knew where he was. But Rodney and Michael have that macho pride. 'No, let him come to us. We don't have to go to him to ask for shit.' They always had that attitude."

Kirkpatrick, a disabled veteran, weighs 230 pounds, is retired, and lives in a public housing development in Bedford-Stuyvesant.

"I don't want Mike's money," he told a newspaper reporter last year. "I don't want Mike to think that, either. It's not that I wouldn't take it, that I couldn't use it. But I'd take it only if Mike wanted to give it out.

"I'm not going to Mike with my hands out. Some people say, 'How can your son let you live in a place like that?' But that don't bother me . . . I think a visit from Mike would be great. That could let us get to be friends. We could sit down and talk."

4

ONCE upon a time the world's greatest boxing professor, Constantine D'Amato, was an impatient young manager-trainer. He'd been raised in the South Bronx back in the days when the people living in the tenements were Italian and Jewish, not black and Hispanic. By the time he was twenty-two, he had gray hair, could only see in one eye, and was color-blind. By the time he was thirty-two, for reasons he never explained, his ability to smell, taste, see, and hear had begun to deteriorate. He'd fallen in love with boxing when just a child and was, by his own definition, "a street fighter." At twelve, he'd fought with a man twice his age and was hit in the face with "an object" that left him virtually blind in the right eye. In another street fight a heavyweight boxer hit him on top of the head with such force that he walked around like a drunk for nearly two weeks.

At twenty-two he joined forces with Jack Barrow, and together they created the Empire Sporting Club to develop young boxers. The club was located at the Gramercy Gym next to Luchow's Restaurant on Fourteenth Street near Union Square in Manhattan. At least three champions, Floyd Patterson, Rocky Graziano, and myself, honed their boxing skills at this club. It was there that D'Amato practically constructed Floyd and myself from scratch.

Cus entered the U.S. Army in the mid-1930s and became a boxing coach. He was discharged as a sergeant just prior to World War II.

Not too tall, not too strong, almost bald with only a few thin, white hairs scattered on his brawny head, Cus D'Amato was an independent man who was driven by his own ideas. He defended them with steely implacability. His basic boxing philosophy was that, at its higher level, victory or defeat in the ring is decided by the mental gears, not by the physical mechanism.

"Boxing," he repeated again and again, "is a contest of character and ingenuity. The boxer with more will, determination, desire, and intelligence is always the one who comes out the victor." The role he played in the gym was that of a master sergeant ordering his soldiers around. Cus commanded his fighters; he didn't advise them.

By 1979, Cus had long ago decided not to rush through life. Boxing—its triumphs, its dreams, and its disappointments—was his world. That was the year that Mike Gerard Tyson first met Cus D'Amato. It was also the year that I met Tyson. Cus and I were neighbors then, living in two small rural towns in upstate New York. Since 1962, Cus had lived in a huge house outside the town of Catskill with his lifelong companion, Camille Ewald; a young, aspiring actor named Jay Bright, who was like his stepson; and a small army of young boxers. I had rented an old summer home about a mile and a half north in Athens, a town of a few hundred people. Cus ran the only boxing gym in the area, where I helped manage a couple of young boxers he trained. The old man was happy and very independent then, despite the fact he was not financially well off. He had declared bankruptcy in 1971 and had been subsidized by his close friend and ex-roommate Jim Jacobs, a versatile former athlete who'd developed a deep interest in boxing. Jacobs had made brilliant investments with the millions he'd inherited from his father.

Cus and I had a father-son relationship and talked to each other several times a week. He'd managed my entire eleven-year (1958–69) prizefighting career, taking me to the world's light-heavyweight championship in the process. Cus had worked with hundreds of young people, including two champions of recent vintage, Wilfredo Benitez and Edwin Rosario. He had helped train them, but had *not* groomed them from pugilistic infancy. In 1979, fifteen years had passed since Cus had produced a champion on his own. Then one cool morning in February, during one of my frequent visits, the old man seemed very excited about a new kid he wanted me to meet. We were in the front yard, talking and inhaling the smell of the greenery when his dogs started wagging their tails and barking. Someone was coming . . .

It turned out to be a stocky, powerful-looking boy with two shiny gold teeth that clashed somehow with his tough, hard-featured face.

"His name is Mike Tyson. This boy," Cus told me, as he placed his hand gently over the youth's head, "is going to be the heavyweight champion of the world someday if he maintains interest and desire in the game."

The youngster, outwardly embarrassed by Cus's remarks, shook my hand sheepishly and looked down at the floor. I took a close look at the boy and decided that he was too short for a heavyweight (5'6"), too strong for a boxer (186 pounds of compressed baby fat and muscle), and too shy for his rough looks. Mike was not yet thirteen, but he'd already had plenty of trouble with the law, I would learn later. He lived at the Tryon School, a tough reformatory for troubled juveniles in nearby Johnstown, New York. The word from Bobby Stewart, one of the prison counselors and its athletic coach, was that the boy was a remorseless predator, thoroughly alienated from society. Just the sort of challenge Cus savored.

"Someday," Mike told me humbly, still eyeing the floor, "I wanna be like you . . . what you were . . . champion of the world." Since his voice was soft with a trace of a lisp, and since Cus's hearing was lousy, the old man, as he did more and more frequently, cupped his right hand around his right ear. Mike, meanwhile, was having trouble expressing himself, and it was obvious that the lost child from Brooklyn was struggling to act respectful and polite. I was probably the first boxing champion he had ever spoken to, although he had once seen Muhammad Ali during one of the former champion's visits to the reformatory. At one point he just walked modestly over to me and felt my biceps, which were not as big nor as powerful as his.

"The power is not there," Cus snapped. "It's right here." He touched the right side of his temple. "Right here." I looked at Mike's eyes and knew he hadn't fallen for all that. A timid smile crept onto his lips.

"That's right," I said, agreeing with Cus. Then I stared at him, searching for his unspoken reply—boxers are masters of body language—but could detect none. Both Cus and I knew that something was on the boy's mind—suspicion, cynicism, something.

"Bobby Stewart wanted me to get paroled because he said I was so talented," Mike would tell me years later. "He told me, 'You're so intelligent it would just be a waste of time if you go back into the streets. I want you to go to Cus D'Amato because he is a great trainer. He could make you a champion.' In my head I was saying, 'Yeah, these big shots at Tryon, you know, the guys running the place, think that's cute; a white guy adopting a black kid. Somebody is going to take this black kid off our hands or whatever.' I think that at that time nobody knew how serious Cus was. Not even me."

A few days earlier, Cus had seen Mike in action for the first time. The old man was amazed. He had told me about a young boy who moved in the ring as if he were an experienced boxer. "I don't know what the hell is going on," Cus told me. "He looks to be older than I've been told . . . twelve." Someone was not telling him the truth about the kid's age, he felt sure; somebody was lying about his boxing maturity. At seventy-four and with a reputation of being one of the wisest boxing men on the planet, the old man was proceeding cautiously.

"When Cus first saw Mike spar with me," Stewart told me years later, "he seemed to be in shock. 'This boy cannot be twelve as I've been told,' Cus said. 'Not with those moves; not with that quickness.' You could see he was doubtful but hoping to be wrong."

The plan had worked. Stewart had known for some time that one of his most troublesome inmates had an incredible talent with his fists. Reform school legend had it that Tyson spent his leisure time knocking out people with his bare hands, including prison guards. Such indiscipline had provoked his transfer from the more easygoing quarters of the reformatory to an area known as Elmwood Cottages, a medium-to-high-security section reserved for the most perverse and undisciplined boys at Tryon.

Stewart was a welterweight boxer from the area who had been trained by Matt Baransky, one of Cus's assistants, who ran the Trinity Boxing Gym in Albany, New York.

"I met Bobby Stewart," Tyson said, "at Elmwood and he was training . . . well, not really training . . . he would put kids to spar just to leave their frustration there. Kids who had beefs and were under a lot of tension put boxing gloves on and just threw punches at each other. No one could have a fistfight there because then you would be in trouble and not be allowed to have visitors for months. . . .

"It was so funny because some of the kids who used to box with Bobby Stewart just threw crazy punches at him and he would cover up and let them take their frustration out on him, and he let them hit him now and then and it helped because the kids were under so much pressure."

So Mike Tyson walked toward Bobby Stewart one day and told him, "You know, I think I can do this thing with you." To which the coach responded, "Everybody here wants to be a punk."

"He said that to me and I was taken . . . you know, I had a reputation and everybody basically was scared of me, but they knew that I would not hit anyone in that cottage because I didn't want my level [rating granting certain privileges] to drop, so they would talk shit. But the kids looked up to me because they knew of my reputation from the other institutions."

The boy wasted no time putting on the boxing gloves and getting in the ring with Stewart. "It was the first time I'd ever boxed in my life," he said, "and I started to throw crazy punches to the body and I thought I was going to wipe this white dude out because he was smaller than me, and here I am bombing away and he was calm, relaxed. Then all of a sudden he hit me in the body and wham!—down I go."

Tyson got up two or three seconds later and resumed his attack but lacked the same eagerness. The boy was not aware then, but Stewart could not have been more impressed with Mike's courage, relentless style, and punching power. Stewart recollected that his sides were sore from the boy's punches for several days.

"He kicked the shit out of me and embarrassed me," Tyson said. "It was Bobby's objective to humiliate me in front of the kids. 'This little white man beat his ass,' kids would say. 'Mike Tyson can't fight shit.' Humiliation . . . that's what I felt." As Stewart took his gloves off, Mike looked straight into his eyes.

"Can you teach me how to fight?" the boy begged. "I wanna fight. I wanna be a fighter."

"That's what they all say," Stewart said.

"So you wanna become a fighter?" Stewart asked Mike a few days later. "If you really want to do it, then pick up your grades and act right around the cottage, and if I hear good reports, you've got yourself a trainer.

"When you go back to classes I don't want you to get A's or be the best student here, but I want you to behave with class and self-respect."

"In about three weeks," Stewart told me, "the teacher started calling up: 'What's happening to this kid? All of a sudden he is behaving. He's trying hard to learn.' So I got a couple of other kids who were there . . . black kids that he could relate to a little better than just teach him . . . you know, he was embarrassed about reading and writing and stuff like that . . . he felt bad. So I figured I could get a couple of the kids who were intimidated by Mike to help him a little bit with his work."

Three weeks later his good behavior earned him the opportunity he desired so much. "And in three months," Stewart recalled, "he went from a second-grade level to a seventh . . . in three months! No one had ever done that in the history of the reformatory. He was not dumb by any means. But when he came to Tryon, he did not know his left hand from his right, let alone know how to box. So we worked together for a while.

"Everything I showed him—he would go back to his room and practice it over and over. At three in the morning one could hear movement and the snorting from Mike's room, learning, perfecting what I'd taught him the day before. The third-shift staff had to put him to bed every night."

Stewart said one counselor at Elmwood was out sick for five weeks, and by the time he got well and came back he could not believe his eyes.

"The guy came to the yard and saw Mike in action. 'Oh, my God!' he said. 'Do you realize how much this kid has improved?' He saw more improvement in Mike," said Stewart, "than I had seen, because he had not been around."

Soon Tyson earned a position as a legitimate spar-mate

and a daily routine was established to teach him some basics. So impressed was Stewart with the way Mike threw punches that he created an intensive training program that included heavy sparring sessions between himself and the husky youngster. He was very much aware that Tyson was a heavyweight (over 175 pounds) and had a thirty-pound weight advantage, but he felt his ring experience would more than make up for the disparity. Stewart had won the National Golden Gloves tournament in the lightweight (135-pound) division in the early 1970s and had turned professional shortly after. As a welterweight he'd lost only three of sixteen fights. Tyson was then familiarizing himself with his new cottage, figuring out what levels one, two, three, and four meant, and getting to know the other inmates.

"I had a reputation of being a killer," Mike remembered. "And let me tell you why. They'd taken me in the middle of the night from Spofford and shipped me somewhere upstate to a place I couldn't escape from. So I just wanted to terrorize the new, faraway place. And I would do anything: throw bottles, hit the staff, hit other inmates . . . just be a nut, treacherous and mean with everybody. So now they took me to Elmwood." Tyson took a deep breath. "It was a locked cottage where you were not free; a security cottage," he continued. "It was like, wow . . . You had to work so hard there. They focused on discipline. The place was spotless. You had to work and work hard to earn your level . . . to even be able to talk. You were not able to talk unless you were at a certain level."

The place had a system to determine an inmate's degree of autonomy, based on conduct and behavior. "When you were at level one you were fucked," Tyson recalled. "You couldn't even move; level two you could at least talk. At level three you could walk around and have some freedom. At level four you could live at the cottage across the street by yourself. It was a trustee system . . . so different."

The cottages and the levels were part of a therapeutic

system in which the youngsters would hopefully exchange experiences and information and learn from each other.

"You just spoke about your personal life," Mike said. "What you were in for, what you ever did, and they would tell you their problems and everybody had to know everybody else's problems. It was like a mind-kick bullshit, but it was good for all the kids. We all talked our problems in the open and we didn't get embarrassed after a while. We knew we were all similar, the black kids, white kids, Puerto Ricans. Only in Elmwood they did that.

"The levels were granted by your peers," Mike said. "If the majority said you belong to this or that level, that was it—popular vote. Your peers and not the staff was with you twenty-four hours a day. The guys knew all the shit you were doing and they would say, 'You do not deserve your level because you did this and that wrong.'

"So, the smart ones formed a buddy system, a clique. Fortunately, the staff got wise to that and they vetoed a bunch of promotions that the guys had given to their buddies."

After a few weeks of sparring with Tyson, Stewart began feeling pain and exhaustion. All his boxing savvy and skills could not stop Mike's furious charges and attacks.

"I couldn't believe it," Stewart told me later. "The boy was extremely strong, very smart, and had a punch like a mule's kick."

Stewart decided to pay a call on Cus D'Amato. He wanted the master to take a look at the boy and also wanted to impress Mike.

Aware of the old man's uncompromising ways, Stewart thought it would be wise for his young prospect to have some blood-and-guts rehearsals before meeting Cus.

"I knew from personal experience what mental and physical skills Cus would be looking for from a novice," Stewart recalled. So Tyson and Stewart practiced moves and punches that Stewart hoped would attract the old man's attention;

especially the all-important side-to-side movement. Bobby called his old boxing teacher, Matt Baransky, who was running the Trinity Boxing Gym in Albany at the time and was also one of D'Amato's assistants at the Catskill gym, to make sure Cus would see the boy.

In the gymnasium of this little town of Catskill, thirty miles south of Albany, Mike and Stewart executed their plan. The most difficult obstacle was convincing Cus that Mike was really twelve years old. Cus was overwhelmed by the kid's natural aptitude and ring savvy and put into motion a plan of his own, one that he would not live to see to fruition.

"If you let him stay here with me," Cus told Tryon's boxing coach, "I'll make this kid rich and happy. In only a few years he'll be the world's heavyweight champ." Tyson, staring meekly at this white-haired stranger, was having difficulty believing what he was hearing, thinking the old man was "bullshitting only to satisfy me." At his age and with his street and reform school experience, it was not easy for Mike to believe in anyone, much less in a blanched outsider with an Italian surname. "Trust" was not a word in Tyson's dictionary, and the small world Tyson had explored as a child brought him into contact with few whites.

Cus, an astute student of human behavior, understood the boy's defensive posture. But he also knew the youngster had no real choice. Either he accepted Cus's proposal and learned the trade that could possibly save his life, or he remained at Tryon.

Unable to hide his anticipation, Cus began to use all his energy and influence to bring Mike to his side. This went on for weeks, a word here, a phone call there. Meanwhile, the boy was at Tryon training under Stewart's supervision and waiting impatiently for his freedom.

Camille Ewald had met the boy a couple of times and one morning Cus asked her casually, "What do you think about this boy, Camille?"

"He is a very nice kid," she answered, "very friendly."

"I'm gonna try to get him to stay over," he said. "I think he's gonna be the heavyweight champion of the world."

After long weeks of bureaucratic transactions, the New York State Corrections Department granted Tyson permission to stay with Cus.

"I don't know if it was coincidental or what," Camille told me, "but on the same week of Mike's thirteenth birthday, he came to stay with us." It would take Cus five more years to finally become Mike's legal guardian.

One year after Mike began living in the house, Camille recalled, an artist friend painted a picture of the boy and gave it to her. "Cus liked it so much," she told me, "that he put an emblem on it that said, 'The Next Heavyweight Champion of the World,' and he told me, 'Show it to Mike the night he brings the crown home.'"

I N 1950, Cus D'Amato took in a delinquent boy named Floyd Patterson and taught him the skills he'd need to win the 1952 Olympic middleweight gold medal. In 1956, Cus saw his exacting lessons pay off further when Patterson became the youngest heavyweight champion in prizefighting history.

Just a year later, while Puerto Rico was not quite finished celebrating the silver medal I'd won in the Olympic Games in Melbourne, Australia, a neighbor came to my home waving a newspaper that proclaimed, "Cus D'Amato interested in becoming Chegui Torres's manager." A week later I flew with my father to New York to become part of D'Amato's boxing stable. I was only twenty, and Cus was waiting at what was then called Idlewild Airport. He figured I'd want to meet the heavyweight champion of the world before starting negotiations.

Once I met Patterson, it didn't take Cus and I long to reach an agreement. Cus said that we didn't need a written document, that I could walk away anytime.

"Whenever you feel I'm not doing the right thing," Cus told me, "you can simply pack and leave." Just like that! We never signed a single piece of paper!

My transformation from amateur to professional began in the same place Patterson's had—the Gramercy Gym, where Cus lived happily in the company of a German shepherd. (Camille Ewald, who preferred not to be in the limelight, was living upstate.)

One of Cus's many strange qualities was his aversion to opulence. Though not a religious man, he felt money was a creation of the devil. He used to quote Gene Fowler's "Money is something to throw off the back of trains." All the cash he received from boxing was put right back into it. He helped young fighters with modest talent; he loaned money to former champions with financial difficulties; he paid the rent for the old Gramercy Gym for more than thirty-five years.

Although he projected strength and a relentless energy, the old man had a delicate, almost feminine quality about him. I remember his telling the story of the time he was giving a speech somewhere after which he received a standing ovation. "I spoke about the psychological force behind every good boxer," he said, "and the people were rather impressed." After his speech a woman, forty to fifty years old, walked toward Cus and said to him, "So, you are in boxing," and without warning, punched Cus in his ribs. "Tell me, how do you like that?" Cus faked a smile and before he could recover, a right cross landed on the same spot.

After the event was over, "I went straight to an emergency room," Cus related. "And after a series of X rays, it was found that I had two, not one, *two*, fractured ribs."

Now in 1979, Cus had his eyes fixed on a new face, a new prospect. He vowed to take one more boy to that special place he'd secured for Patterson and myself. "This kid Tyson just can't miss," he told me repeatedly as he watched the boy's daily improvement. "You must keep an eye on him. He's gonna go all the way."

The young Tyson was not so sure.

"I doubted Cus the first minute I laid eyes on him," Tyson told me once. "But somehow I always trusted Camille . . . from the beginning."

Camille Ewald was Cus's companion for more than forty-five years. A pale Ukrainian woman of seventy-three when she met Tyson, she helped take charge of Tyson's nurturing.

Mike's new home was a large, three-story, seven-bedroom, turn-of-the-century, English-style house built a few yards from the Hudson River. It was regal white and situated between Athens and Catskill. Mike saw his new home and called it "a mansion." Only two miles separated it from the gym above the police station on Main Street in Catskill. The new living situation represented a radical change for the boy who'd for so long called a reform school home. "This is *your* house," Cus told Mike. "You have to watch it and protect it to the end."

Camille was aware that rearing someone of Mike's background and disposition would take a lot of energy and patience. "Straightening him out is not going to be easy," she told me after a few days of dealing with Mike, "but I have a lot of confidence in Cus. He lives his life convinced that every problem has a solution."

Neither Mike's sister, Denise, nor his senior brother, Rodney, nor his mother, Lorna, had so far been able to solve the puzzle.

The basics of Mike Gerard Tyson's boxing education consisted of physical drills and lots of conversation with Cus. Mike tolerated such training, but not without moments of frustration. He was working under a man who required hard labor and demanded perfection—a tall order for a boy accustomed to going his own way. Since Mike needed to be housebroken, domestication became part of Cus's many lessons. Nothing new for the old man—teaching young men discipline was a task he'd labored at for years.

Every night Cus would engage the boy in extensive dia-
logues aimed at probing his intelligence. There was little discussion of boxing technique. Cus believed that the development
of the physical side of a champion was "incidental" during both
the first and last stages of his career. "To teach a kid how to
throw punches and how to move away from them is easy; anybody can do that" were Cus's first words to me when we met.
"Winning and losing is decided by the brain, not by strength,
speed, or physical power." I remember searching his face for a
sign of humor but there was none. He was dead serious.

For Tyson, accepting Cus's priorities was not easy. Though
the boy never complained about the evening talks, it was clear
that he preferred physical training to character building and
psychological therapy. It took little prodding to get him up at
five o'clock each morning to join the other fighters in a six-
to-seven-mile run among the rural hills. He spent every afternoon in the gym, punching the heavy and speed bags, jumping rope, shadowboxing, and doing extensive calisthenics.
Mike's work ethic made Cus even more sanguine about his
prospects. "If he keeps this up," Cus told me after a few
months working with Mike, "he'll be champion sooner than
later." I had not seen Cus as ebullient in years.

This change in Cus's disposition tickled Camille and Jay.
A happy Cus D'Amato meant a happy home. And with Mike
in the house it was as if the family was now complete.

"Mike had never seen a bat before," recalled Jay, "and
Camille had a nest of bats over the living room. You should've
seen his face when he saw them. We had to get rid of it."

"Yeah," added Camille, "there were a lot of bats around the
area and we always left the windows open and they got into the
house. We had lots of fun with them. The first time Mike saw
one, he said, 'There is a bird in the house flying around!' He
was very excited. I said, 'Mike, what kind of bird?' and he said,
'It's black and very fast.' I said, 'Mike, that's a bat.' "

Cus's chief trainer at the time was another former street
kid with a troubled past who'd been straightened out by the

old man. His name was Teddy Atlas, a former boxer who, like the others who'd come in contact with Cus, had been taught about boxing in particular and life in general. Forced to quit the ring because of an eye injury, Teddy quickly learned to teach the training methods Cus had carefully designed.

Atlas became Mike Gerard Tyson's first trainer. Together with the old man, he supervised Mike's every move. Cus believed that most boys caught up in the tough street life of the ghetto emerged with an antipathy toward cerebral training. "They tend to resent intellectual or psychological lessons." He figured Tyson was one of those boys and, consequently, instructed Atlas to work harder on him.

Since the opening of the Gramercy Gym, youngsters by the hundreds had received Cus's mental training. "Not every kid turned out to be a champ," Cus said, "but the boxing discipline they developed in the gym helped most of them deal with life outside the ring." It was the rare youth who clung to his ghetto mentality after coming under Cus's tutelage.

Thus it was that D'Amato set out to change Tyson's outlook. The boy was angry, distrustful, wild—good qualities to have if you intend to make your living in the ring. But he would have to learn that there is a time and a place . . .

"Boxing is a sport of self-control," Cus told Mike. "You must understand fear so you can manipulate it. Fear is like fire. You can make it work for you: it can warm you in the winter, cook your food when you're hungry, give you light when you are in the dark, and produce energy. Let it get out of control and it can hurt you, even kill you. . . . Fear is a friend of exceptional people."

The lesson sunk in. After his first professional match, an impressive one-round knockout over Hector Mercedes, Mike was asked by a young reporter from a small, suburban newspaper: "Were you concerned when that bell rang and you saw this big man coming at you?"

"No, I was not concerned," Mike said. "I was afraid. No normal boxer can enter the ring fearless. Fear is a friend of every good and reasonable athlete." The sportswriters were taken aback.

One night after the ritual therapy/lecture was over, Mike went upstairs to his room. He was still having problems with the old man's concept of fire and fear. The telephone rang and Cus picked it up downstairs. Mike tiptoed down from his third-floor room and heard Cus talking into the phone. "I don't know who he was talking to," Mike told me years later, "but he was saying, 'I have a kid here who's going all the way. He's only a kid, but one day he's going to be the heavyweight champion of the world.' Everybody was in bed and not a soul was listening. I said to myself, 'This guy is not really bull-shitting. The motherfucker is serious.' "

After the first few weeks of training, D'Amato felt it was time to enroll Mike in school, to expand his knowledge and expose him to something besides boxing. But after only a few days Tyson had slapped a girl, beaten up two or three of his classmates, and thrown a book at a teacher. Each time, Cus defended his ward with skill and passion.

"Whenever Cus went to school," Tyson told me, "he first read books about law . . . Clarence Darrow or something . . . and prepared himself to put up a good fight in my behalf. And there I was praying for him to lose the case so I would be kicked out of school"—which was what Mike really wanted anyway. "I had no fucking use for the damned place. I was doing good in the gym."

Every time Cus won a dispute with the principal, Mike came home disappointed. "He acted like a fucking lawyer in a murder trial. He paced himself like a big-time lawyer, making sudden stops and pointing at the accuser as if *he* was the one making trouble.

"If there was one thing Cus wanted for me more than the championship, it was my school graduation. Isn't that a fucking bitch. He wanted that more than the fucking championship. Give me a fucking break! He had planned a huge, very high class party for the day of my graduation."

That day never came. The frequency of Cus's school visits increased by the week. Finally, he had no recourse but to hire a private tutor. The people counting Cus's money accepted it as necessary; Jim Jacobs and his partner Bill Cayton trusted the old man implicitly.

After several weeks of talks and training, the serious sparring began. It was time for Mike to translate theory into practice. Boys his age who had as much or more experience couldn't offer Mike the proper level of competition: he punched too hard and too fast and was too smart—the trait Cus admired most.

Willie Campudoni, twenty-three, had the muscles of a well-bred athlete and the looks of a movie star. The 190-pound heavyweight was part Italian and part Puerto Rican and lived with me, my wife, and my two children in Athens. He had a black belt in karate and quickly sized up Mike as just another tough punk from Brooklyn, a ghetto bully. "I think he's suffering from the 'Napoleonic syndrome,'" said Campudoni, whom I managed. "He has a complex with his size . . . too small to make it as a heavyweight."

Campudoni decided to expose Tyson as a fake. "The time will come," he said, "when I spar with him and then Cus and everybody else will see." The six-foot-three-inch fighter could talk a good game. Months earlier, Atari Games executives had been so impressed with his looks and confidence they'd decided to bankroll us. A deal was cut right on the spot.

Mike and Campudoni took to watching each other's every move, planning for the day when they would be swinging at each other in the ring. A month or so went by before Cus phoned to tell me it was time for Tyson and Campudoni to spar. By now, my family and I had moved back to New York and I was commuting to Catskill on the weekends. "I'd give them specific instructions, but you know how anxious they are to be in the ring together," Cus said.

Later that night, Cus called. "They behaved surprisingly good," he said. "I'm proud of both of them. You know, if Willie applies himself, he can be a good fighter."

Mike's and Willie's sparring abilities were a lot closer to equal than either wanted to admit. The two heavyweights were the camp's stars. Although Kevin Rooney was the only boxer in camp supporting himself as a prizefighter, we all thought it unlikely he'd reach the top. He was already losing interest in the sport, and Cus had been subtly turning him into a trainer.

Mike and Willie were sparring almost every day, both fighters learning from each other. A month later I visited the camp and watched the young man and the boy working on the floor, hitting the bags and jumping rope, shadowboxing. When I saw Mike hit the heavy bag, move to one side, punch again, and move to the other side, I realized how extraordinarily difficult it would be to withstand this kid's sledgehammer punches.

I shook my head in disbelief.

Cus's grand plan was to register Tyson in the amateur ranks but well outside New York City (even though his first real fight would be in the Bronx). If Mike were registered in New York City's boxing programs, he would have to fight whatever opponent came up on a bureaucratic role of the dice. Such randomness was anathema to Cus. At this time he regarded the selection of Mike's opponents as his sole and exclusive responsibility. Thus, he preferred that Mike fight upstate and in the small towns and villages in the adjacent states of Massachusetts and Connecticut, where boxing is limited to only a few programs a year and the supervision is not as inflexible. There Cus would have a better chance at safeguarding Mike Tyson—his way.

As Mike began to defeat strangers in "unofficial" competitions, his confidence and desire grew immeasurably and he learned to function under pressure. Gym workouts are no more than practice sessions. There have been several instances in which a boxer looks exceptional in training and appalling in actual competition. Cus D'Amato was forever conscious of this, especially as it pertained to the difference between fighting in the amateur and professional ranks.

"In the amateur ranks," he often said, "matches are made to find out who's the best boxer at a particular moment. It does not matter how they conduct themselves in the ring so long as they do not violate any rules. An amateur boxer can, and many do, just slap and run, slap and run, and still win a match. In the pro ranks promoters try to impress the boxing fan with a thrilling performance." And that meant pro boxers needed a different set of skills—skills Cus was trying to inculcate in a young boy named Mike Gerard Tyson.

Under Cus's tutelage Mike would skip the amateur courses and instead be instructed in moves, punches, turns, blocks, and riposting until they became natural habits. He would learn to be a boxer-puncher who would provide plenty of punishment, take little in return, and cheat, deceive, and lie in the ring.

Tyson was thirteen when he had his first official boxing match. It was in a Bronx gym, owned and run by Nelson Cuevas, a former club fighter whom Cus once managed. "I had to fill out papers in Mike's behalf," recalled Atlas. "When I put down that he was thirteen, weighed 190 pounds, and had no fights, the guys started to laugh.

" 'Come on, Teddy, stop fooling around,' they said. 'We love you and all, but you've gone too far.' The guys just looked at Mike and thought I was just putting them on."

This was not Mike's first real fight. Prior to this Atlas had matched Mike against kids his own age in small exhibitions that were not under the auspices of the United States Amateur Boxing Federation. This fight in the Bronx, however, would be his first "official at bat." When the time came to step up to the plate, he did so with gusto and was rewarded for his efforts. He knocked out a boy four years his senior in the third round. "He looked like a little Henry Armstrong," said Atlas, referring to the first man to hold three titles at once (featherweight, lightweight, and welterweight—in the 1930s and 1940s), a fighter whose style reminded one of a tank plowing forward in high gear, its guns firing nonstop.

Soon, Mike entered the Junior Olympics, a program designed for children no older than sixteen, in which bouts are set not only by weight but by age. There are three age classifications: ten to eleven, twelve to fourteen, and fifteen to sixteen. Mike qualified for the middle group, but the officials could not believe what they were seeing and checked and rechecked Mike's age and experience as he battered the competition. He became the bogeyman of the Junior Olympics. He was too strong, too powerful, and knew too many moves.

At the 1981 Junior Olympics, the heavyweight division had been narrowed down to four boys, one of whom was Mike Tyson. He won his semifinal match with ease. The other semifinalist match was fairly even, and when the decision was announced both the winner and the loser jumped around the ring with joy.

Atlas overheard the defeated boy say to the winner: "You think you were smarter than me because you won. Look who you have to fight next: that black animal. I was the fucking smart one."

Some of the young men in Catskill were not pleased by Mike's rapid ascension in the boxing world. One was Campudoni, who had gone from respectable heavyweight prospect to a fair sparring partner for Mike.

One night, Cus telephoned me to report on Willie: "Your kid has shown that he has the ability to become a good fighter," Cus said, trying not to laugh. "But he's been chickened out by Mike's publicity. On Monday, Mike hit him with a left hook to the body and Willie went down, making all kind of noises. On Tuesday, Mike hit him with a right to the head and Willie went down and remained on the floor for a long time, complaining of the punch. On Wednesday, he was hit with a left jab, not a hard punch, and again he went down.

"But that's not the entire story . . . This afternoon [Thursday] Mike missed him by about six inches with a right uppercut and Willie went down. . . . You'd better come and talk to him."

The next day I paid an unannounced visit to Catskill and got to the gym just minutes before the Tyson-Campudoni sparring session started. "Hey," Willie greeted me. "What's been happening?"

"I have a fight for you," I said. "We gotta talk."

"Yeah," Willie said as a cornerman stuck a mouthpiece in his mouth just before the bell rang. Tyson came toward Willie, and for three rounds I saw a wonderful workout between two good prospects, one somewhat superior to the other but both with great potential. Afterward Cus looked at me and shook his head in disbelief. "A metamorphosis," he said. "And believe me, Mike didn't look that bad." Translation: Willie looked good.

That night Willie and I had a long conversation. He said he needed a rest. "I have to go home and get my head together."

"But you looked good today," I protested.

"I'm not feeling comfortable here," he said, emphasizing his words. "Every time we eat together that damned Mike Tyson bothers me. He knows that when Camille serves us chicken with spaghetti I like the thighs. You know what that son of a bitch does? He waits until I'm about to take the thigh and beats me to it. Then the bastard tells me, 'Tomorrow we are going to box.' He tells me that while sucking on spaghetti. You wanna know what happens when he does that to me? I'll tell you the truth: I get fucking diarrhea on the spot.

"I'll tell you something, I am beginning to hate . . . the smell of leather."

A leather-covered fist would never again touch Willie Campudoni's nose. He was the first but certainly not the only fighter to be retired prematurely from the ring by Mike's punching power.

6

MIKE Tyson was not unbeatable. The boxing instruction he was receiving from D'Amato and Atlas, which focused on the skills he'd need to succeed as a professional, ironically hurt him in amateur competition, which did not prize deception and concealment—two staples of the D'Amato art.

And there was yet another difference between amateur and professional boxing that made it possible for Mike to suffer his first loss. Amateur fights are limited to no more than three three-minute rounds or five two-minute rounds—hardly enough time for superior mental training to assert itself.

In November 1981, Mike fought an experienced amateur named Ernie Bennet in Rhode Island. Due to Mike's age, fifteen, the bout was unofficial. Mike had a fifteen-pound weight advantage. The fight was a tight one and not easy to judge. Mike had pursued Bennet with relentless fury, connecting with sporadic bombs, while Bennet moved and flicked continuous left jabs that hardly bothered Tyson. The judges voted for Bennet.

"The fight was very close," recalled Teddy Atlas, "but I thought Mike put on a great performance, taking into consideration the other guy's long and successful record."

It was the only fight of twenty-one that Mike would lose under Atlas's meticulous tutelage.

Mike had been nervous before the fight and was aware that he had not controlled his fear. Eight months later, though, there was a more dramatic instance of Mike's wrestling with fear when he defended his Junior Olympics title. A few minutes before his final bout, against a boxer named Celton Brown, Mike had an anxiety attack. He hugged his trainer Atlas on a terrace outside the arena in Colorado Springs and began to sob. A television camera recorded it for posterity.

"No one will like me if I lose," Mike said as he buried his face into Teddy's shoulder. The rest of his words were lost in heavy sobs.

Teddy told him reassuringly, "You've done it before, done it a hundred times in the gym, in Catskill." Gradually, Mike mastered his fear, turned his anxiety into controlled rage, and pulled his emotions together. He pounded his gloves and began walking toward the ring in a hip-hop, Brooklyn swagger. With tears barely dried, Tyson annihilated Brown in a single round.

Soon after that bout, Teddy had a disagreement with Cus and left Catskill. D'Amato lost no time assigning Kevin Rooney to Mike's pugilistic education. The progress continued, but after a few more inconsequential victories, Mike, Cus, and Rooney traveled to Binghamton, New York, where Al Evans caught Tyson in round two with a left-hook-right-cross combination on the head. Mike's legs wobbled, enough for the referee to step in between the fighters and signal that the match was over. It was Mike's first and only loss by the sleeping route—although a "technical" one. Mike was not hurt, but at his age no amateur official would have subjected him to unnecessary punishment.

Cus was not happy with the referee's impatience, but he understood it. Despite the loss, he and Rooney were satisfied with their fighter's performance.

"He was controlling the guy before he was nailed," Cus said.

"It was a learning experience," said Rooney. "He'll be a better fighter because of it."

Tyson continued winning national Junior Olympics titles, knocking out almost everyone he faced. *And* pummeling adults into submission in bootleg fights. But these victories made it difficult for Cus to keep Mike's domination a secret. The boy developed a reputation as a wild animal, and his notoriety spread like a brushfire through the boxing community. Rather than have their young fighters face this monster, trainers began pulling them out of tournaments.

Mike was ready to fight the best amateur heavyweight boxers, but Cus couldn't find any sparring partners. He decided to contact his benefactors, Jacobs and Cayton.

"We need sparring partners," Cus pleaded with Cayton. Even heavyweight champion Larry Holmes's sparring partners had refused to come to New York and spar with the teenager. They wanted more money than Holmes was paying.

"How much?" Cayton asked Cus.

"One thousand a week . . . for each."

These hired guns were the only ones willing to face Mike in practice. He would wear 20-ounce gloves while the sparring partners wore the regular 14-ounce mitts.

"No one can take this kid," Cus told Cayton.

By now, Cayton had learned many of the fine points of boxing from D'Amato and agreed unhesitatingly to the extra costs. Jacobs, who had a thorough understanding of the sport, possessed a small stable of fighters, including welterweight champion Wilfredo Benitez and lightweight contender Edwin Rosario. Both partners knew Mike was no ordinary prospect.

"Jimmy [Jacobs] and I would never hesitate to give Cus

whatever he asked for," Cayton would say later. "We knew how economical and careful he was with money."

By most estimates, Mike had fifty-two amateur bouts, of which he lost five, one by technical knockout. "No one knows exactly how many fights Mike had," said Bruce Silverglade, national director of the Junior Olympics, "because Cus D'Amato took him to bootleg fights . . . barnstorming all around upstate New York, Massachusetts, Connecticut, and even to some gymnasiums in the Bronx where there was no official supervision."

By the beginning of 1983 Mike had moved up to a new level. How many amateurs have $1,000-per-week sparring partners? These journeymen boxers came to camp with vast wisdom in the art of self-defense, then lost it when the teenager opened up on them. Top prizefighters who were having problems getting sparring partners suddenly began coming to Catskill for free practice. They included cruiserweight champion Carlos de Leon—"I miss my family in Puerto Rico too much," he said, after only two days with Mike—and top heavyweight prospect Carl "the Truth" Williams ("That's a boy we'll have to contend with very, very soon," he told me about Mike).

At the same time, Mike's past was beginning to haunt him. Loud voices from the streets of Brooklyn called out to him in his thoughts, beckoning him back. Though his boxing skills were improving daily, he was still plagued by a feeling of dislocation and frustrated by the stagnancy of his personal life.

"I'm just not a good-looking guy," he told Cus during one of their nocturnal therapy sessions.

"Mike," Cus said, "I'm going to buy you a baseball bat so you can keep away the hordes of women who will be begging to be with you."

Cus bought Mike a Louisville Slugger, and though the young man would have frequent occasion to use it in the years to come, he decided early on that there was a certain kind of attack you *didn't* want to fend off.

One day Mike packed up and headed for Brownsville. I

got a call from Cus four days after Mike had disappeared. No one knew his whereabouts. Supposedly, the boy had gone to visit his mother and was scheduled to be back in two days—on Sunday. It was Tuesday.

"Hey, don't panic," Mike told Cus when he returned on Thursday. "I do no bullshit out there, man. I only see my family and friends. I'm a cool dude. No shit. If you just gave me permission to go home and see my mother and my family more often, you wouldn't have to worry."

A few days later, Cus, Camille, and I were downstairs in the living room, chatting. It was before 8 P.M. and Mike was in his third-floor bedroom, watching fight films. The other boys had gone to town. Only a Puerto Rican lightweight prospect named Hector Espada was around.

"I don't know," Camille said, "but this is the second time Mike goes to the city and he comes back a changed person. He talks different. He acts weird." Cus, his right hand cupped to his ear, stared at the white wall. "I really don't like it," Camille said.

Hector peeked in and smiled. I suspected that he knew something that we didn't. Later, Hector and I drove to Athens and I told him a few jokes to get him talking. "I don' know wheah Mike go and whah he do, but I know he no angel," Hector said, practicing his new English on me. "He smokes grass and drinks beer," he said in clear English this time. "And he do it a lot."

Hector had grown up in a slum in Ponce, Puerto Rico, and like Mike, he had been exposed to drugs and liquor before abandoning them for boxing. I helped manage Hector, who sometimes stayed at my house in Athens. Like Cus, I had strict house rules: no women, drugs, or alcohol on the premises. "If you break these rules, you are out," I told my fighters. And I never checked on them.

A few weeks later, I got an anonymous tip that activities were going on at my house that were "not apt for boxers."

So one night I made a surprise visit and discovered several empty liquor bottles, a woman, and a few marijuana cigarette butts. I gave the two boxers their walking papers—Hector was one of them—and closed the house for good a few days later. My wife, Ramona, cried; she loved Hector.

When I told this to Cus, he asked me to investigate whether Mike was involved in the same activities.

"Yeah," Hector once again confirmed, "Mike smokes reefers like mad. More than all of us put together. He also likes to drink lots of beer. And when he goes to the city, he goes wild . . . I am telling you the truth, and you better believe me."

I passed this news on to Cus, not to hurt Mike, but to help him. "I think now is the time to deal with this situation," I said. "The boy has to be confronted."

Cus seemed to agree and a few weeks later I noticed that Mike had started staying close to home, reading boxing books and magazines.

"There was actually a period of time when Cus tried to kick me *out* of the house," Mike told me the night before the Spinks fight. His wife, Robin Givens, was in Atlantic City with him. "At first he had convinced me that I should dedicate my entire time doing and thinking boxing. So that's what I did. Then he changed. 'Get out of here and get a girlfriend,' he told me. I thought he was just bullshittin' me. If he was always criticizing the distraction in fighters, why then have a girl? Aren't women distracting?"

Mike thought for a moment. "I'm going to tell you something . . . I was fifteen, maybe sixteen, and he wanted me to marry a girlfriend I had, Angie. She was a very nice and very intelligent girl. Robin reminds me a lot of her. That's how come I know Cus would've loved Robin. He loves that type. Not naive but smart. A girl that would fight for her man. Just like your wife, Ramona. He said, 'Mike, I think you should marry her.' And I would say, 'Do you think this is a good idea?' And then I would think, 'Are you out of your fucking mind?' "

Camille would listen to Cus's advice to Mike and then get him alone. "First of all," she would tell Mike, "don't trust them women and don't you dare listen to Cus about marrying anyone. You date as many girls as you want, then you select the best."

Then, when Cus would tell Mike to stick to one girl, Mike would say, "Camille's opinion is that I should date a bunch of girls."

Mike laughed at the memory. "Man, Cus would go absolutely crazy. 'Camille, come here right now!' Cus would yell. 'Don't fill Mike's mind with that kind of junk about dating many girls.'

"You know," Mike continued, "Angie was the first girlfriend I had. But then I began to fight and I started to change . . . not being nice to her, and moving around with other girls, and Cus got mad at me.

"He said, 'You're asking for trouble . . . When you've got a girlfriend and you start fooling around with other girls, trying to be a big shot and dropping your original girlfriend, that's the first sign of trouble with your character.' He told me I had to change. You know something? He changed my head and for a while there I didn't go out with other girls."

His eyes rolled up at the ceiling and he burst out in laughter.

"I'm bugging out," he said, "but the truth is that if Cus had been alive today and he had met Robin, that's it, man . . . that would've been it. He would've been taking her side all the time over me. He would've loved Robin for the same reason he liked Angie: She's got guts."

In any case, the monastic lifestyle Cus imposed on Mike did not last long. Six months later, Mike was allowed to visit his family in Brooklyn. Cus insisted that Camille's worries about such trips were just paranoia.

"If he only knew," Mike said. "I was a spoiled brat," he admitted. "I could get anything I wanted from Cus, and I had a large, big room in a beautiful mansion. I think it's funny when people talk about me having a hard life. I did have a hard life when I was a child, but I was so young then. After I met Cus, I lived the life of a little rich kid. I was a very spoiled kid and that's how come I could relate to spoiled kids, like I could really understand a spoiled kid from a rich family or a poor one. I was spoiled in both."

A willing participant in Mike's drinking and carousing was Rory Holloway, a chubby, introverted youth who was four years older. Born in Hartford, Connecticut, and raised in Albany, he was a $12,000-a-year counselor at the Berkshire Farms Juvenile Detention Center near Albany when he met Mike. They were introduced by Rory's younger brother, who, at the time, was Mike's closest friend.

"I used to watch TV all the time in a back room at home," Rory said. "So every time Mike came to visit Todd, he always saw me there. One day he said to my mother, 'Mom'—he always called my mother Mom—'what's wrong with that boy? Why is he always sitting in the dark?' And my mother said, 'Well, he's a quiet boy. He don't like to do much.' "

Todd started going out with a girl, so Mike shifted his friendship to Rory. "Then," Rory said, "Mike used to visit my home almost every day, taking me out of the house . . . 'Mom, Rory is always home. He must be sick or something.' Little by little he started to take me out."

After they started frequenting Mike's hangouts around Albany and Catskill, Rory wondered whether Mike might not be his cup of tea. "Being wild," said Rory, "that was Mike . . . wild! The word around places like September's and The Playroom was 'Don't mess with Mike. . . . Don't you dare fuck with Mike Tyson.'

" 'Who's this fucking guy?' I started to ask myself. I was seein' him every day and I was afraid of him, nothin' that he did, it was just his image. But he was very nice to me. I stopped listening to the bullshit and we became very close."

Although he didn't have a license, Mike frequently borrowed an old car from a neighbor. He would find Rory and throw the car keys on his lap and say, "Let's go." They they would hang out in clubs and bars, places where people under eighteen were not allowed. Mike was just sixteen. "The Playroom," said Rory, "they were real strict with the age limit there, but Mike was so big they would never ask his age. And we would hang out there and Mike would drink beer. He loved to drink beer. Then, he would be wild. When he gets a drink, he starts talking loud . . . and he talks shit to the girls. Like, 'Hey, baby. Hey, come here.' And then they didn't wanna talk to him. Some would call him 'big head' or 'fat boy.' I remember one girl saying to him, 'You stink.' And Mike would get upset. He would say, 'I'll kick all your asses. One day when I'm champ, I'll get you!' "

Rory said Mike would befriend almost anyone. "Guys got close to Mike and Mike would get vulnerable," Rory said. "Mike would let them come in his car and drive around with them. Many times that happened 'cause if he came for me and I was not around, then he would just pick somebody else to hang out with. These guys were no good; they was into negative things . . . into drugs and crack."

Rory said this disturbed him and he became more protective of Mike. "I would go to Mike," Rory said, "and say, 'Mike you can't, you just can't do that . . .' I was like Mike's overseer. 'Mike, those guys are assholes. You can be their friends but don't hang out with them . . . keep away from them.' "

As Rory spoke to me of his most frightening moment with Mike, his eyes and body language communicated the strength of the bond that exists between them. One night he and Mike had dates with two girls and Mike got "wasted" on beer.

"I'll never forget that night," Rory said. "Mike got real drunk and I tried to put him in his car so I could bring him to my house. He's pulling on me, hitting on me, saying, 'Don't bring me home, motherfucker. Don't you bring me home, motherfucker. I'll kick your fucking ass.' I helped him get into the car and we just rode for a while. But then he remembered the girls and said, 'We gotta go out and get the girls.'

"I stopped for a red light and he got out of the car and I

started to chase him around the car. 'Come on, Mike,' I'm begging him. And he's running around the car saying, 'Fuck you, motherfucker, you are not taking me home.' So he ran toward a grocery store and there were some girls and he starts chasing them inside the store. The owner, a lady, told him to calm down or get out. You know what Mike said to her: 'One day, I'll buy this motherfucking place.' Then I bought a hot chocolate, you know, to sober him up a little, and put it on the dashboard. Finally I got him into the car and when I pulled out, the hot chocolate fell right on his lap and he didn't even wake up . . . he was so drunk!"

Mike's demons were pulling on him and he never seemed to try to free himself from their grasp. Still he dreamed big dreams.

" 'Just me and you, man,' " Rory remembered Mike's saying about their future together. " 'I'm going to be rich someday and we won't have to take shit from nobody.' This was before Mike's first professional fight. It was a cold January day and there was a blizzard. And we used to go to this place and rent this old car. This guy let us get the same car dirt cheap. I think their regular charge was a hundred per week and he would let me have it for half that."

The car had no floor mats and there were big holes in it. "But it had a rusted tape deck that we thought was cool," Rory said. Mike liked to prop his feet up on the dashboard. "The car was a piece of shit," said Rory. "It was not worth a fucking dime." But the jalopy never failed them.

One January day Mike decided to drive with Rory to work, a forty- or fifty-minute ride.

"So, we're going to my job," said Rory, "and it was a blizzard out there and snow coming up through the bottom of the car, hitting Mike in the face, and Mike said, 'Man, there gotta be a better way.' And I said, 'Hell, yeah, man!' Then he said, 'Don't worry, come next year at this time we're gonna have Roll-Royces, we gonna have limousines and all that.' I said, 'Mike, shut the fuck up. I'm freezing my ass off.' And sure enough, a year later everything Mike said came through. And I used to get into fights back home because I was the only one who believed in him. Everyone else said his arms was too short and I said, 'Fuck you, man, Mike is gonna be champion.' "

He was right.

7

UNLIKE most fight people, Cus D'Amato did not subscribe to the notion that sex and boxing are incompatible. D'Amato taught his fighters that objectivity, impersonality, coldness, and detachment are essential to a professional boxer. If occasional "relief" can foster those attitudes, so much the better.

In 1962, five years into my professional career, when I was training for a fight with Al Hauser, Cus told me that he was surprised that I had not seen my wife in camp. "Joe, how come I haven't seen Ramona?" he asked. "Is this place too ugly for her to visit?" I was taken aback and as I struggled to make sense of what he'd just said, he added, "She can come on Friday and leave on Sunday."

Two minutes later I was on the telephone telling my wife to drop everything and come up to camp "tomorrow, Friday, and come early in the morning." I tried not to sound too excited. "Cus suggested it," I added.

So Ramona came to my training camp the next morning, and to our delight Cus told her to return the next few weekends—an invitation she accepted with mock hesitation. Maybe it was just modesty.

Soon there was a new addition to my training schedule: ten rounds of sparring every Sunday, a change I welcomed but thought somewhat peculiar. Every Sunday, though, I looked significantly better.

One morning, three days before the fight, Cus asked me casually about my mental condition, the upcoming fight, and whether I'd been happy with my training. I told him that everything was under control. Then he asked, "Have you noticed anything different in you?"

"Well," I answered, "I guess I'm improving each day."

"You've improved in the last three weeks beyond all bounds," he said happily. In the fight I knocked out Al Hauser in less than three rounds.

By 1984 Mike Tyson had accepted Cus's baseball bat to keep girls away from him, but he wasn't making use of it. Women by the bunch, some more beautiful than others, some black, some Hispanic, some white, had begun stampeding in his direction. He was barely eighteen, had a name and money, and was able and willing. When I saw him, Mike seemed cool about his new macho-man image. He talked a good game.

"They're all chasing me because of my fame and because they think I've got lots of money," he said more than a few times. "They feel important being with me." At the same time, Mike would sneak off to Times Square and to Brownsville, his old haunts. It was as if he had to measure his progress by returning to his grim past.

"I'll tell you something," he said to me after I accused him of going to a house of ill repute in Manhattan. "I've never been in a whorehouse."

"But I thought you once told me that—"

"I have never been inside a whorehouse."

"But remember when you told me—"

"I have never gone to a whorehouse!"

I believed him because he had told me worse things about himself. Besides, every time he walked around those four corners of ropes, poles, and canvas under the steaming lights he was the classic gladiator. He fought his heart out and always emerged victorious. Such magnificence could excuse a lot.

This was the year of the XXIII Olympiad in Los Angeles, and those who'd followed Tyson's ring career thought the boy would be a sure gold medal winner. Cus wanted him in the super-heavyweight division. He felt Tyson was too fast and punched too hard for the big fighters in that weight class. But the United States Olympic Boxing Committee had other ideas. Tyrell Biggs was eventually seeded in the Olympic trials in the super-heavyweight class and Tyson entered as a heavyweight. D'Amato blamed the state of affairs on Committee official Bob Surkheim, with whom he'd had a long-running feud. But there was nothing to be done about it.

D'Amato's fears seemed justified by events. At the trials held in Forth Worth, Texas, to select the U.S. Olympic boxing team, Tyson lost a disputed decision to Henry Tillman. I saw the film a few days later and thought Mike had won the bout. Tyson's professional style had not impressed the judges, however, who scored the fight by amateur rules that equate a glancing jab with a thunderous hook. Tillman fought like the amateur he was. Tyson pressed the action, trying to take Tillman out, but Tillman just moved away, flicking an occasional left jab that did no damage but scored points.

"That's okay," Cus told a depressed Tyson in the dressing room after the fight, which at that point had been the most important match of his life. "You'll get another chance at the son of a bitch. You're still going to represent this country in the Olympics."

"But I already lost," Tyson said. "I already lost."

"You'll be there to avenge that armed robbery you were

victim of the first time," Cus responded. "Next time you won't need the judges; only a referee who can count to ten."

The "next time" Cus was talking about referred to a new gimmick devised by the United States Olympic Committee to give Olympic boxing more television exposure. Instead of a one-fight-and-you're-out format, the elimination format was two of three. In the upcoming "Olympic Box-Offs" Tyson needed to score two consecutive wins over Tillman if he was to represent his country in Los Angeles.

Several weeks later, at the Caesars Palace Sports Complex in Las Vegas, Nevada, Tyson faced Tillman again. Before the fight I told Mike to forget about trying to trick or outsmart Tillman. "Just walk in and throw punches. Lots of punches," I said. "You're in tip-top shape."

At the end of the Box-Offs there were four upsets: four fighters who had lost at the trials had redeemed themselves. They now had to defeat their opponents one more time. Three did, including Evander Holyfield, who lost in the trials to James Womack but defeated him twice in the Box-Offs.

Many thought Tyson had also redeemed himself, including myself, but not the judges. Mike chased Tillman around the ring, hitting him with jabs and an assortment of other punches while getting tapped with a few inoffensive jabs in return. It was a dull fight, but I thought Mike had won all three rounds and I jumped in the ring to tell him so. "This one cannot be stolen," I said. "This time you kicked his ass every minute."

When the announcer told the world that the judges disagreed with me, I began to share Cus's belief that something was not on the up-and-up.

Pat Nappi, the head U.S. Olympic boxing coach, a friend and my first boxing teacher, came to me. "Between you and me," he said earnestly, "you know that I prefer Tyson to Tillman. Mike is more exciting, and I'm sure no one could resist his punching power. But Tillman understands the amateur rules and style better than Tyson." He added that from the "amateur point of view," Tillman had beaten Tyson. Tillman went on to win the gold medal at Los Angeles.

Following his elimination, Tyson was angry and gloomy, but his bad mood didn't last long. He befriended Israel Acosta, a featherweight from Milwaukee who had lost a disputed decision at the Box-Offs to eventual Olympic champion Paul Gonzalez. As an act of goodwill, the Olympic Committee designated both Tyson and Acosta alternates. So they remained in Las Vegas as guests of the Committee. If the fighters who had defeated them were unable to compete, they would take their places.

While in Las Vegas, they began frequenting a discotheque called Chi-Chi's in the downtown area. By the second day Tyson had become the most popular man in the disco—with the women, at least.

"Tyson was a ladies' man," said Rose Trentmont, a current New York State Athletic Commissioner who at the time was assistant to the United States Olympic Boxing Committee. "I went a couple of times with them to Chi-Chi's, and Tyson had girls around him like hungry mosquitoes."

When Tyson got back to New York, his managerial triumvirate, D'Amato, Jacobs, and Cayton, presented him with a new Cadillac Seville with a white body and a navy-blue top. It was the teenager's first car, and he eventually smashed it up. Mike was a fighter, not a driver, and was more interested in the women the car might help him attract than watching the road.

At about this time Jim Jacobs commented on Mike's new attitude toward women, which he thought natural and to be expected. Activities and dinners with Tyson now always included women, whose faces were rarely the same. None of them were contenders for a serious relationship. With all the talk about AIDS and other diseases, I thought I should warn Mike about the price he could pay for his promiscuity. I tried to scare him, just a little.

"If you want to avoid an abominable death," I told him, "don't go to bed with girls you don't know."

Mike seemed to believe, though, that freewheeling sex conferred adult status. With his new car, he felt he had the freedom to come and go as he pleased. He was a man now and no longer needed strict supervision. Tyson started telling Cus he was going to spend his weekends in Brooklyn. Instead, he would hang out with his childhood friends and then return a week or two later. Near the end of 1984, Mike left on a Friday and told Cus he would be in the gym on Monday. He stayed away for an entire week.

"This is it," Cus said. "He has to make a decision about what he wants to do with his life."

When Mike finally came home, he tried to con Cus by exaggerating his usual baby-voice excuses about his sister and her problems. Cus cut him short.

"You've got to make up your mind as to what you wanna do with your life. If you wanna be a fighter then you listen to me. That's the only way. You can never become the fighter I want you to be unless you do as I say. If you want me to help you in other things then speak up, I'll help you. But you can't keep doing these disappearing acts anymore. I will not tolerate them."

Then he unloaded a real bombshell.

"Next time you leave here without permission," Cus said, "you just stay wherever you go. I wouldn't want you back. I'll give you a couple of days to think about it."

When I spoke to Camille in October 1988, she remembered that confrontation "as if it was today."

"Mike would not wait," she said. "He told Cus right away that he wanted to be champion of the world. 'I went back to my friends,'" Camille quoted Mike as telling Cus, "'and I saw them and I decided that's not the type of life I wanna live. I wanna fight and go to the top.'"

By the spring of 1985, Tyson already had his first professional match under his belt and his managerial triumvirate was quietly working to develop their fighter into a bigger phenomenon than even Jack Johnson, Joe Louis, or Muhammad Ali. It was easy to understand why this managerial team worked so well:

• No one understood the technique and politics of boxing better than Cus D'Amato. Even the mob could not intimidate him. Cus bucked and fought the mob with all his might. In fact, several mobsters were jailed after a probe by the United States Senate that had partly been instigated by D'Amato. "Even the mob," said the late Dick Young, "respected Cus for that. He beat them fair and square."

• Nearly forty years before he met Tyson, Bill Cayton had been dealing with boxing's entrepreneurial fat cats. His boxing connection started in 1947 when as president of Cayton's Advertising Company he decided his main account, a hair-tonic company, needed a new television commercial. Anticipating the success of sports on television, he evaluated all the team sports—baseball, hockey, football, and basketball—and realized there was a problem. "They looked like midgets in the small television screens," he said, alluding to the five-inch screens that were the norm at the time.

"Then I saw a boxing show and it looked like the perfect match," Bill told me many years later. Soon, in 1948, the famous "Greatest Fights of the Century" was born. The show's popularity caused Cayton to comb film libraries around the world, buying up film rights to classic bouts. Because of the nature of his business, Bill struck deals with some of the same people who, a decade later, would become D'Amato's sworn enemies.

• Jim Jacobs was the son of a California businessman. Instead of participating in his father's many productive ventures, he decided to become a collector. He started with comic books and once owned more than 800,000. But his interest would later turn to fight films. Jacobs met D'Amato first and then Cayton, with whom he formed a business in 1960.

By the time they became Tyson's comanagers, Jacobs and Cayton owned more than 17,000 fight films, including every one involving the members of the Madison Square Garden Hall of Fame.

These three experts, whose skills and experience embraced nearly every aspect of boxing, put together a list of fighters whom Mike would confront on his trek to the top. They'd already set up Mike's second and third matches and were making a long list of future opponents. The heavyweight division traditionally suffers from a lack of quality fighters, and D'Amato, Jacobs, and Cayton were trying to find boxers whose styles would offer valuable experience for their fighter.

Keeping Mike busy was of prime importance. The more he fought and won, the more he wanted to fight. But in order to maintain the momentum, the right opposition had to be found.

On April 10, 1985, Trent Singleton, a fighter with a poor record but an impressive physique was coolly waiting to fight the relatively unknown Tyson. He would be Tyson's second opponent. I had visited Singleton, wished him good luck, and told him, as I tell all boxers, to protect himself.

Tyson, tense and anxious, was not too far away in his own dressing room, throwing punches at an invisible opponent. He was trying to put into practice D'Amato's teachings: relaxation, emotional control.

"I don't have to tell you," I told Mike as he paced the large dressing room he was sharing with a few other fighters, "that the feeling of wishing to be somewhere else at this moment is normal. The other bastard in the next dressing room is as much or more afraid than you." Mike, his head down, never looked up; his face remained expressionless. "You know this, but I must remind you that if you didn't have those feelings I would tell Cus that you're a dumb, crazy kid not worth keeping."

No response. "Are you listening?" I asked.

"Uh-huh."

"At least you're not shaking like I always did," I said.

Before my first professional fight I couldn't control the trembling of my hands or the butterflies in my stomach. I remember my teeth chattering so loudly that my opponent, Gene Hamilton, who was standing next to me, asked if I was cold. I gave him a nervous laugh for an answer because I had noticed that *his* stomach was quivering out of control. I couldn't control my own trembling, but I felt my energy level increasing as the fight approached.

"Just try to relax," I said now. "And when you walk in, don't forget to keep your hands up, your chin down, and punch always in combination."

Tyson nodded a couple of times and then I told him to stand up and show me. He did, and I thought he was loose enough. I said, "Now, you're ready to search and destroy." He managed a spiritless smile.

Minutes later, as referee Sid Rubenstein gave the usual instructions in the center of the ring, Mike stared at the canvas, biting down on his mouthpiece. Fifty-two seconds after that, Rubenstein made Tyson stop punching. The referee had probably prevented Singleton's brains from being scrambled. The fight was suddenly over and Tyson was a happy, beaming teenager. He looked at me as if he was surprised with the ease of his triumph. Rubenstein's instructions had taken longer than the fight itself.

Six weeks later, on a hot May night, Mike returned to the Empire Plaza Convention Center in Albany for a six-round bout with Don Halpin, a run-of-the-mill journeyman who realized after a few seconds that about all he could do with Tyson was fight to survive. Halpin was what is known in the boxing business as "an opponent" whose only purpose in the ring is to concentrate on not getting hit too solidly. But Tyson connected to Halpin's jaw and Halpin hit the deck for the full count in the fourth round. Tyson had never fought more than three rounds but felt comfortable after this match.

As his reputation and confidence increased, the fights became easier. Many of his opponents gave up before fight time. You could see the horror in their faces as they stepped through the ropes. That worried me. I felt that the easy victories might lull Tyson into a false sense of security. In boxing, that is dangerous. And there was still so much to be done. Mike, only nineteen, was not yet making the big money. Jacobs and Cayton were bankrolling most of the promotions, which involved Rooney in the main event and Mike on the top of the undercard.

Names like Mercedes, Singleton, Halpin, Spain, Alderson, Sims, Canady, and Johnson raised no heads among boxing experts as their owners fell like dominoes before Tyson's punching power. But when twenty-seven-year-old Donnie Long was mentioned as a Tyson opponent, boxing ears perked up and sportswriters started to speculate. They considered Long the first true test for the up-and-coming youngster. Teddy Brenner, Madison Square Garden matchmaker for many years and the boxing mind behind promoter Bob Arum, was one of the many who felt D'Amato had probably moved a little too fast matching Mike against Long. Although it was true that Long had failed to beat any major leaguer in the heavyweight division, he was a fine boxer who'd garnered twelve victories in fifteen bouts, scoring ten knockouts in the process. Two of the losses had been against top contenders James Broad and John Tate, neither of whom could put him down. In fact, Donnie was a mature enough boxer to provide the nine-fight Tyson with a few headaches.

When the bell for round one rang at the Trump Plaza Hotel's ring in Atlantic City on October 9, 1985, Tyson simply rushed toward Long with the confidence of a future champion. He connected with the first left hook he threw and Long, a look of surprise on his face, went down. As the referee counted to eight, Long's pride forced him to his feet. He was painfully aware that this was not his night, that he did not belong in the ring with Tyson. And before he could sort his thoughts, Tyson was in front of him launching the heavy artillery. Long went down twice more before referee Frank Cappuccino stopped the one-sided match. The fight lasted a minute and twenty-eight seconds.

C US D'Amato had not been feeling well for some time, something I had noticed when the New York State Athletic Commission (NYSAC) held a three-day (September 27–29) boxing symposium at the Stevensville Country Club in Swan Lake. Boxing people from thirty-five states and Canada took part. As part of the program, D'Amato, my mentor and former manager, was being honored for his lifetime devotion to the sweet science. "How much money," I asked, "do you think Cus D'Amato made of the one million dollars I earned in my eleven-year career?" People shouted out various numbers, the lowest being $50,000. They were all wrong. D'Amato had not touched a single penny of the money I earned as a boxer, a revelation that brought a collective sigh from the audience.

Then Cus got up to speak. He couldn't stay long on the podium. His breathing was difficult, and after a few words my wife and my sister-in-law took him to his room. The old man refused to get in bed and paced from one end of the room to the other, attempting deep breaths and complaining of chest pain.

"I'll be all right," he said. "Go ahead and have a good time."

A few days later, Jim Jacobs learned that Cus's condition had worsened. The old man had no use for hospitals, and it took Jacobs, Jay Bright, and Camille to persuade him to go to one. It was a struggle, but he finally agreed to go to the Albany Medical Center where he was treated first for asthma and then bronchial pneumonia. He had been given a room that Jay Bright referred to as "the worst hospital room I have ever seen in my life.

"It was a mop closet that had been converted into a hospital room," Bright said. "It was truly a shame to see Cus there." When word got to Jacobs about the room, he came to the hospital in a stretch limousine and drove Cus to Mount Sinai Hospital in New York City. At Mount Sinai, the diagnosis changed from bronchial pneumonia to interstitial pneumonia, a more serious ailment that involves the hardening of the lungs. His condition did not improve. I went to see him every day and his deterioration was obvious.

On October 31, 1985, my wife and my brother went to his room while I parked the car. By the time I got upstairs in the hospital, Cus had been transferred to the intensive care unit. He had tubes in his nose and intravenous tubes stuck in his arms. When he saw me, he raised his head and I saw his eyes were filled with fear.

"My boy," he said as he grabbed my hand. There was a minute of silence that seemed to last forever. "My boy," he began again in a raspy, barely audible voice, "yesterday I thought that was it. I just couldn't breath and I said to myself, 'Old man, this is it.' I'm surprised to be alive today, Joe." I told him not to talk.

"You know," I said, "Mike should be making you very proud. That kid is you. He is the fighter you envisioned, the perfect machine you were looking for." Cus smiled, his expression telling me that his job on this earth had been finished.

"That kid took care of Donnie Long and Robert Colay, each in one round like they were nothing, and tomorrow he'll demolish Sterling Benjamin the same way."

On November 4, 1985, Cus D'Amato died of interstitial pneumonia. A few hours after Cus's death, I went to see Jacobs at his apartment on Second Avenue in mid-Manhattan. When he opened the door, neither one of us could utter a single word; we embraced and cried. Then Jacobs, his wife, promoter Mickey Duff, who had an apartment in the same building, and I went to dinner at a nearby restaurant. At the table we reminisced about Cus. "I liked the story in *Sports Illustrated*," said Duff, "when Cus was asked about Bob Arum and he said, 'Arum is the worst man in the Western Hemisphere, and if he lived in the Eastern Hemisphere, he would be the worst there, too.' And then, when the writer said, 'I guess Arum is his own worst enemy,' Cus said, 'Oh, no. Not as long as I am alive.' "

I talked about the time Don King's boxing operation had come under a massive attack by the news media and Cus chose to blast Arum. "And how do you compare Mr. Arum with Mr. King?" he was asked.

"Well," Cus answered, "I have not dealt with Don King yet. But I assure you one thing: God cannot make the same mistake twice."

Jacobs's most vivid memory was of a time Cus attended a fight at Madison Square Garden. "We were crossing the street," Jacobs recalled, "when a young beggar came straight toward me and demanded a couple of bucks. Cus stepped in between me and the man and told him, 'You are not getting anything. Keep walking.' Cus then proceeded to take me by the arm and we just kept going."

Jacobs told Cus, "We could've had serious trouble for nothing, Cus. I would have given the man the two dollars and prevented any problem."

"Oh, don't worry, Jim," Cus responded, "I was just bluffing; I had no intention of hurting the guy."

Jacobs had broken the news of Cus's imminent death to Tyson as gently as possible. "It didn't help," he said. "Mike was devastated."

"I was in Cayton's office," Tyson recalled, "and Jimmy said, 'Mike, I have bad news. They don't think Cus is going to make it through the night and I have to arrange the whole thing for the funeral.' I couldn't take it. I ran outside. I didn't want no one to see me cry. I just went crazy and took a subway to Brooklyn. I knew he was going to die, but one can never tell, you know, miracles happen."

The next day a friend of Tyson's heard about D'Amato's death on the radio. "They saw me in the street," Mike said, "and said, 'I have bad news; they say Cus is dead.' I said, 'I know.' "

A few days later, Mike was asking himself, "What am I going to do? I should take care of Camille . . . make sure she is all right. They don't have no money. So much responsibility. I felt real bad, but Cus told me that if anything happened to him I should depend on Jimmy [Jacobs]."

Jacobs was concerned that Mike might be too upset for his fight with Eddie Richardson, which was scheduled for November 13, nine days after D'Amato's death. "We can call it off and reschedule it as easy as drinking a soda," Jacobs told Mike.

"Do you think Cus would want it that way?" Mike asked.

"I don't think so. He wouldn't want anything to interfere with your career, not even his death."

"I feel the same way."

"It's up to you."

When the press interviewed him, Tyson was prepared. "The only way I could make Cus proud of me is by becoming champion of the world," he told the writers. "Nothing should interfere with that. I'm going to fight in a week and am going to fight better."

A few days later, Cus was buried in Catskill not far from the house he loved so much. I delivered the eulogy to a multitude of Cus's friends, speaking through my tears about how much Cus had helped young fighters and how the only thing he really wanted in return was saving young lives. The three most successful fighters he developed—Floyd Patterson, Mike Tyson, and myself—and Rooney, Jacobs, Bright, and Tom Patti, a light-heavyweight in Cus's stable, were the pallbearers.

Tyson, now nineteen, was truly desolate. "You know," he said to me in tears, "I really feel like taking my own life. If I really had any real guts, I would just kill myself. That's the way I feel. But I have no fucking heart."

"You know deep down that you have to realize what Cus set out for you to do," I tried to console him. "You have to work hard, and I promise you in two to three years Cus will come to you again. He wants to see Mike the champion."

He leaned on my shoulders and cried. "Did you ever see Cus cry?" I asked.

Mike nodded his head.

"When?" I asked.

"When Joe Louis died," he said, wiping his eyes with his shirtsleeves, "and last week when he felt he was not going to make it and might not be able to marry Camille as he planned."

After the funeral Mike went home to rest. He had to travel to Texas in a day or two. On November 13, 1985, he stopped Eddie Richardson in the first round. The first time the six-foot-six Richardson did not move his jaw fast enough from one of Mike's lethal left hooks, he was hit and his body went down—hard. When he got up eight seconds later, another left hook was patiently waiting for him and finished the job, one minute and seventeen seconds into the first round.

A memorial for D'Amato was held in the old Gramercy Gym in Manhattan six days later. "We should celebrate Cus," Jacobs suggested. "It should be a memorial to make people happy . . . about what Cus was able to accomplish . . . all his generous achievements in behalf of the young. All that should be celebrated, and now is the time."

Floyd Patterson, whom Cus helped put into the record books, was conspicuously absent. A previous engagement, he said, "prevents me from attending." But Pete Hamill, Gay Talese, Norman Mailer, and Budd Schulberg were there, and so were Dick Young, Bob Lypsite, Georgie Colon, Simon Ramos, Joe Shaw, Nelson Cuevas, and dozens of others, famous and not so famous, who were touched by Cus. We ate and drank and cried and laughed, bonded together by our love for an old man.

That day Mike sat quietly next to Camille and Jay Bright until he spotted a tall, slender girl—a friend and neighbor of my older brother's family, who lived in Brooklyn. She thought Mike was "cute." And he wasted no time setting up a date with her. She was a teenager who believed in serious relationships and was genuinely impressed with the undefeated boxer's growing fame. She began seeing Mike between fights and eventually sex became a part of their relationship. She was taciturn about her friendship, except with my wife, to whom she confided that Mike would show up unannounced at her home in Brooklyn, say he was hungry, and soon her mother would whip up a colossal Spanish meal that he would wolf down as if he had just ended a two-week hunger strike.

It was hard for Tyson to spend much time with her. He was fighting every two weeks or so and had little time for a normal social life. But somehow he found time for this pretty Puerto Rican girl from Brooklyn. With Cus and his counsel gone, no one could predict what Mike would do with fame, fortune, and women. For the time being, though, the priority was boxing.

Mike's training was now being carefully supervised by Kevin Rooney and Matt Baransky, who found themselves trying to measure the effect of Cus's death on their charge. Nine days after the Richardson fight, at the Colonie Coliseum in Latham, New York, Tyson disposed of Conroy Nelson in about three-and-a-half minutes. If you asked his opponents, Tyson was unstoppable. But a few boxing writers, whose expertise often seemed to be based on an obligation to be clever, were still skeptical.

From December 6, 1985, through February 16, 1986, Tyson traveled from New York City to Latham to Albany to Atlantic City to Troy, New York, for a scheduled 144 minutes of boxing, one eight-round and four ten-round fights. But the fans only saw Tyson for about thirty-nine minutes, barely thirteen rounds of action.

The fight on February 16, 1986, against Jesse Ferguson established Tyson as a true drawing power. No other boxer, with the exception of champions like Marvin Hagler, Sugar Ray Leonard, and "Macho" Camacho could spark the same enthusiasm. The 12,000-seat R.P.I. Houston Field House in Troy was filled to capacity. It was Mike's first exposure on national television. And the crowd behaved just like the wild fight fans of yesteryear. No one could hear the announcer call out Ferguson's name. It was drowned out by deafening boos. And it was almost as hard to hear Tyson's name because of the cheers.

In the first round, Tyson rushed Ferguson and was greeted by a cool pro who knew what he was doing. Tyson missed with a jab and a right cross and got hit with a jab in return. Mike walked in again. Ferguson just waited for him. There were a few inside exchanges. Both fighters felt comfortable in close. Mike was forced to think because Ferguson was countering every time Tyson missed a punch. Suddenly, Mike threw a right-hook-to-the-ribs-right-uppercut-to-the-chin combination. Ferguson went down and remained there for the obligatory eight count. From that point on the fight was not the same. His confidence buoyed by the knockdown, Mike chased Jesse around the ring. Every time they came close, Ferguson would hold Tyson with all his might, making it difficult for referee Luis Rivera to separate them. Rivera warned Ferguson several times. After struggling to untangle Jesse's hands from Tyson's arms in the sixth round, he turned toward the judges and crisscrossed his hands vigorously, signaling Ferguson's disqualification. The audience roared in approval, and Tyson loved it.

In the postfight press conference Tyson was asked about the vicious uppercut that floored Ferguson in the first round. "Well," Mike said, "I was trying to push his nose bone up to his brains."

By then, Jacobs, Cayton, and Rooney knew that the teenager from Brooklyn had reached boxing adulthood. Tyson's busy boxing schedule had escalated the level of his competition. Now, he had to fight legitimate contenders, and if he really had the right stuff, the time had come to prove it. He was on the road of no return—make-or-break time.

THE scarcity of good heavyweights and the resulting probability of a mismatch whenever Tyson was in the ring scared most boxing commissioners to no end, myself included. As commissioner, I'd asked Peter Della, NYSAC's supervisor of officials, to assign only the best referees to Tyson's matches. I also told Dr. Frank Folk, our chief physician, to watch Tyson's rivals closely and not to hesitate to stop any match when in doubt. I've always thought it preferable to stop a bout too soon rather than too late.

Several days before his death, Cus and I discussed what would be a major problem for Tyson during the early part of his career. Basically, the teenager was much too powerful, smart, and sharp for heavyweights who matched his limited experience, but he could be very vulnerable to guys with know-how and seasoning. Before he stepped in the ring with this higher class of opponent, he would have to be exposed to a wide variety of boxing styles, but in a manner that allowed him to correct his weaknesses without incurring risk. The problem, therefore, was finding "ideal opponents" who were limited enough to represent a probable "W" in Mike's win column, but skilled enough to expand Mike's repertoire— opponents who wouldn't be defeated so convincingly that Mike would be catapulted to the next level. Finding and securing these ideal opponents often boiled down to politics— back-room game playing. Sometimes, though, the politics carried over to the ring itself.

That had been brought home to me dramatically years earlier when I'd fought top middleweight contender Al Andrews on the undercard of the Floyd Patterson–Ingemar Johansson match at Yankee Stadium. There'd been rumors that Andrews was way over the hill and that he wasn't skilled enough to fight a young boxer like me. I was concerned with Andrews's boxing experience and trained extra hard to get my body and mind in tip-top condition.

When the bell rang for the first round, I moved in with care and threw a fast left jab that landed flush on his mouth. Then I moved to the side, and a punch he threw passed two feet away from my face. I threw a left-jab-right-cross combination and both punches hit their target; I bent at the waist immediately after landing and his return punch passed way over my head. I hit him with such ease that I thought he was playing possum. But when I hit him with a left hook to the body and heard him shriek, I knew he was not deceiving me. He was a boxer on his way out, ready to leave the business that had given him some distinction.

When I went to my corner after the first round, my trainer, Joey Fariello, acting on Cus D'Amato's instructions, told me not to show my superiority over Andrews and ordered me to hit him on the arms and gloves and to miss some punches deliberately. "Just practice," my trainer said. I followed the instructions but did such a lousy job that even some in the crowd booed. So I moved around and flicked left jabs aimed at Andrews's forehead, and surprisingly, the veteran boxer was incapable of escaping them.

Next came the real shocker.

"Let him hit you a couple of times," Joey told me between rounds four and five. "We have to justify your counter that will finally put him away." I finally did so in the sixth round. The plan worked fine and apparently fooled many people. I learned later that such strategy was designed as a "political move" to make boxing regulators think that I was not yet ready to move up the skill ladder. Cus wanted more fights for me but against fighters of similar ability. "I want you to confront every possible trouble there might be in the ring by fighting all sorts of styles," he told me. "That's what experience is all about."

It was March 1986, not June 1959, Cus was not around and Tyson was not Torres. Mike was an explosive young man who understood that boxing yielded up too many surprises for anyone to take unnecessary risks. His philosophy was: the sooner Mike leaves the ring intact, the better; if there are politics involved, then let the comanagers deal with it. *His* job was to dispose of the bodies in the ring.

As it turned out, Jacobs and Cayton had been able to hold off the procession of "ideal opponents" for one more fight that promised a respectable payday and not much work. Mike's nemesis would be a fighter named Steve Zouski, and the bout would be part of a pay-television doubleheader that featured the Marvelous Marvin Hagler–John "the Beast" Mugabi world middleweight title bout. Although the Hagler-Mugabi fight was being staged in Las Vegas, Nevada, and the Tyson-Zouski bout at the Nassau Coliseum in Uniondale, Long Island, the television audience, supposedly tuning in to watch the championship fight, would be enhanced significantly in New York, where Tyson had become boxing's biggest attraction.

Tyson had trouble sleeping the night before this bout, and

at five o'clock in the morning he asked his assistant, Steve Lott, if he could go to the gym and do some training. Steve in turn asked Rooney, who thought it was a great idea.

"So we went to the gym at six," Steve recalled, "on the morning of the fight, and Mike loosened up a bit, went on the bike for about twenty minutes, did some calisthenics, shadow-boxed for a while, and then jumped rope."

That night, as was his habit, Tyson jumped at his opponent, forcing him to use his hands and legs as defensive tools rather than weapons. The first and second rounds followed the same pattern: Tyson chasing, Zouski backing up and then grabbing until the referee separated them. Now and then, Zouski would throw desperate punches and one or two would graze Mike's face, delighting the few Zouski fans at the Coliseum. Then, during the third round, as Zouski tried to formulate an effective attack, Tyson threw a few soft right hooks to Zouski's hanging left ribs and with the same hand, launched two powerful uppercuts, following through with a vicious left hook. Zouski's large frame collapsed over his inanimate feet. As Mike walked to a neutral corner—his white trunks with red stripes spotted with his opponent's blood—Arthur Mercante, one of the sport's best referees, completed his ten-second count. Zouski had expired with eleven seconds remaining in the third round.

This was to be the last time Tyson would fight someone at this level. Jacobs and Cayton knew that the degree of competition would have to go up several notches, but not so much, of course, as to constitute a grave danger to their fighter.

Tyson had fought nineteen times in the past twelve months, many times twice a month and sometimes more frequently, knocking out most of his adversaries in the first round. Now he would face the first of his "ideal opponents," James "Quick" Tillis, who would also become Tyson's first formidable rival.

In this fight, both boxers were looking to advance their ratings, although Tyson was the main attraction, the hot item.

His reputation was overwhelming and that meant good business. So the fight had been scheduled to take place in Tyson's backyard—the Civic Center, in Glens Falls, New York.

People came by the busload and Glens Falls transformed itself into a huge carnival. The theme was the Tyson fight, and every one of the mostly white faces was rooting for their favorite son. Quick Tillis became public enemy No. 1. This was Tysonland. And when the two fighters entered the ring to settle things, the electrified atmosphere at the arena brought memories of the old noisy, brawling club fights in New York City in the 1940s, 1950s, and 1960s, a time when fans were divided into neighborhood or ethnic factions and extra cops were always needed.

Quick Tillis was definitely not from this neighborhood, and the fans, their faces beet-red, booed him with real venom. Some of them appeared to want to jump into the ring to take on Tyson's opponent themselves. At 215½ pounds, Tyson—dressed in black shoes, black trunks, no socks, and no robe—looked fit. But he was aware that Tillis had a reputation for being wily in the ring, and consequently, he was on guard.

At the sound of the first bell there was a solemn silence. The fans were very much aware that Tyson had a habit of dispatching his adversaries in a matter of seconds, and they expected him to score a knockout in the first round.

After the first two minutes of the fight, with Tillis evading Mike's punches skillfully and throwing some leather of his own, punches that at times made contact with Tyson's face and body, the fans began chanting, "First round! Come on, Mike. One! One! One!" And then the bell sounded to end the first round and the crowd sighed in disappointment.

I couldn't hear what Tyson said to Rooney, but his eyes and expression showed concern. Mike had connected with some of his best shots, and Tillis had taken them without batting an eye. Obviously, Mike would have to work harder —much harder. And most important, he couldn't allow his emotions to get the best of him. This was probably the first time in his short career that he'd have to appeal to the various psychological switches Cus had installed in his head.

As the fight continued, Quick Tillis maintained a consistency in moves, punches, and attitude, and at times, he even outpunched Mike in the in-fighting. For the first time in twenty bouts, Tyson had lost more than one round. But at the sound of the last bell, though some were displeased by Tyson's performance, everyone knew that the teenager had prevailed. A few boxing writers, notably Mike Katz and Wally Matthews, still groused that Tyson was a myth invented by Cus, Jacobs, and Cayton, but they didn't find much support.

Seventeen days later, Don King Productions and Madison Square Garden were copromoting Tyson against Mitchell Green, a six-foot-five-inch hulk who was managed by Don King's son, Carl. It was the first fight in which Tyson would make a substantial amount of money. Home Box Office (HBO) was bankrolling this match and two more Tyson bouts to the tune of half a million each. As a matter of fact, HBO was paying Tyson directly, the first television-to-fighter transaction in boxing history. The only stipulation was that Mike had to fight one of the three or four contenders from any of the bonafide international organizations.

I'd seen Mitch Green in action some years back. If there was a heavyweight in 1980–82 with real potential to challenge for the top, it was this giant of a man. I hadn't watched him fight recently but had heard about his troubles with the law and wondered if perhaps he was one of those prospects too wild to be tamed. In any case, Green was a fighter who scared me. Cus had been dead for six months, but I was trying to connect with him in my thoughts and learn what would he think of a Mitch Green–Mike Tyson fight. Then I remembered the day Cus conceded to me he wasn't perfect and was liable to make mistakes.

"I think," he had said, "that I know of another person who would probably make less mistakes than me in boxing at this stage of my life . . . Jimmy Jacobs."

"If I was not absolutely convinced that Mike is going to take care of Green with ease," Jacobs told me seriously, "I wouldn't have made the match." For my part, I thought Mike was ready to fight the best in his division, even those with higher ratings than Green. But still, something about Green's size and tenacity worried me.

The morning of May 20, 1986, was hot and humid, and the Tyson-Green weigh-in was being held in the ring of Madison Square Garden rather than at the usual small room at the New York State Athletic Commission. The venue gave promise of high drama—or at least more drama than usual—and consequently, a large contingent of press was on hand.

As NYSAC chairman, I purposely kept myself a safe distance from both fighters. I was a friend of Tyson's and an acquaintance of Green's. Since Tyson was big news and whatever he did was good copy, there were some sportswriters who weren't above making something of my closeness to him if the opportunity presented itself. That's one reason why, whenever Tyson fought in New York, I always prayed for a knockout. A close fight going Tyson's way might have provided a field day for the press.

It looked as if the press would have its field day anyway when, just before stepping onto the scale, Green, in the company of his mother, claimed to have just discovered that he was only getting $50,000 for that evening's bout while Tyson was guaranteed half a million. He argued that the disparity was unfair. And the fact that Green's manager, Carl King, was the adoptive son of the promoter and seemed to have no clear explanation for the disparity added to the controversy.

I was forced to join the melee when Green began shouting insults and threats against the two Kings and said he wasn't going to show up for the fight.

I told Green that he would have to honor his contract. The agreement had been signed some time ago, I pointed out, and Mitch had known the numbers long before the weigh-in. It took another heated argument between Carl King and Green to resolve the matter, but by now it was no secret in the boxing world that the Kings were rooting against their own man, maybe even hoping he'd get knocked out.

That night Madison Square Garden was not filled to capacity, but the crowd was excited and noisy. With Muhammad Ali out of the limelight and Larry Holmes lacking the charisma and aura of a superchampion, boxing fans were hoping to witness the birth of a new era. They'd missed those special moments that could only be produced by the likes of Jack Johnson, Jack Dempsey, Joe Louis, Rocky Marciano, and Muhammad Ali.

Holmes, a formidable champion, failed to achieve legendary status because he'd followed Ali to the throne. Holmes suffered from "the Ezzard Charles syndrome." (Charles, one of the greatest boxers of his time, followed Joe Louis and his overpowering popularity. Consequently, he never achieved the recognition he deserved.) Another problem Holmes faced in his time was the resurgence of the various international boxing organizations. The organizations' refusal to consolidate their rankings resulted in at least three different "champions" in each weight class, devaluing the worth of any one title.

The night of the Tyson-Green encounter, my older brother, Andresito, was more nervous than usual. He had gone to the Gramercy gym, where Mike had trained the past week, and had noticed that Mike was "unnaturally scared."

"I would be too," I said.

Andresito, whose opinion Tyson respected, told me that Mike had asked him whether he'd looked okay in sparring. "Did I make any big mistakes?" Mike asked him.

"You're not busy enough inside," my brother told him. "You've become too lazy in the in-fighting." Mike nodded thanks. The next day Tyson tried to fight inside more and was much more active. Again he solicited opinions on his gym work.

The night of the fight I visited both dressing rooms. Mike was quietly sitting in a chair. He was tense and I didn't want him or anybody else to think that the commission would give him special treatment. So I told him, "No one can guarantee you just and fair treatment better than I can. But if you want to win, no one but you must do it." Then I lowered my head and whispered in his ear, "But I'm sure you can and will. Good luck." I shook his hand and he winked at me.

In the other dressing room I told Green that there was only one way he would carry some weight in this business. "And that is by winning fights," I said. "You beat Tyson and you'll get lots of attention . . . and money." I also wished him luck and shook his hand. He had a nonchalant attitude and seemed unafraid. To be honest, I hoped my impression was wrong. A fearless person had no chance against Tyson. No one could take gratuitous chances with him and survive. Against Tyson a boxer needed the protection of fear.

When referee Luis Rivera called the fighters to the center of the ring, Mike appeared to be angry. His upper lip was contracted and his mouthpiece was covered with saliva foam. He was breathing hard through his nose. Across from Tyson, Green was not timid either. He was moving around and moving his lips, trying to unnerve Tyson with insults.

The first punch was thrown by Mike, who, like most D'Amato fighters, would try to catch his opponent cold, unprepared for a quick, hard blow. Cus had taught that most heavyweights draw confidence from their size rather than talent: at heart they're just big bullies. Tyson was hoping Green fit that profile.

But Mitch was moving smartly, and remembering how able and efficient he'd been in the past, I worried that Mike could find himself in a very tough fight. Eventually it became clear that Tyson had decided to throw bombs until one of them hit the bull's-eye. But at the end of ten rounds Mitch was still there, and Mike had failed to knock out his second rival in a row.

Tyson detractors were quick to tsk-tsk over the fact that Mike had permitted Green, and before that Tillis, to finish on his feet. They were so exultant at seeing their low opinion of Tyson confirmed that they failed to notice that Mike's vast superiority had prevented either fight from being close.

MIKE badly needed to relax so that before—and during—his fights he could achieve that state of mind Ernest Hemingway called "grace under pressure." The obvious solution was a confidence-building fight that would restore his belief in himself, and for that reason I encouraged Jim Jacobs to "get Marvis Frazier." I told him: "He has an incredible name, but he's also made to order for our style." By "our style" I meant the so-called peekaboo appearance Cus's fighters projected by carrying both hands high with the gloves resting over the cheekbones and moving, blocking, and punching from that position. "He wouldn't go over two to three rounds with Mike" was my belief.

Though Frazier wouldn't be slotted in immediately, perhaps that conversation was what convinced Jim to match Mike against three "fair" but unknown fighters. He needed to build up Mike's confidence and he chose the summer months of 1986 to do it. Of the three boxers scheduled to fight

Mike—Reggie Gross, William Hosea, and Lorenzo Boyd—I was most concerned with Gross. I had seen him in a vicious battle in Pennsylvania against a boxer named Jimmy Clark just a few months before D'Amato's death and was so impressed with both fighters that I urged the old man to keep an eye on them and put them on his list of possible opponents for Mike.

The first of this not-too-dangerous series of bouts would pit Tyson against Gross on June 13, 1986, at Madison Square Garden. When I told Jim about my chat with Cus regarding Gross, he smiled.

"As a matter of fact, every single fight we've selected for Mike is from a list given to us by Cus; he thought that by now Gross would be just right for Mike."

Mike entered the ring to thunderous applause that in itself had to revitalize his confidence. Some sportswriters had begun reporting that Tyson's unconventional boxing gear—no socks, no robe, black shoes, black trunks—was some sort of ghetto superstition. After Rooney put his arms around Mike's immense shoulders and whispered final instructions in his ear, he planted a big Irish kiss on his fighter's mouth. Was this something new in the mystical world of prizefighters?

Tyson walked menacingly toward Gross and opened up with a barrage of swift and powerful punches that forced his opponent into a defensive shell. Some of the punches found the intended target, mainly the ones to the body, but there was no indication that Gross was ready to sign off. Mike persisted with his cannonball shots until Gross returned one of his own—a piercing right uppercut that landed flush under Mike's jaw. The crowd let go a collective murmur as if they'd shared the pain. It did not diminish Mike's relentlessness. He kept up his attack, and as Gross connected with another uppercut, Mike let go a left hook to the jaw. Gross's legs folded under him. Referee Johnny LoBianco started to count and Gross looked up with sad eyes as if to announce that he'd had enough. But his pride got him to his feet. Tyson did not wait;

another left hook was already on its way toward Gross, who did not see it coming. The punch exploded on his right temple, sending him back to the dusty canvas, his coordination gone for the night. A look at the fighter's eyes prevented LoBianco from starting the count, and he signaled instead the end of the fight. Tyson was the victor by a technical knockout (TKO). The match was only two minutes and thirty-six seconds old.

Two weeks later, William Hosea, a rough-looking boxer from somewhere out west, came to Troy's R.P.I. Houston Field House to challenge Tyson. Two minutes into the first round, Hosea was on the soft floor, holding on to his right side, screaming with pain. He tried to say something, but nothing came out of his mouth. Referee Harry Papacharalambous made clear motions with his hands that the fight was over.

Fifteen minutes later, Hosea, his pain somewhat subdued, said a few words to the media. His breathing still heavy, he said, "I was hit with a sledgehammer." He held his right side, his face full of sweat. "The bastard hits like a sledgehammer."

Two weeks later on July 11, 1986, Tyson was back in a boxing ring. The venue was the Stevensville Country Club, Swan Lake, New York, and the fight was billed—privately, of course—as "a preparation match" for Tyson. His rival was Lorenzo Boyd, a youngster—just like Tyson—with a decent record but with no experience. Boyd's manager didn't deserve a medal for accepting this bout.

It had been labeled a "preparation match" by Jacobs and Cayton because an important fight had just been negotiated for Mike. On July 26, 1986, his opponent was going to be a youngster from a tough boxing town named Philadelphia with a legendary last name: Frazier . . . Marvis Frazier.

"So you wouldn't bother us anymore with Marvis, we made the match," Jacobs told me jokingly. "If anything happens to Mike, nobody but you is to be blamed."

Stevensville, because of its limited capacity, was the perfect spot for a tune-up fight. Also, since it was located in Tysonland, the crowd was highly partisan. For those who preferred lengthy bouts it was fortunate Mike was not up for this fight. He was probably fighting Boyd with his fists and Frazier in the back of his mind. The battle actually lasted four minutes and forty-three seconds. It was the second-longest time Sid Rubenstein had had to work in the seven Tyson fights he'd refereed.

To say that I would be a disinterested observer of the upcoming Tyson-Frazier fight because of my position as chief of boxing in New York would be a falsehood. Tyson had slept in my house and was loved by my family as if he were a relative. We always wanted him to win. Everyone in the boxing business was aware of our friendship. However, as far as I knew, no member of the boxing community had ever doubted my honesty and integrity regarding Tyson's matches. Thus, when Papa Joe Frazier made public remarks criticizing my friendship with Mike, I called him to the side. "The one who should be concerned about my relationship with Mike is Mike himself," I told him. "My officials are human beings and just by nature they would bend over backwards to be objective. That may affect Mike much more than his opponents. So, don't worry."

The former heavyweight champion of the world smiled and walked away. A few days later, however, he repeated his concern publicly. This time when the press approached me with the question, I was a little angry.

"Mike Tyson," I said, "needs help from no one. And much less against Marvis Frazier."

This fight would be in the heart of Tysonland: the Civic Center in Glens Falls where Mike had lost his perfect knockout record after nineteen straight KOs about twelve weeks before. The referee would be Joe Cortez, one of the top referees I'd asked Peter Della to designate for Tyson's fights. Meanwhile, because of Joe Frazier's comments about my closeness to Mike, I decided to stay away from the boxers as much as possible. Still, just before the match, I visited both dressing rooms and wished each fighter good luck. I must admit that

I reminded Mike about his need to keep cool. "Don't you get excited," I said. "Keep your mind clear at all times and the rest will come automatically."

Mike nodded and gave me the thumbs-up sign. He was concentrating fully, a sure sign he'd matured. "Oh, God," I reassured him, "are you looking good." I went out and told Jacobs I had not seen his fighter in a better boxing disposition. For this fight, Steve Lott, an assistant trainer, had gotten hold of two patches displaying the colors of the American flag— one with the letters "Go America," the other "USA"—and sewed them on the front of Tyson's trunks.

As we waited for the opening bell, I thought of all the misfortunes good fighters had been subjected to by one punch; the sure winners whose one foolish mistake had gotten them knocked out. I hoped Mike was not having these same thoughts. I stared at him from my first-row seat, studying his eyes, and concluded he couldn't be readier. As Cortez repeated what the boxers already knew in the middle of the ring, Mike's legs moved in anticipation. His belly, just like Marvis's, was trembling involuntarily. Marvis had his father next to him, staring insults at Tyson while massaging his fighter's back. And then the fighters walked back to their corners and we heard the first stroke of the bell.

By the time Joe Frazier ushered himself into a position where he could shout instructions at his son, Tyson had backed Marvis into a corner and was throwing nasty bombs from every angle. The crowd, anticipating the inevitable, rose to their feet. As Marvis looked for refuge in his own corner, close to Pops, Tyson dispatched a murderous right uppercut that landed perfectly on his opponent's jaw. Marvis's superb condition kept him on his feet, but though his limbs and body maintained a semblance of consciousness, his eyes indicated a lack of brain function. Tyson, sharp as a laser beam, threw a five-punch combination. Three caught the falling body of his rival, and Cortez rushed in to prevent Frazier from being unnecessarily injured. The fans went crazy, their demand for a first-rounder fulfilled. Marvis Frazier had been pounded so soundly that the referee did not have to give the ten count. Instead, Cortez called the fight doctor into the ring as Marvis struggled to regain consciousness. While still in the ring just after the knockout, Cortez told me he'd never seen a greater puncher than Tyson in all his years in boxing.

Immediately after the postfight press conference, Tyson called his sister, Denise. "He was very happy," she recalled. "The first thing he said was, 'Did you see how fast I got rid of this guy? It was funny how his father, Joe, stood next to him during the instructions, looking at me like he wanted to hit me. I thought he was going to take a swing at me.' Then we laughed." Denise said Mike told her he would probably be fighting for the championship soon. "He said it made him scared to think about fighting for a world's title."

Three weeks later, Mike was at Trump Plaza Hotel in Atlantic City, preparing to take another step toward the heaviest of all crowns in the sports world. His opponent was José "Niño" Ribalta, not a great threat, but good enough to expose flaws in any fighter. Niño, not the easiest man to hit cleanly, was the type of awkward boxer that could make any boxer look awful. And in fact, there were a few rounds in the fight that Tyson's detractors loved. Mike missed punches like an amateur, some of the sportswriters claimed. But when he connected, he connected solidly—no less so in the tenth round, when Niño put his jaw in the way of one of Tyson's right-uppercut-left-hook combinations and dropped to the canvas. He went down twice more, forcing the third man in the ring, referee Rudy Battle, to stop the match and declare Tyson the winner by TKO—at one minute and thirty-seven seconds of the last round.

The third bout in the deal HBO had struck with Tyson would be in Las Vegas against Alfonso Ratliff, a six-foot-five-inch giant. This time Don King was involved in the promotion but not on the most favorable terms. He would get a fixed fee, instead of a percentage. While Tyson and his crew had been busy in the East, Don King, ever searching for huge profits, had formed a partnership with pal Butch Lewis, which he'd dubbed "The Dynamic Duo," and in conjuntion with the Las Vegas Hilton Hotel and Home Box Office he was promoting something called "The Heavyweight Unification Tourna-ment." In effect, Don would get all the international boxing organizations together and induce their respective heavy-weight champions to be part of an elimination contest; the one left standing would become the "Undisputed Heavy-weight Champion of the World." This was the appropriate answer to the grim confusion the general public had about the multitude of champions. It made lots of sense, although I'd been truly distressed to see that for some mysterious reason Tyson had not been included.

But to the surprise of many boxing fans, King agreed to embrace the Tyson-Ratliff match as part of the "Unification Tournament." Since he was classified as the No. 1 challenger by the WBA, Tyson was a rightful and deserving contestant. But Tyson's sudden good fortune was not due to King's good heart. The promoter already had an elimination match set for the Las Vegas Hilton between WBA heavyweight champion Michael Spinks and Norwegian Steffen Tangstad, the Euro-pean heavyweight champ. The trouble was that the advance sale for that fight amounted to only a few thousand dollars— a situation that augured financial catastrophe. Tyson was the best ticket in *any* town. One can only imagine Seth Abraham of HBO and the two Johns—Giovenco and Fitzgerald—of the Las Vegas Hilton, putting pressure on Don to change things around.

Once Tyson's name was added to the program, sales went through the roof, making King and everyone involved in the promotion cheerful. King also realized that without Mike Ty-son, the death of the "Unification Tournament" was almost guaranteed, so he needed little prodding to get Tyson involved.

It was Tyson's first professional appearance in Las Vegas, and King and Lewis had said in private that Mike's next fight, "if he beats Ratliff," would be against Trevor Berbick for the WBC crown. I knew right then that this kid so close to my heart was going to be the youngest heavyweight champion in boxing history. Mike called me at the Hilton to say that in just weeks he was going to fight for the title. I didn't want Mike to have added pressure on him. And yet as the professional he was becoming, he should be concerned not just with defeating Ratliff but with looking sensational and exciting in the process. I felt that to do that he couldn't afford to fight two bouts at once in his mind—against Ratliff *and* Berbick.

"Just think about Alfonso Ratliff and forget about any other fight," I told him. "Take this guy out first, then we talk about the next one."

Increasingly attentive and watchful as the fight drew near, Tyson rehearsed moves and punches with me in flawless fashion. How in hell he was able to be so calm was beyond me. "Man," I told him a couple of days before the Ratliff fight, "you are a much better liar than I ever was. You can hide that anxiety and fear much better than I could ever do." Mike would give me only a very deceptive smile.

As I was to learn later, on the very first day Mike trained at the Johnny Tocco's Ringside Gym in Las Vegas, the boy seemed surly and uncomfortable, the pressure of being in a different environment getting to him. No one had noticed that the new pugilistic sensation was there with his crew, so the place was deserted. As it turned out, it was for the best since there were no outsiders to witness the anguish that overtook Mike during that first day of sparring. At the close of the session, Rooney and Tyson, as they always did, walked together into the dressing room and suddenly Mile spoke.

"I wanna go home," he declared. "I don't like this place here. We are packing today." Kevin was shocked. Unable to say a word he went to Steve Lott and gave him the bad news.

"I started to walk into the dressing room," said Lott, "and I'm thinking, 'My God, what would Jim or Bill say to Mike in a position like this?' I gotta do whatever they would do, shit!" As he walked into Mike's dressing room, Tyson was just getting out of the shower. Steve spoke first.

"Mike, how you doing?" Tyson didn't say a word. This was followed by a second gambit. "How ya feeling?"

"I don't like it here," Tyson said. "I wanna go home."

"Why?" Lott asked.

"I just don't like it in here." Tyson stood up. "Let's go home."

"Mike, this is normal. Sit down for a second. You think that coming to Las Vegas is like going to prison, but that's not true. It's a reward. Don't you think that everything Cus told you has come true—that you'd become an exciting fighter, that you'd become a great fighter?"

"Yes."

"Well, now you are bearing the fruit of all that. You've been rewarded with the luxury of coming to Las Vegas and fighting before this large audience. How do you think Spinks feels knowing that he had an advance ticket sale of only eighty dollars and when they added your name on the marquee outside the hotel they sold nine thousand dollars' worth of tickets in two days? Isn't that a credit to what you and Cus have done?"

"Yes."

"This is a reward. Fighters go their whole life praying and hoping to be invited to Las Vegas to fight before a world audience and exhibit their skills, but they are never asked. And here you are, twenty years old . . . the entire world is saying, 'We love to see you. We want you.' And because everything you've got is so exciting, they want to see it.

"Besides," Lott continued, "you fought in the most famous boxing arena in the world: Madison Square Garden; and you went to Atlantic City and to Houston, Texas, and you had nothing but tremendous success in those places. You've already faced the pressure and the turmoil and you overcame. Did you do that before?"

"Yes."

"You just have to do it again. Particularly with this guy. You know that as soon as you hit him he's gonna go."

"Yeah, I know," Mike said. "That's not the problem. It's the place, the moment . . . the circumstances."

"Let's see how you feel in a couple of days," Lott said. "Can you give it a chance?"

"Yeah," Tyson answered, "I can do that."

"Great," Steve said, his insides ready to burst.

In the early evening of September 6, 1986, in the privacy of his dressing room, minutes before fight time, Mike Tyson, as usual, soaked his entire body in Aboline, a heavy moisturizing cream—and started to put on his jock strap and protective cup. It was then that Lott noticed the boy was having some difficulty pinning a dime-size, metal Jewish charm to the tongue of his left boxing shoe. "What are you trying to do?" Steve asked.

"Just trying to put this thing in here," Tyson replied. Lott took the charm and pinned it to Mike's shoe. It was a lucky emblem that became part of the all-black, no-socks, no-robe boxing uniform Mike would wear for every fight.

A few minutes later, the floodlights above the boxing ring at the Las Vegas Hilton shone on referee David Pearl, Alfonso Ratliff, Mike Tyson, and the boxers' cornermen. Pearl repeated some of the rules that most boxers hear wherever they fight. Then the bell sounded and Tyson marched forward. His intimidating steps were followed by even more intimidating punches that established his bad intentions. Ratliff quickly decided that the possibility of victory was too remote to take stupid chances and that the best route to take was the practical one. Let's survive, Ratliff figured. Tyson, for his part, did not want to put on a boring performance and give the media more ammunition to use against him. At the same time, he wasn't willing to risk the opportunity of his life.

Mike put extra pressure on the tall man. Instead of chasing him as most boxers do with a moving opponent, Tyson cut the ring short by moving in the same direction as his opponent moved and then moving in quickly with brutal combinations. It didn't take long. A left hook put Ratliff down for the eight count. A second later he was up and Tyson was next to him with another swift left hook combined with a right cross that sent Alfonso down again. Pearl took a fast look at Ratliff's eyes and stopped the match at once.

Mike Gerard Tyson had secured his opportunity to fight for the world's heavyweight championship in only eleven weeks.

He was twenty years old.

11

ON November 15, 1986, seven days before the biggest match of Mike Gerard Tyson's life, the WBC world heavyweight championship against titleholder Trevor Berbick, I went to see Tyson train at the Johnny Tocco's Ringside Gym in Las Vegas. When he saw me, he jumped with genuine happiness and hugged me. He'd been under a lot of prefight pressure, championship tension, and had been driving Rooney and Lott up the wall. They were staying with Tyson at a house in Vegas's Spanish Oaks section, a mile from the Strip. It was owned by Dr. Bruce Handelman, a member of the D'Amato-Cayton-Jacobs extended family. Tyson had been uncooperative and contrary and prone to wild mood changes. At the gym he tormented assistant trainer Matt Baransky, who stayed at the hotel to manage Tyson's army of sparring partners: James Broad, Mike Williams, Oscar Holman, Walter Santemore, Mike Jameson, and Licous Kirkley.

Tyson was sparring that day, and Jacobs wanted my opinion. Actually, watching Tyson spar was like seeing him in competition. He had no mercy for these men, whose main function was to help him stay sharp and in shape. Their job was thankless. It was in gymnasiums, I'd learned long ago, that fighters get their noses flattened, their faces cut, and their bodies worn. Tyson pounded his sparring partners as if he were a soldier caught behind enemy lines and they were the enemy bent on killing him. These six men were receiving the equivalent of combat pay for their one-sided wars, $1,000 a week. Broad was paid $1,500.

Tyson was like a tiger and looked real sharp, I told Jacobs. The one habit that concerned me was Mike's tendency to stay in close, holding on, an imperfection that could be easily remedied by Rooney. After the workout Mike and I decided to walk from the gym to the Las Vegas Hilton, two or three miles away. I didn't want to offer Mike any advice in public—especially in front of Rooney, who knew Tyson's strengths and weaknesses better than anyone. I'd seen a few other mistakes and mentioned them to Mike as we walked to the hotel. He said very little. At times we would stop while I illustrated some technical point.

Then he changed the conversation to what had become his favorite topic: women.

"You know something," he said, "I like to hurt women when I make love to them." He stopped, searching my face for a reaction. But there was none. "I like to hear them scream with pain, to see them bleed," he said as he put his right arm around me. "It gives me pleasure."

"Why?"

"I don't know."

"You mean to tell me that you don't have any idea why you do that to women?"

Mike shook his head.

"You want me to believe that you always thought this was just natural behavior? You're full of shit."

"José, I am that way and I don't know why."

"Well," I said, "did it ever occur to you that men who behave that way probably hate women; that deep down they simply don't like them?"

"You may be right. You're the first person to tell me that. . . . You know, you may be fucking right. Holy fucking shit!"

We'd almost reached the hotel. Tyson grabbed me by the arm and told me to stop walking. He wanted to talk in the open air where it would be harder to overhear, where he could yell and curse. It didn't matter to him that in the street passersby would stop to salute him and motorists would blow their horns. Cus D'Amato had been dead a little more than a year, and Tyson seemed to miss their long rap sessions. He was a young man who wanted to understand affection, passion, lovemaking. Most of his short life had been steeped in violence, dedicated to doling out pain, and he wanted to learn and hear more about the other side of himself. Playing psychologist was not one of my favorite pastimes, but I tried.

"Let's go back to the shit about me not liking women," he said as we leaned against a pillar. "You're the first person who probably hit it right on the head."

I made one last effort to change the subject, but he persisted. "Come on, man, expand on that shit."

"I'm no fucking psychologist," I said, "but I may say something you wouldn't like at all."

"Speak up."

"Some men who dislike women at an unconscious level," I said, "could be considered latent homosexuals."

"What the fuck is that?" He was smiling and probably had an idea of what that meant.

"A state of homosexuality that may never manifest itself overtly."

"Explain that. I don't get it."

"A fag by implication, not by actual acts of homosexuality. . . . If you are a latent homosexual, you will keep making love and hurting girls. And you may hate them, but you may never engage in lovemaking with a man."

There was a blank expression on his face, but he nodded as if he finally understood what I was saying. A photographer materialized out of the dry desert air. Tyson and I posed for some pictures and then went up to my room in the hotel.

Inside, he forced a tight-lipped smile and moved his head as if he was trying to say something but couldn't think of the right words. "Hey, man," he said finally, "if you only knew."

I told him to tell me what was on his mind. "If you don't tell me, I may imagine anything."

"Like what?"

"Like, you are a homosexual."

He laughed hard and gave me a brotherly punch in the chest, then kissed me on the cheek.

"Girls, pussy, butts, women's butts," he said, "that's what I like."

He wanted to tell me something else but didn't. It turned out he was being treated for gonorrhea that he'd probably contracted in Vegas. This kid could have almost any woman he wanted, but he preferred to take risks with strangers.

A few days before, he'd been in his car inside a car wash with Lott and pulled down his pants. "Look at this," he said, revealing patches of dried pus on the front of his underwear.

Lott, hiding his concern, told him not to worry. "It's not that serious," he told Tyson. But back at the hotel, Lott rushed to his room and telephoned Jacobs.

"We have a small problem," Steve told him. "Mike seems to have an infection." After getting the details, Jacobs told Lott to take Tyson to the fighter's personal physician—immediately.

So a week before the fight, Tyson had needle punctures in his buttocks and antibiotics in his blood. I'd fought many times with penicillin in my system, mostly because of colds brought on by prefight pressures. I related my own experiences to him.

"Mike," I said, "you're just recovering from a serious eardrum infection that was treated with antibiotics. Too much of that shit could do you harm. Do you feel strong?"

"Chegui," he said to me, using my nickname almost sarcastically, "nothing and nobody is going to stop me from winning this fucking fight. I refuse, I refuse. The doctor said it would make me weak and I say he's full of shit 'cause I want that title so bad. There is no way I would give up that title."

"That's not the point."

"That's the only point."

"Yes, but when you—"

"*When*," he interrupted, "they raise my hand in the ring as the youngest heavyweight champion of the world, all of yous are going to be very proud of me. That's the fucking point, my friend."

Who could dispute that? Cus's spirit was with him, and I felt it would do more harm than good to argue the point further. After all, there was a rightness to what he was saying. In effect, he'd been quoting Cus's mind-over-matter theories. I took a long, hard look at Tyson and I saw Cus. His head and face somehow seemed to resemble Cus's, and there were similarities in the way the two walked and talked. It was not a mystical transfiguration. Cus and Mike were so close in body and soul that Tyson had adopted some of his mentor's physical peculiarities.

November 22, 1986, arrived too fast. It was the twenty-third anniversary of President John F. Kennedy's assassination, and most of the country was commemorating it with solemnity and sadness. But in this self-involved land of entertainment, gambling, and prostitution, it was all Tyson and WBC champion Trevor Berbick. The memories of Kennedy, Lee Harvey Oswald, and Jack Ruby did nothing to diminish the hoopla.

Mike had gotten up that morning somewhat restless. As usual, he'd eaten some fruit for breakfast and had gone back to bed, leaving the television on and videotape movie cassettes all over the floor. When I arrived in the afternoon, he was in the living room chatting with Lott. He was quiet and in a no-nonsense mood. The war of nerves was on. I took him out on the back porch and showed him some basic moves and punches I didn't want him to forget that night. He started to relax. At 3:30 P.M. Steve cooked some spaghetti that Mike ate with a large New York–cut sirloin steak from a nearby res-taurant. Before he sat down to eat we embraced, and I assured him he had nothing to worry about.

Jacobs had called Lott from his suite at the Hilton just about the same time Tyson sat down to eat and told Lott not to forget to be at the hotel by 6 P.M.

"Don't worry," Steve said. "I'll be there just before six." Tyson went straight to bed and in a few minutes was fast asleep.

At five-thirty Lott started to pack. All of a sudden Tyson woke up hungry. "Steve," Tyson yelled, stretching his arms and making an animal noise, "I'm hungry. Make me some dinner." Lott ran into the kitchen and put more spaghetti on to boil and continued to pack.

"I couldn't say, 'Hey, Mike, your manager wants you at the arena in fifteen minutes. I can't cook now, it will take too long,' " Lott recalled later. "Neither could I call Jim and say, 'Boss, Mike wants to eat now, what should I do?' "

His instincts went with Tyson. Lott continued packing, periodically going back to the kitchen and fixing the food, which Tyson wolfed down. "We got there just a few minutes late," Lott said, "and nobody said anything except for some stares from Jacobs."

Mills Lane was the referee that night—good news for Mike, given his fighting style. Lane was a complete referee, a professional who allowed boxers to fight inside as long as there was some action. He understood, like most good referees, that the boxing fan paid to be entertained. Accordingly, when a bout became dull and boring, Mills demanded activity. That night's boxing crew—the fight doctor, the inspectors, the judges—was, in fact, as efficient as any I'd seen. And I'd always thought that Sig Rogish was one of the most knowledgeable boxing commissioners in the business. Rogish, who two years later would work hard to elect Bush president, was a conscientious overseer who skilfully blended political savvy with boxing knowledge.

I was talking with Rogish when the bell sounded. Tyson walked toward Berbick, his gloves snug against his cheeks, his torso in perpetual motion first to one side, then to the other, then down. Each movement was perfectly choreographed. Jabs jutted out with the force of Mack-truck pistons between Tyson's moves. Berbick moved and missed, in succession, a couple jabs, a left hook, and a right cross. Then he was hit with a stiff left jab that snapped his neck back. In only a few seconds Tyson was solidly established as the man in charge. I rushed over to Jacobs and embraced him in celebration. "It won't go past three," I told him. He put his right arm around me in acknowledgment, but his eyes were fixed on the ring. He wanted to see what I'd seen. "Mike is the new champ," I screamed.

Just before the bell, Tyson landed a right hand to the forehead that stunned Berbick. When Tyson sat down after the round ended, he and his crew—Rooney, Lott, and Baransky— knew the fight was not going to last long. They were all trying to be nonchalant but couldn't. The heavyweight championship was in reach, right under their noses.

The second round started not much differently from the first, and Tyson, perceiving the inevitable, marched in with relentless jabs, constantly moving his head to avoid being hit by a stray punch. Berbick knew what was about to happen, but he tried not to make it too easy for the challenger. He threw a fast, desperate jab, stepped to the side, and came in with a five-punch combination. Tyson, extremely relaxed and controlled, saw every punch and moved out of danger, bobbing and weaving in synch with each stroke. After the futile combination,

Berbick's eyes were glazed with shock, broadcasting distress. Tyson forced the issue. Berbick went inside and bent his waist forward as if bowing. Tyson loosed a deceptive left hook that landed on Berbick's right temple, and the champion dropped to the canvas. As Lane started the count, Trevor attempted to straighten up but was caught in a torturous conflict between body and mind. Berbick's 230 pounds zigzagged from one side of the ring to another. He fell twice more, got up, and was prevented from falling out of the ring by the ropes. Berbick's last dance as champion had the look of a death rattle. Lane chased Berbick around and held the big heavyweight still, telling him it was over, that he was no longer champion.

I jumped into the ring, and Tyson was talking to himself. "I can't believe this, man. I'm the fucking champion of the world at twenty," he was saying. "Shit, the champion of the world at twenty. This fucking shit is unreal. Champion of the world at twenty. I'm a kid, a fucking kid." Then he embraced his boxing family one by one.

I knew how he felt, overcome with joy, happy beyond belief, stuck between tears and laughter. Back in 1965 when I knocked out Willie Pastrano to become the light-heavyweight champion of the world, the first Hispanic to capture a heavy division, I jumped aimlessly around the ring like a chicken with his head cut off, screaming at the top of my lungs.

Minutes later came the official announcement from Chuck Null, who said: "The winner by a TKO in two minutes and thirty-five seconds of the second round, and the new WBC heavyweight champion of the world . . . Mike Tyson."

For me, the announcement was anticlimactic, but that didn't diminish my enthusiasm. This happy ending—a ghetto kid having his destiny and fortune forever changed by the wonderful, magical world of boxing—was almost a cliché, but as I stood outside the ropes everything about it seemed unique, special, wondrous. I'd witnessed a moment in history that had been foretold back in New York, and I felt very much a part of it.

* * *

While his managers set themselves to the task of negotiating his financial future, Mike began capitalizing on his championship in another direction. As champion, his circle of female friends quickly expanded. The girl from Brooklyn was still there, but she had become "one of them," her demotion, she felt, due to her low social level as compared with that of most of the women Mike was now seeing.

His next match in the Unification Tournament would take place March 7, 1987, fifteen weeks after the Berbick fight, the largest gap between fights he'd so far experienced. That much free time can be dangerous for any twenty-year-old, especially for a well-to-do young heavyweight champion.

It was during this hiatus that Mike told me about the night he and his friend Rory Holloway had gone to bed with twenty-four women somewhere near Philadelphia. He tried to elaborate, but I thought it was an invention of his imagination and changed the subject. Later, though, when Mike was married, I found myself interviewing him for this book in his bedroom. The tape recorder was running, Holloway was at his side, and Mike was dividing his attention between a movie called *Super Ninja* and me. I remembered his story about the twenty-four women and asked him about it.

"There were twenty-four," Mike confirmed. "We fucked those bitches in Pennsylvania."

Rory jumped up from the end of the bed and joined the conversation.

"They were whores," Rory said. "The first bunch of girls came and they were beautiful. Mike was in his room and I was sitting there with one girl. So I walk in the room, right? Mike had two bitches at one time in bed. He was fucking them. No shit, fucking both of them.

"He was fucking the bitch so hard that the bitch hit the wall and Mike said, 'I made the bitch faint! I made the bitch faint!' " Tyson was listening quietly, snatching glimpses at the television and nodding in agreement.

I turned toward Mike. "Did you have an orgasm with each one of them?"

"Yeah."

"You came twenty-four times in one night?"

"You know, after a couple of times, you just stay hard for a while, and—"

"He was fucking girls," Rory interjected, "like this . . . 'Come here, it's your turn,' fuck them . . . 'Now it's yours' . . . 'Next!' Then the girls would come to me and I would fuck them. We had the house full of bitches. We stayed all day long fucking, from five in the afternoon till one o'clock in the morning."

"How do you know," I asked Rory, "that your supermacho friend had an orgasm with every one of those women?"

"That," he said, "I cannot swear to. But I know he put his dick in every one of them. I was there and I know because I was a participant."

Rory said he invited one of the women to come back with him and Tyson to Albany. She accepted without hesitation. "That was the best-looking one of them all," Rory said. "Mike was driving and I was with her in the backseat, fucking her. And Mike said, 'Is it good? Is it good?' And I said, 'This shit is good, man.' Mike said, 'Pull over, pull over, man. Let me get back there.' "

"Then," Mike added, "I said, 'Naah.' "

"True," Rory agreed, "he said, 'Naah,' and then he said, 'Yeah, yeah. Why not?' " Rory said Mike pulled into a gas station to get the tank filled and more important, to change seats —Rory up front, Mike in the back.

"I was butt naked," Rory said, "and so was the girl. I just put a jacket over me and the guy from the gas station was trying to look inside the car. And I said, 'What the fuck are you looking at, motherfucker?' "

The trip home ended at September's, the club in Albany that had become one of Mike's favorite hangouts. "A friend came to us in the club," Rory said, "and asked, 'Where the fuck are you guys coming from, man?' We just laughed."

A T the beginning of the new year Tyson was back in camp, readying himself to defend his WBC title and acquire the WBA crown. He was scheduled to fight WBA king James "Bonecrusher" Smith on March 7, even though the gonococcus bacteria had reappeared like an old friend. His obvious unconcern about sexual dangers was disturbing. I'd begun worrying more and more that his promiscuity made him a perfect candidate for herpes or AIDS.

How could he be so perfectly relaxed and in total command in the ring and so out of control away from the four ropes? That question was asked repeatedly by his managers and friends. I decided to have another fatherly discussion with him. "Mike," I said, "as Cus would have said, your head downstairs is controlling the one upstairs. Shape up. You can die. You're taking too many chances."

The agenda for Smith was the same as it had been for Berbick: arrive at Handelman's house in Las Vegas four to five weeks before the fight, in the company of Rooney, Lott, and Baransky; train daily at noon at Tocco's Ringside Gym; trade punches with sparring partners Broad, Holman, Jameson, Santemore, and Williams (as well as Tyron Armstrong and Jesse Ferguson).

Tyson was not fond of Las Vegas; he complained of the "spiritless atmosphere" of the place. But he now knew that fighting in Vegas was a required part of the business and that he had to deal with it.

No other place in the world had hosted as many super-fights in the 1980s. This latter day Sodom near the Mojave Desert horrified many boxing purists who were convinced that the gambling casinos and the people who ran them would further tarnish the already tainted image of the sport. But there was no denying that the commercial possibilities Las Vegas offered were unmatched, even by its kid sister, Atlantic City, and so it continued to be the most popular big-fight venue.

When living with Tyson became unbearable for Rooney and Lott, Tyson's supposed hatred for Las Vegas took the blame for it. I showed up at Tocco's a week or so before the Smith fight and found Tyson to be warm, cordial, and attentive. Surprisingly, the one acting strange was Lott. Normally quite affable, Lott, then thirty-six, had become curt and dismissive. Puzzled by the metamorphosis, I asked, "What's eating you?"

Tyson's assistant didn't look me in the face. Finally he said, "Come and spend five weeks living with Mike, then you'll know what's wrong with me."

"What do you mean?"

"Mike, Kevin, and I come to Vegas five weeks in advance of a fight. During the first week of training Mike is fairly calm and relaxed. Then the trouble begins."

At that point, Lott told me, the prefight pressure starts to become unbearable for Tyson. "He becomes surly, mean, and difficult to deal with. He goes into some sort of isolation and then it's as if me and Kevin don't exist," Lott said. "When either one of us asks Mike to come have lunch or dinner, it's as if we're talking to the wall."

Mike's foul mood manifested itself at the gym as well, I learned.

Rooney would try to explain something technical to Tyson and the champ would simply ignore him and walk to another corner of the ring. Or Tyson would brush by Rooney, take his gloves off, throw them on the floor, take a shower, dress fast, and walk the few miles home without saying a word to anyone.

"When you people come to see Mike," Lott told me, "he's over the mood crisis. Now you, Bill, and Jim will get this delightful attention from him, while Kevin and I had to take all the bullshit."

There probably was much truth to what Lott was saying. By the time Jacobs, Cayton, and I arrived in Las Vegas, the bout was around the corner and Mike had resigned himself to the fight despite his inner turmoil. Some of his earlier moodiness may have been attributable to loneliness: Cus was dead, Rory and I were in New York. Some of it may have been more deep-seated, the manifestation of psychological traits that had become ingrained during his early life in the Brooklyn streets.

I know I wasn't impressed with what I saw in the gym. Tyson's inclination to get in close with his sparring partners and do nothing, allowing them to grab his arms and elbows and prevent him from punching, was becoming a sloppy habit. Despite Rooney's instructions, Mike remained practically inactive when in close. He obviously felt comfortable doing that, which was a bad sign.

I'd seen "Bonecrusher" Smith in action several times and had been impressed with his punching power. Fortunately, D'Amato's better fighters had the ability to prevent their opponents from landing "clean" punches. For that reason it came as some relief that Smith's best asset was his ability to hit hard.

When I visited Mike in his dressing room a few minutes

before the fight March 7, 1987, he seemed in control of his emotions. He got a pretty good "chiropractic" treatment on his neck from the chairman of the New York State Athletic Commission—me—and some basic advice. "Keep your hands up," I told him, "and chin down and punch in combination. One more thing: do not stay idle inside—punch, punch, punch."

Tyson changed the subject. "You know," he said, "I saw the most beautiful girl in the world on television . . . tall, elegant. Her name is Robin Givens."

"Another one?"

"Well, I haven't met her yet. . . ."

Had he finally learned a way to alleviate the tension? Why hadn't he mentioned her before, and why now? A few minutes later Tyson's name was called, we embraced for good luck, and in what seemed like seconds, the fight was on. . . .

One round, two rounds, three rounds—for twelve monotonous rounds the WBA champion and the WBC champion pushed and pulled at each other in a style that more closely resembled sumo wrestling than boxing. Though the booing wouldn't begin until the third round, the pattern was established in the first when Tyson charged Bonecrusher, only to throw his left arm around Smith as if they were dance partners. Smith, in no hurry, clamped his elbow down, locking Tyson's left glove in place, depriving Tyson of his left hand and making it difficult for him to get leverage into his right, which Mike was forced to use as a defensive shield. Tyson seemed too complacent with the situation. I figured he mustn't be in the mood tonight, that he'd decided to do just enough to win the match. Even so, it was frustrating to see two big, powerful men pushing and pulling while the small referee did most of the work, constantly separating them.

I was sitting just behind Smith's corner, right behind Carl King, who screamed instructions at his fighter. To my alarm, King was offering the correct coaching, shouting, "Please punch, just punch. Throw that right hand . . . straight." If

Smith had followed his manager's advice, my young friend could've been in some trouble. "Follow the jab with a right cross," King was yelling. "Come on, Jim, the straight right."

Rooney was annoyed. His coaching was being ignored, and he didn't like it. Tyson was showing the same laziness as in training. Smith had adopted the same tactics, realizing that although he couldn't hurt Tyson, it was equally difficult for Tyson to hurt him. I was convinced that Smith's disregard of King's instructions was deliberate.

Round twelve began just like the other eleven, but about fifteen seconds before the end Smith shot the punch King had been begging for all night. It caught Tyson between his eyes, causing his legs to buckle and momentarily disorienting him. Emboldened, Smith rushed toward Tyson to finish him. But Tyson's brief confusion had already dissipated and he opened up with a flurry of vicious punches that could possibly have stunned Smith. The crowd was on its feet as the bell sounded the fight's conclusion. With a unanimous decision, Tyson gained his second title in four months.

A few days after the Bonecrusher fight, Mike called John Horne, a thin, handsome actor he'd met in the Albany area. Horne was in California auditioning for parts.

"I want you to get me in touch with Robin Givens," Mike told him. "I wanna meet her." Horne called Givens's publicist, and in a day or two Mike had her telephone number.

But Mike's timing was a little off. He was scheduled to travel to England to promote a possible match against Frank Bruno that would tentatively be billed as the "Ten Million Pound Super-Fight" and be held at Wembley Stadium in London.

On his second day there, Mike discovered that the hotel where he was staying—the Grovesnor House Hotel—was hosting a major film-award ceremony. He suggested to Lott that they go downstairs and see the movie stars. They went

The Tyson team circa 1985. *From left to right:* Cus D'Amato, Kevin Rooney, Tyson, Bill Cayton, and Jim Jacobs. Four years later, D'Amato and Jacobs would be dead, Rooney would be banished, and Tyson would be calling Cayton "a horrible, wretched guy." *(Big Fights, Inc.)*

Camille Ewald, the mother figure Tyson often turned to during rough times, sees the champ off at the airport. *(Big Fights, Inc.)*

Cus D'Amato *(far left)* poses with, *from left to right,* Floyd Patterson, former world heavyweight champion; Mike Tyson, current world heavyweight champion; and the author, José Torres, former light-heavyweight champion. All three boxers were trained and managed by D'Amato. *(Big Fights, Inc.)*

Tyrell Biggs, a highly touted ex-Olympian, tenses up to receive a punishing blow from Tyson's right hand. *(Big Fights, Inc.)*

At a post-Biggs fight party, Mike and friend Rory Holloway discover the perks associated with being a top contender. *(Big Fights, Inc.)*

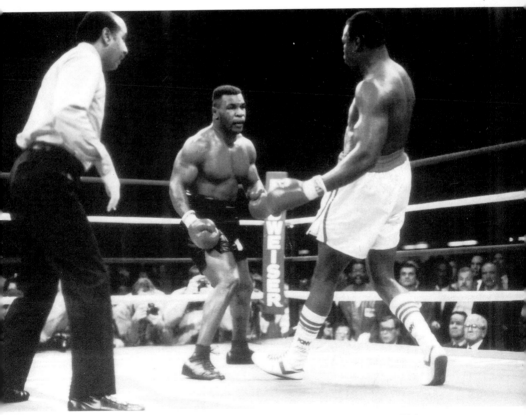

Larry Holmes staggers back as Tyson moves in for the kill in their 1988 bout. This one would go barely four rounds. *(Big Fights, Inc.)*

Trevor Berbick wilts under a massive Tyson assault. The referee raised Mike's hands at two minutes and thirty-five seconds of the second round. *(Big Fights, Inc.)*

Immediately after his victory over Tony Tucker for the undisputed heavyweight championship of the world, Mike accepts the championship belt from the Reverend Al Sharpton as, *from left to right,* promoter Don King, Jimmy Binns of the WBA, and José Sulaiman of the WBC stand in the background. The gaudy robe and crown were reported to be King's idea. *(Big Fights, Inc.)*

At a ceremony at New York's Municipal Court, lovebirds Mike Tyson and Robin Givens *legally* tie the knot—after a religious ceremony in Chicago forty-eight hours earlier. *(New York Daily News)*

From left to right, Donald Trump, Tyson, Michael Spinks, and Spinks's manager Butch Lewis pose for photos at a press party promoting the upcoming Tyson-Spinks bout. *(New York Daily News)*

Mike takes a short break from his training prior to the Spinks bout to compare Atlantic City's sea gulls to the pigeons he raised in Brooklyn. *(Big Fights, Inc.)*

In a fight that earned Mike Tyson and Michael Spinks almost $34 million, Spinks was only able to stay on his feet for one minute and thirty-one seconds of the first round. *(New York Daily News)*

The champ gets a kiss from his wife, Robin, following his knockout victory over Spinks. (New York Daily News)

Presidential candidate Jesse Jackson offers the champ a few inspirational words.
(Big Fights, Inc.)

One legend meets another—Mike and Muhammad Ali.
(Big Fights, Inc.)

The two biggest draws in boxing—Sugar Ray Leonard and Tyson.
(Big Fights, Inc.)

Mike appears to be teaching New York Yankee slugger Dave Winfield some of his fancy footwork in the ring. *(Big Fights, Inc.)*

Mike clowns with New York Giants linebacker Lawrence Taylor and New York Mets first baseman Keith Hernandez. *(New York Daily News)*

A disgusted Tyson leans against his silver Bentley while waiting for police to write up the fender bender. Later, he would "give" the Bentley to two Port Authority security officers who would be reprimanded for accepting it. *(Greg Chamberlain)*

A pensive Mike Tyson answers questions about his fistfight with former opponent Mitch Green in front of a Harlem clothing store. The champ's hand was broken in the altercation while Green emerged with a black eye. *(New York Daily News)*

Robin Givens motions to photographers to stay back as Mike is taken away in a stretcher *(lower right corner)* following an auto accident in Catskill, New York. The next day the *New York Daily News* reported that the champ had tried to commit suicide by driving into a tree. Mike vehemently denied the story. *(New York Daily News)*

As part of a *20/20* segment broadcast on ABC, Mike sits and listens as his wife, Robin, answers questions from Barbara Walters about the couple's relationship. *(New York Daily News)*

Two weeks prior to his bout with Frank Bruno, Mike poses with the author at the Golden Nugget Hotel in Las Vegas. *(Heidi Spitz)*

down and ran into Joan Collins. A short while later another familiar face came into view.

"I'm a great admirer of yours, Mr. Tyson," Omar Sharif said.

"And I'm a big fan of yours, Mr. Sharif," Mike replied.

In London, Mike discovered that he was a true international celebrity. He drew crowds wherever he went, and at the prestigious National Sporting Club in London hundreds of corporate heads honored the champion. More than two hundred of them stood in a line that spilled out into the street.

Mike would tell me later that Robin Givens was on his mind at the time. However, these romantic thoughts didn't stop him from avidly pursuing female companionship among the Brits. Mike's carousing surprised Lott, who thought that without his friend Rory Holloway next to him, he'd likely keep to himself. Only Cayton and Cayton's wife, Doris, had accompanied them. "The truth was that we decided against Holloway coming," Steve told me, "because we didn't want Mike going wild in London and creating a bad image."

One morning Mike decided to call Givens. "And when I heard her voice," he told me later, "I hung up the phone. I think it was by the third time I called her that I said to myself, 'What the hell is wrong with me?' "

He stayed on the phone with her for nearly an hour.

"I'm very charming," Mike explained to me. "And I'm making her laugh. And I'm thinking, 'This is my girl. I've got her, I've got her.'

"Basically, when you talk to women, they love to talk about themselves. So I spoke about her, about how much I admired her beauty, acting . . . just pouring it on. And then she said, 'Why do you want to meet me? I'm flattered . . . but I'm sure you'll find somebody.' I said, 'Maybe I will.' You know, I didn't want to push the issue."

A few more calls followed, and when Mike got back to his home in Catskill, he told Rory about his conversation with

Givens and decided it was time to meet her. It was toward the end of March that he and Rory began making preparations to go to California.

"First," Mike told me, "Rory and I got into the car and drove to New York City. We took like ten thousand dollars out of the bank and went to Gucci's and spent it all there." When they walked out of the Fifth Avenue boutique, Mike realized he didn't have any money to spend on his dream date and the banks were all closed. "I said to Rory, 'Oh, shit, we can't go to California tonight, we got to wait until tomorrow because all the banks are fucking closed.'"

The next day Mike went back to the bank, withdrew a few thousand dollars, and took a limousine to the airport. "Everything I wore—black-and-white jacket, black shoes, white shirt—was from Gucci's," he reassured me. "I wanted to impress her, you know."

They got to California later than they thought they would. John Horne was waiting. They calculated that by the time they got to the restaurant where Givens was waiting, they'd be three hours late. Mike remembers that he was so ashamed he thought it might be best not to show up. "I really felt I shouldn't go, but my friends made me go," he said.

At the restaurant, Robin was with her mother, sister, and a few friends. "And they were finishing their dessert," Mike recalled. She was everything he'd thought she'd be. His first impression was: "Holy shit, this girl looks good." He figured that if she'd waited for three hours, it was "because she wanted to meet me bad."

At the restaurant they made small talk, and after a while everyone left, leaving the young champion and the young actress alone.

"We hung out that night and I was a complete gentleman," Mike said. "Then the next night I took her out again and her mother was not very happy with me." He said Givens invited him into her house, and after a while he got very tired and laid his head on her. "I fell asleep with my head resting on her legs—oh, God, she has great legs—and I drooled on them. Shit, that was so bad. I got very nervous. When I woke up, I first tried to cover it up and stick it back into my mouth. But, you know something?" he continued. "She loved it; she thought it was great."

After that, they saw each other every single night for a week. "Then I had to go to New York to accept an award and she had to go to Aspen to host a show." At their first farewell the young heavyweight champion was heavyhearted. "I told her, 'I should come and see you in Denver tomorrow, but that place is too cold.' And she said, 'If you really love me you'll come and visit me.' And I said, 'I love you.' I felt like a puppy on a leash."

As soon as he arrived in New York he had Lott make reservations for a flight to Denver and, from there, a flight to Aspen. "You know," Steve told Mike, "the plane from Denver is a small one and you don't like—"

"I don't care," Mike said. "I'm in love with this girl and I wanna see her."

A day later Mike called Steve from Aspen to say that everything was great. Lott wanted to know about the weather in Aspen. "Cold as a motherfucker," Mike said, "cold as a motherfucker." But the new romance was apparently enough to keep him warm.

On April 16, 1987, the New York Amateur Boxing Federation held a banquet to honor my appointment as chairman of the New York State Athletic Commission. It was held at the Marina del Rey club in the Bronx and attended by scores of boxers, promoters, managers, commissioners, and trainers as well as by Mike and Robin Givens; Jacobs, Rooney, and Cayton—and their spouses; and Lott. It was the first time Tyson's boxing family had met Mike's new girlfriend.

When I was introduced to her by Mike, I thought she was beautiful, determined, and intelligent and that they were enthralled with each other. I was perhaps the only one in the place who thought she was more than just a sexual conquest.

"This is marriage material," I told Mike right in front of her. I thought that she'd force him to settle down, keep his roving eye riveted on her.

At the end of April, before he and his crew left for Las Vegas to fight top contender Pinklon Thomas, Mike and I spoke at length about Robin. "It's no secret that she knows about the multiple women I go out with," he said. "She told me she'd seen me on television with a bunch of girls. But now she is very possessive."

By now, Mike had practically moved into Steve Lott's East Side apartment. They'd become virtual roommates. No one could gauge how Mike really felt about Robin, but judging from the number of young women calling the apartment for him, the young champion was still not ready to commit.

Robin Givens didn't operate like the other girls in Mike's life. While most of Mike's women discreetly kept themselves out of the limelight, Robin seemed to enjoy the exposure. And Mike didn't object—to me, a sign of new and better things to come.

When I told this to Lott, he laughed.

"José," he said, "Mike's interest in women as a group has not subsided one iota. He's still screwing half of the town."

I was disappointed; maybe Robin was not as special to Mike as I'd hoped and as she projected.

13

MAY 30, 1987, was exactly twenty-seven days after my fifty-first birthday. It was also the day of Tyson's second defense of his WBC title and first defense of the WBA crown. Again, the promoter for this match was Don King. It was no secret in the boxing community that Tyson's opponents in the Unification Tournament—Ratliff, Berbick, Smith, and now Thomas—were connected to King, either through exclusive promotional contracts or through his son Carl.

This night, cornerman Angelo Dundee would not allow Carl King to work in Pinklon Thomas's corner. The legendary trainer of Muhammad Ali and other great fighters had been boasting that only he had the formula that would finally destroy Tyson, and that Thomas was the only man alive ready, able, and willing to apply it. Dundee viewed Carl as a distraction.

"José," Angelo told me very seriously, "Pinklon is going

to upset Tyson." I wished him luck. Everyone else saw the bout as a tune-up for Tyson's final Unification Tournament encounter against IBF champion Tony Tucker, tentatively scheduled ten weeks hence. But there were few empty seats at the Las Vegas Hilton Outdoor Stadium. No one in the sports world had Tyson's drawing power. He was the new Ali, the new Pelé, the Michael Jackson of boxing. The Don Kings and Bob Arums of the boxing world don't argue with boxers of such magnitude, they approach them on bended knee. Tyson was no exception, but they couldn't seduce Tyson's comanagers. Cayton and Jacobs negotiated with all comers but only approved the best offers. The fact that King was promoting Tyson's recent fights only meant that, as far as Jacobs and Cayton were concerned, King was providing the longest numbers.

The perception was that the Cayton–Jacobs–Don King alliance was a happy one, and that they were all making a bundle in the process. I knew differently.

Unlike the deals signed by many other boxers, the deal Tyson had signed for his recent fights resulted in huge profits for himself, instead of the promoters. Consequently, King, the game's premier promoter, was not receiving his customary huge piece of the pie. And he was fuming.

As Jacobs and Cayton explored ways to increase Tyson's income, King's rule changed in a most interesting way. In effect, King was slowly becoming an employee of Tyson and company.

"We'll have him [King] on a fee very soon," Jacobs told me privately, "if he wants to continue promoting Mike's fights."

"They're looking to emasculate me," King said to me when no one else was listening.

King beamed and waved in the ring when announcer Chuck Hall called his name. The prefight introductions, which in decades past had been reserved for boxing greats, had in recent years fallen victim to a politics of inclusion. Now movie and television stars, politicians, singers, and comedians were introduced as if they were some integral part of the pain, work, and struggle of the two boxers waiting in the wings. King was partly to blame for the circuslike atmosphere; especially galling was his distribution of free tickets for "special" patrons. While high rollers and entertainers dominated the ringside seats, some former champions—proud exemplars of the best the sport has to offer—were obliged to watch matches from afar.

It was no different now as announcer Hall read from his long list of stars seated comfortably nearby, and Tyson and Thomas moved around the ring, looking down at the canvas, then out into the sea of faces.

As referee Carlos Padilla bored the fighters with a recitation of the rules, Mike and Pinklon stared at each other in intense concentration. Dundee's face reflected the most confidence in the ring. Seated almost inconspicuously in the large crowd was Robin Givens. She'd spent a few days in Las Vegas with Tyson and her presence had helped ease his usual prefight anxiety.

The bell proclaimed the first round. After planting a kiss on Rooney's lips, Tyson walked out of his corner toward Thomas. He took a few steps to his right, then turned a little to his left. A left jab thrown by Pinklon failed to reach the intended target. Tyson flicked a straight left in return that landed just above Thomas's protective cup. Thomas was an experienced prizefighter and was trying not to expose his fear. However, his refusal to take the initiative or to counter some of Tyson's wild punches seemed motivated by terror, not caution. Tyson was well aware that his last fight—the twelve-round decision over Bonecrusher Smith—had been dreadfully dull, and he was looking to take Thomas out with one good shot or hurt him enough to knock him out with follow-up punches. Of course, this is never the right way to box. A good fighter always takes his time in setting up knockouts.

D'Amato's fighters were taught that a knockout is a bonus for hard work. I always tried to outpunch my rival every round, every minute, every second; if in the process I could connect hard enough to deprive him of his senses for at least ten seconds—fine. If not, then I wouldn't have to worry about losing a decision.

When I won the light-heavyweight crown in 1965, against a masterful boxer named Willie Pastrano, Cus D'Amato said to me, "I'm very proud of you, not because you won the crown, but because of the way you did it. You didn't lose one single minute of the fight." D'Amato certainly wouldn't have appreciated what was happening here as Tyson moved forward like a howitzer, swinging wildly for a one-punch KO. In the corner, Rooney was cursing, trying to pound some boxing sense into Tyson's head. "It will come if you fight your fight," Rooney yelled between rounds.

When Tyson came out for the sixth round, his left jab became like a spring, darting into Pinklon's face and retracting immediately. These jabs are difficult to counter and cause terrible headaches. Thomas changed his defensive pattern and came inside, expecting Tyson to hug him with his left arm. But the challenger was met with a right uppercut to the jaw and a devastating left hook to the temple. Thomas reeled backward. Tyson was on him like a hungry wildcat as Pinklon tried to recover. Mike unloaded punches from every imaginable angle, not stopping until the big challenger hit the canvas with the seat of his pants, his eyes unable to focus. As Thomas struggled to get up, I looked at Dundee's face droop into disappointment. After exactly seventeen minutes of fighting, referee Padilla declared the war over.

Back in the dressing room, before the postfight press conference, Tyson, who never complained, told me that he had a wicked headache and was nauseated. "I feel like throwing up," Tyson exclaimed. Panicked, I ran for Tyson's private physician, Gene Brody. The young champion was feeling the effects of twenty minutes in the ring with a top boxer, absorbing punishment and exerting himself. A few minutes later, after a talk with Brody, Tyson was feeling fine; me, too.

Mike would have eight to nine weeks of free time now, which was especially valuable to him because he could spend much of it with Robin. Whenever I saw them together, I wished they were married. I reminded them often that I wouldn't mind being the best man.

Mike still wouldn't admit, though, to being in love with the beautiful young television actress, who was two years older than him, and in a macho mood he'd even describe her as just "another girl after my fame and money." I didn't believe him. And sure enough, he began spending more and more time in California where Robin worked and he played.

On the night of June 21, 1987, he went to the Greek Theater in Los Angeles to see Run-D.M.C. and The Beastie Boys, two rap groups. Robin wasn't with him. Maybe if she had been, a misunderstanding over a hug and a kiss would not have resulted in a lawsuit.

Around ten-thirty, Tyson was in the parking lot and saw Tabita Gonzalez, who worked at the theater, and asked her for a hug. She complied. "I patted him on his shoulders," she said, "and gave him a hug . . . I thought he was a bodyguard for the band." Tyson misconstrued her polite affection as an invitation to go further.

In a legal deposition, Gonzalez gave this version: "In a friendly and nonthreatening manner he asked me for 'a little kiss.' I was friendly and smiling at him during this time. However, I declined the kiss . . . He was in a friendly mood, and actually, so was I."

Jonathan Casares, twenty, the theater's parking lot supervisor, was making his rounds and must have been a little surprised to see Gonzalez, a coworker and good friend, in the huge arms of the champion. By now, she claimed in a deposition, Tyson was getting a little rough and scaring her, and "I quickly tried to free myself from the hug."

"I inquired of her if she was all right or if there was any problem at that time," Casares said in legal papers. "A brief conversation took place between Mr. Tyson and myself . . . It appeared that Mr. Tyson was getting upset that I was butting into his business. As I moved about inside the parking attendant's cart that I was driving, Mr. Tyson threw a T-shirt at me and pushed me back into the cart with the palm of his hand in my face." Casares claimed Tyson caused "a contusion and/or laceration [on] the inside of my mouth or lip." He'd retained an attorney, Andrew Shapiro, for his suit against Tyson. Gonzalez had also retained counsel, Joyce Mendlin.

Cayton and Jacobs wanted to put a lid on the incident and avoid as much bad publicity as possible. They hired David Wood, a prominent West Los Angeles lawyer, who quietly settled the case out of court. Casares got $75,000; Gonzalez, $30,000. The settlement satisfied Los Angeles prosecutors, who'd contemplated filing criminal charges. Jacobs kept Tyson abreast of the legal proceedings to show the champion how important good conduct was for a public figure—especially one of his wealth and prominence.

I believed that Robin was fast becoming the most important person in Mike's life, and if anyone could contain his wildness, it was her. After all, she seemed intelligent and gracious, and being an actress, she had experience conducting herself under the watchful eye of the media. To my surprise, though, when I told her some of my concerns about Mike, she became angry and aggressive—almost insulting.

"These people [Cayton and Jacobs] don't understand Mike," she declared. "They don't understand him at all. They don't have the slightest idea what's really bothering Mike. They will never know how to deal with him. They just can't."

I couldn't believe my ears. She was questioning how Cayton and Jacobs, two white multimillionaires who'd known Mike since he was twelve, subsidized his nurturing and boxing education, and helped him turn his talents into wealth, could understand? But then again, maybe she had a point. Maybe Mike needed a black on his boxing team. For years I'd exhausted myself trying to help my fellow Hispanics—quite a few of them boxers—with the sociopolitical problems heaped on them by American society. The more I thought about it, the more Robin's outburst made sense.

I sincerely believed Cus, Jacobs, and Rooney were colorblind, and I had no reason to believe that Cayton and Lott were not the same. But I decided not to confront them with my idea of "integrating" the team when I realized that Robin might soon be, in a sense, joining the team herself. At the very least, she and her mother, Ruth Roper, could provide a new perspective—one that Jacobs and Cayton might actually appreciate.

Just before Mike's fight with Tony Tucker for the undisputed world heavyweight crown, the final round in the Unification Tournament, he spent a few days at Lott's Manhattan flat. Tyson was apt to show up at the apartment anytime with young women he'd picked up in bars or at parties, even though Lott, a bachelor, often had one of his own friends there. It didn't matter. To Lott, having the heavyweight champion at his place was "an incredible experience."

The first night Tyson brought Robin to the apartment it was late, and Lott went to bed "very tired." But at around four in the morning, Lott recalled, he was awakened by a loud noise, followed by a woman's screams and curses. Then there was a knock at the apartment door. Lott said he put on a robe and opened his bedroom door to see what was going on.

"Standing at the entrance to the apartment," Steve said, "was the uniformed doorman—who obviously had been summoned by a neighbor—asking both Robin and Mike if he should get transportation for either one of them; Robin was still complaining of being struck by Mike; and Mike was telling the doorman to calm down and to leave."

Then the champ turned to Lott.

"Steve," Lott recalled Tyson saying firmly, "everything is okay, get back into your room and close the door."

"I got back in," Steve said, "and closed the door."

Much later, just before the Spinks fight, I asked Mike to tell me about the best punch he'd ever thrown in his life. A broad smile covered his face and his answer came fast and abruptly. "Man, I'll never forget that punch. It was when I fought with Robin in Steve's apartment. She really offended me and I went bam," he said, throwing a fast backhand right into the air to illustrate, "and she flew backward, hitting every fucking wall in the apartment. That was the best punch I've ever thrown in my fucking life.

"The bitch wanted to call the cops from my own fucking telephone. Was she fucking crazy or something? She had some fucking balls. She wanted to call the fucking cops from my own phone."

A few days after Tyson's first official match with his lover, Mike went back to Las Vegas to prepare for Tony Tucker, a tall, lanky boxer with an exceptional punch. Tucker, from Grand Rapids, Michigan, was not as well known as the other champions involved in the Unification Tournament, but anyone who'd seen him in action knew that this youngster was a true professional, cool in the ring with dynamite in both hands.

Mike came to town five weeks before the bout, wearing a cap to cover his growing bald spot, a stress-related condition that can go away as suddenly as it appears. Mike's hair loss also had some family ramifications.

Roger Anderson, Denise's older child, was only four years old when he saw his favorite uncle, laughing and being praised on television, a role model to be emulated. So one morning little Roger went to the bathroom and came out with a bald spot right on top of his head.

"Mommy," the boy said to Denise with the scissors still in his hands, "look, I'm Uncle Mike, I'm Uncle Mike."

Everything began smoothly in Las Vegas. Tyson's sparring partners were already there, so he could start his boxing drills immediately at Johnny Tocco's gym. As usual, he'd live at Handelman's home and mess up the place. Robin was expected about a week to ten days before the fight and would be staying at the Las Vegas Hilton.

After several weeks of sparring, and at a point in his career when most of us felt he'd learned to control and exploit the prefight pressures, Tyson pulled Lott aside in the gym and told him that this was it.

"I want to retire," he told Lott, who'd heard the line from many boxers, heard it in the movies, and heard it from Mike a few times before. "But this time *before* the fight, no bullshit. I don't want to fight anymore." Not waiting for a response, he left the gym to walk to Handelman's house.

"Let's leave him alone," was Steve's strategy. "He's said that before. It is the same old story."

At the house, Mike changed clothes and took off to see Robin at the Hilton. Lott had been at the hotel the day before and heard Mike giggling and joking with Robin in her suite. He figured her presence was a positive force in Mike's boxing life, a counter to the growing tension, so he ignored Tyson's threats. It was not until Robin called him at Handelman's house later that day that he became concerned. She'd slipped out of her room and gone downstairs in the hotel to call Lott. She told him that Tyson was packing and that she'd heard him making a reservation to fly back east. Lott got Rooney and raced to the hotel. The champion was gone.

Everyone assumed he'd gone home to Catskill, New York. The next day Camille called Rooney and told him that his fighter was in Albany with Holloway. Rooney called Holloway, who gave him the impression that Tyson was beginning to change his mind about retiring. The day after that Tyson himself called Lott.

"He was very apologetic," Lott said. "He said he was sorry for leaving camp and told me to arrange for his trip back to Vegas." There was one more call. Tyson had missed his flight. He called again and apologized again. "Don't worry," he said, "I'll take care of that Tucker."

Three days after "quitting," the champion came back to his natural habitat. "He came straight from the airport to the gym," said Lott, "and boxed eight tough rounds and looked even better than before the escape."

Rooney was angry, but understanding. He told Mike that every boxer goes through this experience. "But the *real* ones don't quit," he told his champion. "You better shape up."

When the gates at the Hilton Center opened on August 1, 1987, Mike Gerard Tyson was indeed ready for Tony Tucker. The WBC-WBA champion received my customary chiropractic correction of his neck and back in the dressing room just minutes before the first bell and nobody seemed concerned. Tyson had us spoiled rotten. Victory was inevitable.

Then, the bell rang. I didn't like the ease with which Tucker moved. He was too relaxed and unconcerned about Tyson. Tucker was going to fight his fight despite Tyson. And Mike didn't realize what was going on right away. My young friend was a little careless and Tucker took advantage of that. Tucker waited patiently, looking for an opening. Tyson had not altered his own plan and was not worried about his opponent—not yet. Suddenly, the two fighters went inside. Tucker was loose but prepared; Tyson relaxed but inattentive. When it appeared that referee Mills Lane was about to shout "break," Tucker let go a devastating left uppercut that caught Tyson under the chin. His legs wobbled for a second, and by the time he realized he'd been shaken up, Tucker was on him, trying to end the fight.

Tyson then went into a brilliant defensive ballet of bobs

and weaves, riposting sporadically with left hooks and straight rights and preventing Tucker from connecting. When the bell ended the first round, Rooney told Tyson, "You can't get careless with this guy. You have to go after him and hurt him. He's too confident in there. You're giving him too many chances. Don't do that."

I knew that now, in the next round, Mike had to exhibit all his toughness to survive. In the previous round I'd seen his teeth clamp down on his mouthpiece when his brain was unexpectedly short-circuited, and I'd said to myself, "Be tough, Mike. Now is the time to be mean and strong and rugged." He'd often talked about his anger as a boxer.

"I was fourteen and going into the ring of the Les Bataillon Hall in Queens," he told me once. "I'm real mad and angry because I'm poor and I wanted to be somebody. I'm angry and mean. Cus used to talk to me about hunger. And about being vicious and mean. 'You've got to be a smart animal, be a tiger and be smart,' Cus said to me. 'You've got to know when to strike, when to let your adrenaline flow, and when to deal with fear properly.'

"Cus used to talk about the good fighters and how they were mean motherfuckers—tigers, fucking mean. Mickey Walker, Jack Dempsey, how they act tough and be mean bastards. 'You can't turn your back or complain to the referee because they hit you low or punch you after the bell,' Cus used to say. I wanted to be like them, mean, savage, vicious.

"I wanted to be like that even when I was in the street. I wanna be a mean motherfucker and kick some ass all the time. I even used to train myself to be wicked . . . I used to walk to school and be mean, snappy to everybody. I don't know, I just had to be disciplined.

"Joe Louis was mean even though he was an introvert. People would never know he was a savage, an animal in the ring. And I wanted to be that way. I used to make it my business to be a mean, ruthless bastard. I knew I had to be mean because if I lose, I'm going to die, to starve to death."

Tyson stood up for the second round, inwardly reciting Rooney's instructions and—I hoped—my telepathic ones. But Tucker would not make things easy for him. Tyson charged and Tucker moved cleverly away, letting go a left jab that kept Mike at a safe distance. That jab was connecting more often than not. Tyson was trying to move his head side to side as usual, but Tucker was timing his jabs with amazing accuracy. Tyson was accustomed to winning rounds by huge margins, and now in round two, Tucker was planting the seeds of doubt. He jabbed and moved around and got out of reach, frustrating his opponent.

After the second round, Rooney tried to explain to Tyson how to solve his problem with Tucker. "You go in there and use *your* jab," he told Mike. "You're gonna go in there and you're gonna move your head side to side so you'll slip his jabs, and then you're gonna counter with yours. You're gonna beat his jabs with yours. Do you understand?"

Mike nodded.

There are times when a boxer is doing his thing in the ring and there is no need to change. When that happens, the coaching falls on deaf ears. A relaxed boxer knows when things are going well and when they are not. D'Amato's fighters knew this, and for obvious reasons, at this point in the fight Tyson was listening to Kevin with more care than ever before.

Just before the bell for round three sounded, Tyson stood up in his corner and looked straight at me. I was standing, throwing jabs over the heads of the people in front of me, and he acknowledged by nodding his head. When the bell rang, he came out, his hands protecting his face, his elbows protecting his torso, his jab resembling an electric hammer. Everyone in his corner seemed to be breathing easier; so was Mike himself.

But the fight turned somewhat boring. Tucker's jabs were coming less frequently and he began moving farther and farther out of danger. The few jabs he threw were being countered.

And from the fourth round on, the fight adopted a pattern

of moves, charges, and misses. Tucker would survive, which was apparently his only intention after the fourth round, and Mike would score his thirty-first victory, but not his twenty-eighth knockout.

At the end, Tucker seemed pleased to be standing. Mike had an expressionless face as if trying to hide his disappointment.

Before the decision was announced, Tucker put his arm around Tyson as Rooney was taking off his fighter's gloves. "You're a damned good fighter," Tucker said to Tyson. "Don't worry, I'll give you a chance to fight me again." Tyson was not paying attention to him, but Rooney was.

"You think you won?" Rooney asked. "Get the fuck out of here."

Minutes later, Chuck Hall declared that Mike Gerard Tyson had become the first real undisputed heavyweight champion of the world since Muhammad Ali ten years before.

A few hours later Tyson was in his suite at the hotel, arguing with Jacobs. The undisputed champion of the world was not in the mood to dress up and go downstairs to the ballroom. The last thing he wanted to do was participate in the corny celebration Don King had arranged for the winner of the Unification Tournament, a Hollywood-like, make-believe coronation. "That's humiliating," Tyson said, "and I'm not going to put up with that shit."

"This is part of the business," Jacobs told Mike, "and sometimes one must do what one is supposed to do and not what one wants to do." Tyson reluctantly acquiesced.

I had mixed feelings about the pageant but had to concede that Don King was a boxing innovator. He'd made himself the world's premier promoter by striking deals such as this one. Who else would have thought to make a few bucks by airing the "coronation" live? King was flanked by the executive heads of the international boxing bodies—José Sulaiman of the WBC, Gilberto Mendoza of the WBA, and Robert Lee of the IBF—and friends that included the Reverend Al Sharpton.

Sharpton, who received the honor of presenting the "crown" to Tyson, was a self-styled civil rights leader from Brooklyn whom the media had labeled a hustler and government informer. New York *Daily News* investigative reporter Jack Newfield had described the Pentecostal minister as "the clown prince of militancy" and a man who had gotten his job (as a minister) "by coming in third in a Little Richard look-alike contest."

Sportswriters who liked King had lots of laughs over the silly affair. But those who constantly quarreled with him and criticized him in print considered the whole thing a sad episode of degradation—an insult to boxing in general and to Tyson in particular. Throughout the festivities, Tyson looked down at the floor in embarrassment. He couldn't wait to be away from the postfight sham and Las Vegas. The next morning he fled the state of Nevada.

14

F REED from boxing for a while, Mike continued his amorous forays, but Robin was there more than most, and the public began to see more and more of her. Tyson seemed to be genuinely proud of her good looks and elegance.

However, by the time Don King and Donald Trump called a press conference in New York City to announce the date (October 16, 1987) and the site (the Convention Hall in Atlantic City) for the Tyson–Tyrell Biggs contest, Mike's extracurricular activities had come back to haunt him. At the end of the conference, he was asked to take the usual physical test that would guarantee he was fit to fight. Tyson refused. "I had a tough night last night," he said. "I drank a few beers and was out late. Could you wait a couple of days?"

He then pulled Lott to the side.

"I think I have that shit again," he said. Sure enough, the man who'd scored victories over Berbick and Smith while recovering from venereal disease had managed once again to make a friend of that pesky bacteria. I warned him not to engage in any type of intimacy with Robin. "It would be an unforgivable sin if you transmitted a social disease to your girlfriend," I said.

By October 16, 1987, Tyson was again ready for ring action. He wanted the tall, cocky Tyrell Biggs in the worst way. Tyson had met Biggs at the 1984 Olympic Games in Los Angeles, where Biggs won the super-heavyweight gold medal, but they never became friends. Tyson was only eighteen at the time and served as a sparring partner for the three heaviest U.S. representatives: light-heavy Evander Holyfield, heavyweight Henry Tillman, and super-heavyweight Biggs. After a day of training with Tyson, the super-heavyweight had to use a special heavy pad around his waist to protect him from Mike's devastating body punches. For whatever reason, Tyson and Biggs detested each other.

Managed by Lou Duva and Shelly Finkel and trained by Georgie Benton, Biggs was now being hyped by them as Mr. Invincible. Retired for more than twenty years, Benton said that Biggs had the same exact style as his and that it was the perfect one to beat Tyson. "Twenty years ago," Benton declared, "I would have beaten Mike Tyson easily."

Duva echoed Benton's braggadocio: "Tyson loves the limelight and the nightlife. No fighter with that type of lifestyle can ever beat my fighters."

Jacobs warned Duva that such attacks on his fighter were dirty and unfair. "If he wants to attack me," Jacobs told the press, "fine. But not my fighter." Duva ignored the warning and continued his psychological warfare.

Jacobs had to fight back. "The man [Duva] who is saying such terrible things about my fighter," he said, "has said worse things about *his* own fighter. Just a few weeks ago, Lou told me that Biggs was 'totally insane' and that he was 'a serious head-case.' He also told me to help him get bums for Biggs because he was 'terrified' to put him with a dangerous opponent for fear he'd be knocked out."

When asked about the attacks on him by the Biggs camp, Tyson shrugged it off. "It's quite entertaining," he deadpanned, "but quite beneath me."

Immediately after the weigh-in, Mike was returning to his penthouse apartment at the Ocean Club in Atlantic City when he told me, "If I don't kill him, it don't count."

On fight night, as referee Tony Orlando explained the rules, Tyson was edgy, wanting the bell to ring. The boxer in the other corner is always the enemy, but this one, Tyrell Biggs, was viewed by Tyson as something to be annihilated. And he intended to do just that—even as Biggs set about the same task.

Tyson walked out of his corner in his usual manner. His bullet-fast hands were steady; his iron legs kept him in the right position in case he needed his torso to uncork a roundhouse; his right foot pushed and dragged forward, moving a huge and versatile physique that had the capacity to dodge and sidestep danger.

At six foot three and one-half inches, Biggs was taller, much taller. When that height differential occurs—and it occurs in nearly every Tyson match—the Tyson corner knows what to expect. Like the other fighters who carried a height advantage into the ring with Tyson, Biggs came out and threw a left jab and moved to his left. Then he threw a double jab and moved to his right. In Tyson's corner Rooney smiled. Even Baransky and Lott knew what was going on. Benton didn't look that disappointed, though, with the way his boxer had started. Biggs was fighting the way a tall guy *should* fight a short man: move, move, flick that left jab, move some more, jab some more, and when the other boxer is confused, open up with flurries—then move some more and throw left jabs.

The world of boxing is filled with trainers and cornermen, but it lacks teachers. Each time I see a tall man boxing his head off, unable to do anything else, or a short one trying to get inside because he can't box at a distance, I think "shoemaker." A "shoemaker," as Cus D'Amato defined it, is a boxing teacher who thinks that tall boys were made to move and jab.

Biggs had apparently been taught early on by a "shoemaker." For the first two rounds Tyson just did enough to get the edge. At the same time he didn't want Tyrell to become too discouraged. He wanted Biggs to feel comfortable before surprising him with the bitter truth. It began in the third round. There was an exchange from the outside and suddenly there was a cut over Biggs's left eye. Biggs no longer moved with the same ease as before. The left jabs that up to this point had kept him out of danger now seemed detrimental to his health: every time he'd let one go, Tyson countered effectively. And no matter where Biggs moved, there was Tyson—"cutting" the ring short, moving right in front of him, throwing a jab in his face.

As round seven began, Tyson and most everyone else knew the end was near. A gloomy, exhausted Biggs, with barely enough strength to lift his gloved hands, could not get away from a vicious left hook that sent him reeling to the canvas, his face a bloody mess. His ego raised him up, and waiting for him was another left hook that put him down for good. When Orlando stopped the one-sided match, there was one second left in the seventh round.

After the fight Jacobs and Lott remembered Benton's pre-fight boast that he would have easily defeated Tyson had they been matched together in the same era. Tyson's comanager and cornerman got hold of some Benton fight films and watched them for a while.

"He's right," Jacobs concluded. "Benton used to fight *exactly* like Tyrell Biggs."

The future was much clearer now. Mike Gerard Tyson was invincible. He was also the biggest money-maker in the history of boxing. Financial experts were saying that the new

heavyweight king had the potential to become the first billionaire athlete in history. They were saying this about a
twenty-one-year-old kid from the dangerous streets of Brooklyn who'd been lucky enough to have met Cus D'Amato nine
years before. The old man had put the boy on the right track,
and with Jacobs and Cayton managing Tyson as Cus had di-
rected, there seemed to be no chance that he would wind up
like many other boxing greats before him—in desolation and
poverty.

Don King wasted no time beginning a search for Tyson's
next "ideal opponent." (The term had been redefined now to
mean an opponent who could offer everyone concerned a big
payday.) Promoting Tyson meant big money, and to share in
that big money King knew he had to keep Tyson and his boxing
family happy. The name of former champion Larry Holmes
eventually surfaced. King saw Holmes as a washed-up, has-
been champion with enough recognition to generate ample
money—and certainly no danger—for Tyson. King had had a
similar brainstorm back in 1980 when he pitted a tired fighter
who'd lost much of his skill, Ali, against a champion, Holmes,
in his prime. Holmes mercifully laid back—Ali had been his
idol—and "the Greatest" could not answer the bell for the
eleventh round.

The master promoter polled the boxing world and discovered that there was plenty of interest in such a match. He
then proceeded to use his charm and promotional skills to
persuade business people, boxing fans, and Holmes himself to
go for it. The former champion would be guaranteed $3.1
million—an offer even a man as rich as he could not refuse.

After relaxing for a couple of months, Mike began to train
in Catskill for Holmes at the beginning of December. He took
off a few days during the holidays, and by the first week of
the new year he was in good shape and had moved into his
Atlantic City penthouse.

Tyson's army of sparring partners was quartered at the

Trump Plaza Hotel. By now, Jacobs and Cayton had decided to allow Tyson to make himself more accessible to the press. And it became routine to see the heavyweight king talking to sportswriters after his midday workouts at the hotel's theater.

When January 22, 1988, appeared on the calendar, he was in tip-top condition. He got up late that morning and had fruits—pears, grapes, oranges, and bananas—for breakfast. I got to the Ocean Club at around noon and found Mike in the kitchen, quietly reading newspapers. He shook my hand, gave me a hug, and invited me to his bedroom. Once again he was doing his best to deal with the prefight pressure, something no fighter can really escape. We began talking about Cus, switched to Mike's childhood, and then to his favorite relaxing subject: women. We laughed, and then I saw him lie back in bed and close his eyes. I tiptoed out of the room. Fighters don't like to talk about it, but the vast majority of them have trouble sleeping the day before a fight.

Later that night, just before making his bid for a thirty-third straight victory, Tyson was in his dressing room, his hands bandaged, waiting for official word to don his gloves, which came as soon as he got up to shadowbox.

I went outside for a while to watch the crowd. In the very first row of the section behind the press tables, I saw Steve Wynn, the Golden Nugget's chairman, being approached by a Trump Plaza executive. They spoke for a minute or so and then Wynn got up and moved a few rows to the back. I found it strange that the casino operator would be in the wrong seat, so I asked Gene Kilroy, a boxing man who'd worked for years with Ali and was now the marketing executive for Wynn, what the story was.

What had happened, according to Kilroy, was that Ali had gotten three tickets from Trump and had asked Wynn to ac-company him to the fight. "When Trump saw that Wynn was going to be sitting next to Ali, himself, and other sports fig-ures," Kilroy told me, "the rich man panicked." Trump didn't want to share the spotlight, Kilroy was suggesting. "I didn't want to cause any commotion," Wynn told me later, "so I just moved."

I went back to Tyson's dressing room where officials from the New Jersey State Athletic Commission and a man from Holmes's camp were inspecting the gloving of Mike's hands. Once that was done, everybody left except for one of the commission's inspectors. A minute later, as usual, Rooney put on the "pads"—thick, oversize, formless mitts for Mike to hit as part of his warm-up. The warm-up was timed so that Mike wouldn't have the chance to cool off before he reached the ring.

Holmes, the former Easton (Pennsylvania) Assassin, decided to be a pain in the ass. He wouldn't leave his dressing room when told to do so, thinking perhaps that the delay would disconcert Tyson. The HBO television crew was not happy. The challenger traditionally enters the ring before the champ.

A bit frustrated, Tyson began shadowboxing in front of a small mirror, working up another sweat. Once again he was notified that Holmes was claiming he wasn't ready to go to the ring.

"Mike started to shadowbox again and to test the firmness of his bandaged hands inside the gloves," Lott said. "And he threw, as usual, a couple of punches to the wall." By this time the HBO crew, two people from *TV Guide* magazine, and four members of the New Jersey Boxing Commission had joined Tyson and his crew in the dressing room.

Suddenly, to everyone's surprise and horror, Tyson threw a jab and followed it with a straight right that went through the wall.

"The chips and plaster go flying all over the place," Lott recalled. "Everyone's jaw drops and then Mike stops, looks at the hole, and turns to his left to look at everyone looking at him. And his eyes are as if he'd just been caught stealing cookies. He was so afraid of having done something wrong. He looked like a little boy saying, 'I'm sorry.' "

The commissioners checked his gloves and asked him if his hand was okay. Mike—still embarrassed—nodded yes, and then they all walked toward the ring where Holmes was waiting, his eyes reflecting panic.

Referee Joe Cortez was no stranger to Tyson's style; this was the sixth time he would be the third man in the ring with Tyson.

And so, the fight began. Tyson came toward Holmes in a crouch, making the former champion look a foot taller. Holmes jabbed and missed by a mile. Right then and there I suspected this fight wouldn't last long, though Holmes still had the skill and presence of mind to get away from the bombs Tyson aimed at his jaw, which all missed by several inches. But as Tyson adjusted his radar, Holmes was not able to do the same. Desperately, the thirty-eight-year-old fighter chased his youth as Joe Louis and Sugar Ray Robinson had before him; just as Wilfredo Benitez, Ike Williams, Johnny Saxton, and Ezzard Charles had. But for the first two rounds at least, the old timing and reflexes stayed hidden.

At the beginning of the third round, Holmes started to move much faster, dance a little bit, and use his snapping left jab. Tyson was not impressed, but from the audience I began to hear murmurs. Holmes *did* land two or three times with the jab, but he missed a few right crosses that were intended to catch Tyson by surprise. This angered the young champion, who started to increase the pressure. Holmes rested for a few seconds against the ropes and suffered for it. Tyson hit him with a couple of body shots that had to hurt. Holmes was too much the professional, though, to let the average fan see his distress. When the bell rang to end the third round, Holmes walked to his corner like an old man. He'd aged many years in those three rounds and knew by now how difficult it would be to give Tyson a respectable fight. Only one course of action seemed left to him: if he couldn't win like a champion, then why not at least lose like one?

As round four began, Holmes tried to play the game his

way. He would not make it easy for Tyson. He would try to bluff, and if that failed, he would gamble it all. Midway into the round Tyson connected with a malignant straight right that barely landed on Holmes's jaw. The former champion went down, but his pride got him to his feet eight seconds later. Tyson, all business, charged with premeditated fury and hit Holmes with a series of punches that sent the taller man onto the canvas again. And *again* Holmes's brain ordered his body to stand up. Tyson went for the kill and Cortez could not stop the slaughter in time. Holmes was down for the third time, more from exhaustion and discouragement than from clean punches. Cortez stepped between the boxers to avert a calamity—at two minutes and fifty-five seconds of the fourth round.

At postfight festivities in the Trump Plaza's large ball-room, Tyson's people thumped each other on the back and hooted with joy. King went quietly to the loser's dressing room to console the man who'd made millions for him. It was the worst thing he could have done. To the shock of those attending the former champion, Holmes started to scream epithets at King, blaming the promoter for, among other things, his "humiliation."

I learned later that King had handed Holmes an agent's or finder's fee bill for $300,000, roughly 10 percent of Holmes's $3.1-million purse, a figure later negotiated down to $150,000 after Holmes threatened to sue the promoter.

SHORTLY before the Holmes fight, on a cold January afternoon in 1988, Jim Jacobs had reached me by telephone. "I must talk to you," he said, "and see what we can do about two very important and serious matters concerning Mike." I detected a sense of urgency in his voice. "The first is personal but very, very important. The second is professional. When can I see you?"

"How about now?"

We met at his office on East Fortieth Street at five forty-five that afternoon. Looking around to make sure no one else was within hearing range, he said, "Mike has a problem that must be attended to promptly. Ruth Roper says—"

"Who's that?" I cut in.

"Ruth Roper is the mother of Robin Givens, Mike's girl-friend."

"I like her . . . I mean Robin, smart, independent."

"This cannot, repeat, this cannot get out of this room.

José, I can't emphasize it more. What I'm about to tell you should remain right here . . . I just want your honest, objective opinion. . . ." After a brief pause, he said, "Miss Roper tells me her daughter is three-and-a-half months pregnant . . . by Mike. She says we must take appropriate action or else."

"Is he willing to marry her?"

"What do *you* think?" Jacobs asked, probing my eyes for more than an answer.

"I think he should. Cus would have loved her."

"Are you sure?"

"My instincts seldom betray me." So much for the first issue.

"The other matter," Jacobs said, grabbing my elbow and leaning closer to me, "is that Bill and I made a serious mistake when we applied for the original manager-assignee contracts." He was whispering now. "If anything happens to us—Bill is not a young man and anything can happen to me—our boxers could all wind up in the wrong hands, including Mike. We must amend the existing contract in order to protect our boys . . . they could be exposed to very serious danger."

Boxing contracts written in the state of New York invariably stated that the demise of a manager ended legal commitment on the part of the fighter, who would then become a de facto free agent. I understood Jacobs's concern in this case and told him that I'd discuss the matter with NYSAC's legal counsel Carl DeSantis and get back to him. Temporarily satisfied, Jacobs smiled and invited me to dinner. I declined and on the way home rationalized telling my wife about the first part of the talk.

"Jesus!" she exclaimed after I'd imparted the news. "That's good. No more fooling around for Mr. Casanova."

A week later I asked Jacobs whether there were any further developments. "No one has mentioned it again," he said, "so I have kept it quiet. Don't forget, Mike is fighting Holmes and we shouldn't bother him with this now; maybe after the fight. By the way, what have you done about the other thing?"

I told him I was working on it.

"It's of immense importance," he said.

Bill Cayton wasn't sure what to do about the pregnancy issue. "Should we confront Mike and advise him?" Cayton asked.

"What if it's a false alarm?" I said.

"Not after four months of pregnancy," Jacobs said. He and Cayton both said they weren't sure what to do if Tyson decided to say no to marriage. They'd been negotiating endorsements and commercials for Mike that had morals clauses pertaining to his conduct and behavior outside the ring. Robin's alleged pregnancy could possibly trigger one of these clauses. And if Tyson refused to marry Robin, they figured her mother wouldn't give up without a public fight. With all that in mind, they decided to wait and see what developed.

Two weeks later, we discovered that Tyson was no longer a bachelor.

"He called me on Sunday [February 7, 1988]," Steve Lott told me, "and asked me, 'What would you say if I marry Robin right now?'" The hypothetical question took Lott completely by surprise. Steve knew more about Tyson's sex life than anyone except Rory Holloway and never suspected that the champ was that serious about Robin.

He told Mike it was a great idea.

The next day, Roper called Jacobs and told him that Mike and Robin had been married by Father George Clements, a Catholic priest, and that it had only been a religious ceremony. She said that if Jacobs didn't arrange for Tyson to marry her daughter legally in New York "at once," she'd take matters in her own hands and fly the young couple to Nevada and do it there. That evening, Jacobs told Lott to make the arrangements.

"I don't want to start on the wrong foot with Roper," Jacobs told Steve.

Tyson had actually decided to take the plunge at the NBA All-Star game in Chicago. "Dr. J [former basketball great Julius

Erving] had called to invite us to have dinner with him [after the game]," Tyson told me, "but I preferred to go to a charity affair instead." Tyson knew that Father Clements, a new acquaintance who'd been at the basketball game, was going to be at the fund-raiser.

"I said to Robin, 'Let's get married,' " Mike related. "Then I turned to the reverend and I said, 'Do you have the power to marry us?' And he said, 'Yes, I do.' And I said, 'Robin, come on, let's get married now.' Robin didn't know. She was in shock, and I said, 'We are going to get married, right now.' We went to the reverend's house—Father Clements's—and right there we got married."

"He married you in his house," I asked, "and you just considered yourself fully married?"

"Definitely."

The first to know was Camille Ewald, Tyson said. "Then Robin called her mother and she thought we was out of our mind. Her family thought it was crazy that we didn't have no big wedding. . . . Camille was happy."

At 9 A.M., Tuesday, February 9, 1988, best man Steve Lott, Mike, and Robin arrived at the Municipal Building near City Hall in Manhattan. Robin had on a dark blouse, dark skirt, and sunglasses. Mike, dressed in a dark-blue suit, was hoping the ceremony would be quick because he was supposed to appear with Larry Hazzard, New Jersey's boxing chief, at a New Jersey school. Jacobs had told Lott to make sure Tyson kept the appointment.

"We had to stand in line behind about twenty other couples," Lott recalled. "The place was so cold that everyone was wearing overcoats."

But soon enough, Tyson was recognized and invited to wait in a warm room. It was while waiting there that the couple discovered they had to have a blood test and wait at least twenty-four hours before they could be married. They were also told that only a state Supreme Court justice could order exceptions. Out they went to look for a judge.

"We went to the courthouse a couple of blocks away and we waited for about an hour," Lott said. "The waiver for the twenty-four-hour wait was signed and we went back to the Municipal Building."

Then with just a handful of people present, they entered the small chamber where their marriage was made official.

"I hugged and kissed Mike," said Lott, "kissed Robin. Then I paid the fee—I think it was less than ten dollars—and then we all went outside where Hazzard was waiting in a black limousine."

After Mike left in the limo Lott drove Robin to her mother's apartment on Manhattan's Upper West Side. "I had the marriage license in my pocket," Steve said, "and I was trying to decide in the car whether to give it to Robin. And I said, no, I better hold on to it, because it could be valuable one day. So I gave it to Jim [Jacobs], who put it in a safe-deposit box."

For Jacobs and Cayton there were nagging questions: Did Tyson know anything about prenuptial agreements? Had he been tricked somehow? Or had the marriage actually taken a heavy load off their backs? After all, Robin was supposed to be nearly five months pregnant, and Tyson had done the most sensible thing under the circumstances. A few days later Jacobs got one answer.

"Mike," Jacobs asked, "is there a premarital arrangement involved here?"

"Do you have one with Loraine [Jacobs's wife]?" Tyson snapped back. "I'm married because I'm in love."

Case closed! This was not Tyson coming back at Jacobs with a straight right to the jaw in the fifteenth round after saving the punch all night. That's a deceit reserved for the ring. But he *was* brief and cutting—not the champ's style at all. Had marriage changed him so soon? Was this the Tyson of the future?

In and out of hospitals for the past several weeks and in the midst of difficult negotiations for the Tyson-Spinks match, Jacobs had no desire to fight back. He could only hope for the best for his friend and fighter. "It's his life," he told me. "We should all help him if he needs help."

By then, NYSAC counsel DeSantis had reviewed the documents in the Tyson-Jacobs boxing-manager contract. In New York, a prizefighter can only be managed by one person. Nevertheless, a third party, called an assignee, can be involved on a limited basis. Assignees, who own part of the manager's share of a boxer's profits, are allowed for two reasons: first, to permit a person to invest in a boxer; second, to have an official record of the investor for his or her protection. The assignee has no official say in contract matters and any renumeration comes from the manager's share.

DeSantis told me he would draw up documents that restructured the system of assignees that was then in place with respect to the Tyson-Jacobs contract, providing protection for Mike in the event of either of his comanagers' dying. The news came as a relief to Jacobs, who continued to be concerned that, in the event something happened to him, Mike might be easy prey for boxing's "sharks." Also, the new contract arrangement would, of course, benefit Jacobs and Cayton and their families.

So that Mike and Robin's entry into wedded bliss would not be totally lacking in pomp and circumstance, Robin's mother, Ruth Roper, decided to give her daughter and new son-in-law a wedding present. On February 14, 1988, St. Valentine's Day, she threw a small but high-toned party at the Library Room of the Helmsley Palace Hotel on Madison Avenue. Mother and daughter both wore black—it wouldn't have been difficult for Roper to pass for Robin's sister—as guests mingled pleasantly and sampled the delicious food. The affair amounted to Roper's coming out party. Though Roper is a small, energetic woman with diminutive features, her guileful smile and disappointingly devious eyes gave me the impression at the time that she didn't trust anyone and might drive insecure people insane.

My wife, Ramona, who's never at a loss for words, pulled me aside at the party. "Tell your friends Bill Cayton, Jimmy

Jacobs, and Mike Tyson himself," she said, "that this is a woman they'll have to contend with from now on." Ramona had chatted with one of Roper's business associates, Olga Rosario, and come away convinced that Roper would not stand idly by in the background while her daughter merged her life with the biggest commodity in sports.

If there were veiled dangers at the party, they eluded me. True, there was not much rapport between Tyson's new family and the old one, but I couldn't detect any animosity between them.

One day after the party both of Tyson's comanagers fell ill. Cayton was hospitalized with endocarditis, an inflammation of the membranes of the heart. Jacobs, who left town supposedly to visit relatives—no one, except those very close to him, knew his whereabouts—was recovering from intestinal surgery. Rumors had him suffering from every type of illness: cancer, appendicitis, AIDS, tonsillitis.

It was while in the hospital that Cayton first faced Robin's wrath. She'd been unable to contact Jacobs and apparently figured Cayton would do, even though he was suffering from a serious illness.

"I'm Mrs. Mike Tyson," she announced over the telephone, "and I'm taking over my husband's affairs."

Cayton was enraged by her manner. "She said those words in a rather abusive, dominant tone as though she had taken over the managership." Cayton was surprised at her tone and told her so.

Cayton, too weak to meet her fire with some of his own, tried to give the young actress some context. "I said to her that Jim and I had been Mike's managers for many years and tried to explain about the long relationship Jim, Cus, and I had with Mike. . . .

"Here she is, married three weeks and she's taking over for people who had been with Mike since he was twelve years old."

Her call was followed, a few days later, by a firm letter from Michael Winston, an attorney representing "Mr. and Mrs. Mike Tyson," who demanded to see every financial document related to Tyson's affairs. Cayton decided not to respond until he'd had a chance to talk to his fighter.

At this point Tyson was in Japan, preparing for his scheduled March 21, 1988, championship bout against Tony Tubbs. Robin had been with him in Japan briefly but returned to New York City to, among other things, check on a mansion in Bernardsville, New Jersey, that she and her husband were about to buy. She also went to Merrill Lynch's office at the Pan Am Building to see James Brady, a Merrill Lynch vice president and Tyson's financial advisor. There she demanded to see her husband's financial records, but she was told that only Tyson could make such requests. Infuriated, she left empty-handed, promising to come back prepared.

I arrived in Tokyo nine days before the Tyson-Tubbs fight. The limousine driver who picked me up had come to fetch another passenger as well: Robin Givens. Her plane had landed just minutes after mine. Even following the long trip she looked great—well dressed, slender, attractive. In the car, we made small talk. She told me her mother was coming in a few days and I told her that Don King was having trouble getting a visa.

"Yes," she said, "I've met him a few times. He's an interesting man."

"You've got to watch him," I said. "He knows the ins and outs of the game as well as anybody . . . maybe better."

"Now that Mike and I are married," she said, "King's paying more attention to me. He thinks I'm a person of major influence in Mike's life. I know better."

A week later, two days before the fight, King resolved his visa problem and arrived in Tokyo.

"You know," I told him, "anyone who talks to Mike's wife should know they're not dealing with a dummy. You'd better watch your ass with her." King looked at me, a coy smile on his big face.

"José," he said, "Robin Givens is a woman with larceny in her heart." He also questioned Ruth Roper's role. "Robin's mother is pretty sharp and she'll be involved somewhere."

Tyson looked good in training—too good for his opposition—even though I noticed a look of worry in his eyes. I thought perhaps Jacobs's absence for the first time in his professional boxing career was bothering him. They'd become much closer as time went by, and now Jacobs was in a hospital unable to see him fight. "What's troubling you?" I asked.

"My wife is having some problems," he told me. "She's throwing up and having pain in the stomach . . . she's really complaining a lot. I think she's bleeding."

Well, that would certainly explain his distraction and uneasiness. Vomiting is usually associated with early pregnancy and midterm bleeding is a cause for real concern and a condition that sometimes necessitates hospitalization. But I learned that the mansion was on his mind as well. Robin had brought photographs of the estate and was excitedly showing them to everyone.

Two days before stepping into the ring, Tyson revealed to the media that Robin was expecting. "We're not sure yet what the baby's name will be if it's a boy," said a beaming Tyson, "but if it's a girl, she'll be named D'Amato."

Meanwhile, Tony Tubbs, former WBA heavyweight champion, was as happy as Tyson about the recent marriage and the news that Robin was expecting. Tubbs thought these distractions played to his advantage. In fact, the people in Tubbs's camp discussed Tyson's sex life at length. Tubbs's handlers were convinced that a healthy Tyson would not skip the pleasures of a honeymoon for anything in the world, much less for a boxing match.

The Tubbs fight could hardly be considered a barometer of the effects of nonfight pressures on Tyson's boxing, however. If anything, he fought that much more fiercely to hurry back to his wife. Tyson scored a two-round, one-sided knock-out victory over Tubbs with hardly any significant effort.

Tyson's entourage flew back to the United States in the first-class section of a Japan Air Lines 747. On the flight Robin took the opportunity to make an open challenge to Cayton. After all, she was the legal wife of a wealthy man who lacked her education and refinement. If I'd been Cayton, I would have expected it.

"We had most of the first-class seats," Steve Lott recalled, "and I made sure to secure the twelve seats available upstairs. Upstairs we had three pairs of seats on one side and three pairs on the other." The large group included Tyson; Robin; Dr. Gene Brody; Roper; John Halpin (Tyson's hypnotist); Cayton; his wife, Doris; Rory Holloway; Rooney and his friend Roe; and Dr. Ira Gelb (a heart specialist keeping an eye on Cayton) and his wife.

Entertaining the rest of the Tyson group downstairs was Don King. With him were Camille Ewald and Jay Bright.

Four hours into the flight, the pyrotechnics began. Tyson and his wife sat in the first two seats on the right side. Bill and Doris Cayton were behind them. Holloway had the third seat of that row. Lott had assigned himself and Roper seats in the second row on the left. But when Ruth entered the plane, she walked past her reserved place and sat in the aisle chair of the first row on the left, across from her daughter. She settled there with the intention of staying put, and Gelb, who'd been assigned the seat, saw her in the chair and without a word went downstairs.

Cayton and Lott were discussing the preparations for the Spinks fight that was scheduled in June. And at the same time, Robin was having an animated conversation with her mother. Suddenly Robin got up and marched toward Bill.

"Bill," she said calmly with no emotion, "as I told you before, I'd like to see the contract you have with Mike."

"As soon as we get back to New York," Cayton said, "I'll

send you a typical New York State contract exactly the same as the one we have with Mike."

"I don't want to see a typical New York State contract. I want to see your contract. I want to see how much money you are making for Mike."

At that point Cayton got up and walked over to Tyson. "Mike, can I speak with you for a second?"

Tyson said, "Sure."

"Now, you tell him to give us those papers we spoke about, Mike," Robin said. "You tell him what I want."

Cayton said, "May I speak with you for a second—alone."

Mike turned to Robin. "I wanna speak to Bill alone."

"But Mike," Robin continued, "you tell him what I want, what we want. You tell him—"

"Please," Mike said, cutting Robin short, a trace of anger in his voice, "give us a few minutes alone."

Robin finally walked away. When she was out of sight, Cayton sat down next to Tyson.

"Mike," Cayton said, "I'll give you any papers you want, anything you want. But it's *your* business, not anybody else's business. I want you to know that anytime you want any papers for any purpose I'll give them to you directly."

"I know that Robin is new," Tyson said. "I just want her to feel that she is part of the team. That's all, that she's part of the team."

"Anytime you want papers, contracts, anything," Cayton reiterated, "you just ask me and I'll give them to you personally."

16

TYSON'S other comanager would never learn of these developments. At that moment he was in New York's Mount Sinai Hospital, dying. He had succumbed to an eight-year battle with leukemia. The day after Tyson and his entourage returned from Japan, March 23, Jacobs died.

"I was on my way to the hospital to visit him," Tyson told me later, "and my wife reached me on the car's phone to tell me that Jimmy had just died. I told the driver to make a U-turn and go instead to [Jacobs and Cayton's] office."

Tyson, according to Cayton, arrived at his office "in tears and out of control."

That same day, Tyson and Robin showed up at Merrill Lynch to shift $1.9 million from his stock account to make the down payment on the couple's new $4-million mansion.

"Robin was not even concerned that Jim had just died," Merrill Lynch Vice President James Brady told the *Daily*

News. "I followed her instructions and made a wire transfer to their account at Citibank."

I saw Mike later that night. He and his wife had come to Jacobs's modest two-bedroom east-side apartment—two floors below theirs—to join the mourners. A few friends of the family were there, and Jacobs's wife, Loraine, was doing her best to be a cordial hostess. "I'm waiting for Doris [Cayton] to help me with the people," she said, trying to hold back the tears. Her fine features and unpretentious manners had become more pronounced in sorrow. She'd been an active participant in her husband's business, but she never relished the limelight and mostly kept herself in the background. Coffee, sandwiches, and soft drinks came out of the kitchen, and that helped ease the tension in the apartment.

Later, Tyson, his wife, and myself went upstairs to the couple's apartment, and after a short while Mike asked me to go out for a walk.

When we left his apartment, he seemed in a deep fit of melancholy. It was as if he'd been hit by a sucker punch. He started crying on my shoulders. "You know," he said, "people think I'm tough. But that's bullshit. I'm a fucking coward. You know something, I feel like taking my own life . . . killing myself. But I don't have the fucking guts to do it, you know what I mean?" We were walking on Second Avenue in the forties against the cool March breeze. "When Cus died, I felt the same way," he said.

"My friend," I said, "you had a commitment when Cus died and that was fulfilled. You have a commitment now and I see no obstacle preventing its execution. You must keep winning until you want the championship no more. You and only you must make that decision. Both Cus and Jimmy will be happier wherever they are."

He started talking about how he could trust them. "You know," he volunteered, "trust and love are two different things."

He thought for a moment then nodded his head as if carrying on some inner dialogue. "I love Robin but I don't trust her," he said. "Not yet, you know what I mean?" He put his hand on my shoulder. "I guess deep inside I think all girls want me only for my money. . . . It took me some time before I really trusted Cus. I guess I'm basically a paranoid person—my past, my background . . .

"Shit," he murmured, shaking his head as if in unbearable pain. We walked the next three blocks in silence.

"Let's go to Brian Hamill's place," he said finally, snapping out of his trancelike state. We turned right on Forty-second Street. The photographer's apartment was all the way across town on Forty-third Street and Tenth Avenue. As we reached the southeast corner of Forty-second Street and Third Avenue, we noticed some sort of a gathering at the Horn and Hardart Restaurant. "Hey," Tyson said, pointing inside the place. "I was with those guys just yesterday." And as he tried to remember their names, he was mobbed by photographers. Inside, Tyson's mood improved markedly, but he still seemed in need of a jolt. I walked to the bar and asked for a double scotch in one cup and a club soda in another. The champ took the liquor and swallowed it like water. His eyes asked for another; it didn't seem inappropriate.

On the way out—about an hour later—a beautiful young woman just arriving wanted a picture with Iron Mike. It was Brooke Shields. I grabbed her by the waist—who could resist?—and told Tyson to get on the other side of her. As we waved good-bye, the melancholy set in again and memories of Jacobs and D'Amato washed over us.

"Life is shit," Tyson said softly. "One minute you're here and the next you're gone."

All thoughts of going to Brian Hamill's place abandoned, we walked back to Tyson's apartment. Robin was already in bed. I wished Mike a good night. When I got home, there were a number of messages next to my bed. One read: "Don King called. Please call him whenever you get home. At any time."

King wanted to know if I was going to Jacobs's funeral in

California. "Yes," I told him. "I'm going with the team." He wanted to know the date, place, time, and flight number.

The following day at New York's John F. Kennedy Airport, the conspicuously large figure of Don King could be seen making its way to the American Airline's terminal. In the VIP room he embraced each of us: Tyson, Loraine Jacobs, Bill and Doris Cayton, Lott, Rooney, Handelman, Brody, and Matty Decatur and Sal Rappa, close friends of the Jacobs family. Neither Robin nor Roper would attend the funeral.

Cayton and Jacobs had never completely trusted King, and Cayton was gradually reducing King's role in the promotion of Mike's fights. Most of us were wondering why he was there.

In Los Angeles, Tyson had some trouble getting a limo right away. "These people don't know how to deal with this kid," King complained, but only loud enough for me and Tyson to hear. "There should have been not one but a couple of limousines waiting for the champ *before* you people got here. I'll tell you something, Muhammad Ali never waited this long in any airport. Never!"

King was a master opportunist, and sowing subtle seeds of doubt and suspicion was just one weapon in his psychological arsenal. He was never averse to using unorthodox methods if it got him somewhere. Although an uninvited guest, he seemed to fit right in with the mourning party. Of course, King himself had no trouble arranging for a proper conveyance from the airport. He even had space for whoever was "careless enough" not to be prepared. After a few idle minutes, we were all on our way to the Beverly Hilton Hotel.

Arrangements had been made to have dinner in the hotel's restaurant, but Tyson spent the evening with John Horne, his actor friend. Horne, whom some suspected of being a conduit to King, and Tyson did not return to the hotel until the wee hours of the morning. At dinner that night Robin and her mother became the chief topic of conversation.

"If Mike Tyson wants to see his papers," Loraine Jacobs said, "give them to him. If he wants to give his wife every single penny he has in the bank, that's his business, not ours. We just cannot meddle with his wishes."

Cayton said there were too many sharks around and that one of Cus's last requests was that "we should protect Mike."

"Look at that girl," Loraine Jacobs said. "She is gorgeous and smart, and she is married to Mike. She sees him every day and goes to bed with him every single night. Let's leave them alone. As I see it, we're in a no-win situation."

The next morning King and I ate at a soul food restaurant a few miles from the hotel. We talked about Cayton and Tyson's future. King seemed to be testing my loyalty to the Tyson crew and again expressed his reservations about Robin Givens and Ruth Roper. He was not sure what steps he should take to secure a position in Tyson's future. After breakfast we went to his West Coast apartment in Los Angeles, which was not too far from the Hilton. He made a few telephone calls. At around 10 A.M. we returned to the hotel lobby where Jacobs's funeral procession would start. A short time later Mike and the others arrived and we all left for the mortuary.

Three thousand miles away, Robin and her mother were not idle. While Tyson and his entire boxing family mourned Jacobs, mother and daughter were visiting the Merrill Lynch office, this time exhibiting power-of-attorney papers authorized by Tyson. Again they met with strong resistance from Brady, and clamorous shouting resulted. "I want my money! Where is my money!" Robin yelled before storming out of the office. "You're one of Cayton's boys. We're going to take our money out of here."

Eventually they did.

In Culver City, California, the temple at Hillside Memorial Park and Mortuary was not a comfortable place for the large crowd that showed up to pay its final respects to Jimmy Jacobs. Cayton, myself, and a rabbi eulogized our departed friend.

Not everyone there knew about Jacobs's athletic past, and

some were in awe of his sports accomplishments. Besides being one of the greatest four-wall handball players in the history of the game, he'd boxed in the light-heavyweight division in the military and was once asked to participate in the U.S. Olympic trials. He'd also run the 100-yard dash in 9.6 seconds and was an outstanding high school basketball player. It was in high school that Jacobs was involved in an incident that showed his concern, compassion, and understanding for his fellow man.

The story is best told by referring to the night, several years back, that he was talking to a few friends in his apartment in New York when somebody asked to use his phone to call a friend in Los Angeles. "My sister is married to David Janssen, [who starred in *The Fugitive* television series]," said the caller, "and I want to say hello to them."

"If you get David on the phone," Jacobs said, "I'd love to say hello." The friend gave him a look as if to say, "Who the hell does this guy think he is?" The call was made, and after a while, Janssen was told that "a stranger" wanted to say hello.

"Hi, kiddo," Jacobs shouted into the phone. His voice had been instantly recognized on the other end. The two men, it turned out, had been close friends back when they'd attended high school the same year Sherrill Luke was told that he couldn't play on the school's basketball team because he was black. Janssen and Jacobs, two leading players on the team, got together and decided that if Luke didn't play, *they* wouldn't play.

"Sherrill Luke," said Jacobs, "played."

Eight pallbearers, including Tyson and myself, carried Jacobs to his final resting place next to his mother—and also, as it happened, a few steps from actor Al Jolson. The King of the Hill, Mike Gerard Tyson, sobbed inconsolably throughout the ceremony.

Back in the hotel, Loraine had arranged a small, post-funeral gathering. King, his wheels spinning, was obviously there to probe rather than to grieve. Shelly Finkel was one of those milling around when Tyson asked him to take a walk with him.

"We were upstairs after we came back from the funeral," Finkel told me later, "in Loraine's room. And then Mike and I took a walk outside and that's when he told me what Don King had said to him earlier:

" 'Don't go through with the Spinks fight. I can give you five easy matches for five million each instead.' And Mike answered, 'Why should I take five easy fights when I can make the same amount of money in *one* easy match.' " What King had failed to mention was that the five matches would be against boxers he and his son controlled.

Shelly went to Cayton. "King is making a move on Mike," he told him. "He is telling Mike to forget about the Spinks fight."

"What a disgusting man," was Cayton's initial response, adding that he had no recourse but to disassociate Tyson from King. "We just can't afford to have this man working with us anymore. He is poison for the business," Cayton said, "and worse for Mike."

Instead of taking the American Airlines flight the next morning, Tyson and I took Pan Am's red-eye the night of the funeral. Mike missed his wife and made his wishes to go back home too loud and too clear for Lott to ignore them. He would have Robin meet him at Kennedy Airport.

At the Los Angeles airport, Tyson met actor Arnold Schwarzenegger, who was taking the same flight. The two hulking stars exchanged some smiles and compliments. Tyson then insisted I shouldn't go straight home to Manhattan but should visit his mansion in Bernardsville.

"You've got to see my house," he said in that childlike voice he uses when he wants something real bad and won't accept no for an answer. "It's a beauty, it has twenty-eight rooms and—"

"Okay, Mike."

No one, including the champion himself, could describe the house properly. Robin kept her excitement under control, but I couldn't help emitting a complimentary expletive when I first laid eyes on Tyson's minipalace.

"That," I shouted to Mike, "is a motherfucker!"

He threw a playful punch to my stomach. With the thoroughness of an expert guide he explained in detail not only what was there (expensive but old furniture, fancy paintings, tennis trophies, and kitchen utensils—all left over from the previous owner), but what he intended to replace it with. "I've got to bring my awards for the trophy room and buy new furniture to change every room around," he said. "And I'm going to fix the fancy edges of the rooms downstairs with gold decorations, real gold. . . . My kids are going to have plenty of room around here."

I asked whether the Tysons believed in large families. "Probably a bunch," he said without thinking. "I think my wife wouldn't mind. I can't wait for the first one . . . it's on his way—"

"Or *her* way," I cut in. "It's going to be a girl, and for her sake, she'd better look like Robin."

Mike laughed and punched me in the stomach again. "Robin and I wouldn't mind . . . either way," he continued. "A girl, a boy; it doesn't make any difference. Lots of kids . . . that's what I want. . . .

"You know," he said, referring again to his house, "I'll spend perhaps over a million bucks adjusting it to *my* taste."

Mike was good to his word, and when I returned a few weeks later, some noticeable changes had taken place and men were still working downstairs. The mansion's front parking lot also played host to a number of expensive automobiles, including a few Rolls-Royces. It was all meant to show the world—or perhaps Mike himself—that he had arrived.

One who had no doubt that the champ had arrived, and was trying his best, now that Jacobs was gone, to ensure continuing prosperity for Tyson was Bill Cayton.

Cayton was not outwardly affectionate. He had a reputation for being cold, distant, detached. There were also those who said his wealth had bred a certain laziness. But no one had ever questioned his honesty and integrity, or his ability to negotiate for his fighters.

With Rooney, Lott, and Baransky backing him up in the boxing department, and with his own business experience, Cayton was ready to continue where Jacobs had left off. But it was vital that he obtain the cooperation of Mike Gerard Tyson.

Unfortunately for Cayton, the champ had switched his loyalties. He hadn't completely conceded to Robin, but unbeknown to Robin and her mother, he'd started to assert himself with Cayton. Right or wrong, he felt obliged to stick with his wife.

"He's my husband and he must stand up for me," Robin told me in Bernardsville early in April 1988. "He's not doing that and he has to learn that standing up for his wife is one of his responsibilities." She was angry and in a talking mood and I wanted to know a little more about her real feelings for Mike. I was bold and direct.

"Was this house bought under your name?" I asked her. "I heard rumors and—"

"Why can't people understand that I'm with Mike because I love him, because I care for him," she cut in angrily, "and that I'm not with him for his money. Why can't they understand that?" She paused. "Of course this house isn't under my name. This is Mike Tyson's home. Mike works too hard to make a living, too dangerously. How can I be so cruel as to pretend I would buy this house with his money—for me?"

"Are you pregnant?" was my next question. I was aware that my queries wouldn't win me any awards for tact, but I asked them for Mike's sake.

"Of course I am," she said unhesitatingly. Somehow I believed her.

I went back to tell Cayton that I felt a reconciliation

between the two groups was possible, and that I thought Robin loved Mike, that she was pregnant, and that she could be trusted. I also told Bill to be warm and compassionate with Mike; to call him and inquire about his health, to show a personal interest not connected to boxing. He was skeptical.

"You should do exactly the same with Robin," I told him. Bill drew the line there. "Why don't *you* do that for me," he joked.

When I went home and told my wife about my talks with Robin and Bill, she was quick to sum up, "I hate to use clichés, but as far as Cayton is concerned, you can't teach an old dog new tricks, and in the case of Robin, like Cervantes said in *Don Quixote*: 'I can look as sharp as another, and let me alone to keep the cobwebs out of my eyes.' "

IN the beginning of May 1988, six weeks before the Spinks fight, the undisputed heavyweight champion of the world, Mike Gerard Tyson, was, to say the least, overweight. He'd been eating an enormous amount and seemed to be wearing it. His twenty-inch neck now seemed part of his back. He was even walking differently. The extra load on his frame had compressed his muscles in such a manner that they appeared ready to explode with his every move. The weight gain was deceptive. The average person might see him as fifteen to twenty pounds over his normal 218-pound fighting weight and think he was trim and fit. And because he was a heavyweight and the champion of the division, he naturally created the illusion that he was bigger than he really was, larger than life so to speak. But the bottom line was that Tyson, who usually labored long and hard in training, was unconcerned about his weight fluctuation, assuming, as did most of those around him, that it was normal. In addition, he had no respect for

Spinks as a boxer, especially as a heavyweight boxer, and consequently didn't feel he had to train very hard.

Tyson felt that Spinks was a fraud as a heavyweight and he was probably correct—when Spinks was compared to Mike. I'd begged Jacobs to get Spinks for Tyson as soon as the light-heavy outsmarted and knocked out Gerry Cooney. My infatuation with Spinks as an opponent was not based on Spinks's shortcomings, but on Tyson's superior mental and physical dexterity. Cus D'Amato, who always warned against predicting the result of a boxing match, made sure his prizefighters were in the gym at least six weeks before a match. It was a sin to do otherwise. He had known too many outstanding fighters who'd become sad footnotes as a result of their own lethargy.

But Cus was no longer with us and Tyson was not in any gymnasium. A sense of uneasiness overwhelmed all of us. It brought to mind the time when Cus was alive and Tyson, still a novice in the professional ranks, disappeared sometimes for weeks without telling anyone of his whereabouts.

"He thinks that because he's a good boxer he can just do whatever he wants here," Cus once told me. "Well, that's lots of bull. He's wrong, and he's going to pay for it." Cus made a fist. "He's going to find out who's boss here. And he is going to find out the hard way." A few days later Cus asked Mike to "come outside and show me how tough you really are." At age seventy Cus had challenged the boy who would become king.

Rooney was justifiably irritated, his mood restless. There were only five weeks before the fight, and Tyson had still not shown up at the gym. No one knew where he was, and the only thing Rooney could do was to sit next to the phone and wait.

"Every time I saw Spinks on TV or in the newspaper, he was training. And every time I saw Michael, he was kissing Robin," complained Mike's sister, Denise. "You know, it's like I say, Spinks is goin' to beat the livin' hell out of my brother . . . kick his ass."

She was not the only person expressing those feelings. The boxing community, the always-willing-and-ready-to-join-small-talk people, and of course, the media were spreading rumors about Mike's private life wherever one went. People in the street spoke in familiar terms about Tyson and Robin Givens; Ruth Roper and her lawyer, Michael Winston; and manager Bill Cayton.

Playing a less publicized role in the Tyson drama—at least, for the moment—was the indefatigable Don King, who was content to watch the action closely. King was flying low, seeing who was doing what, talking to both sides, making sure he was with Tyson all the way, feeling here and there to see on which side of the fence he would finally land. A man accustomed to maneuvering tough men in a rough game, King had to be careful this time. Robin and her mother were not puppets to be tossed around; they had minds of their own and they knew how to play hardball.

On May 8, 1988, Tyson, in the company of Robin, was driving his silver Bentley on Varick Street in downtown Manhattan when he lost control of his car and hit two parked cars. Two cops who were employed by the Port Authority of New York and New Jersey quickly arrived on the scene.

Incredibly, Mike gave them his $185,000 automobile in an attempt, some would say later, to smooth things over. Reporters had a field day speculating about the reason for Mike's largesse as well as the reason for the accident itself. I waited until he was under the pressure of a fight to ask him about it.

"Tell me the real story behind the car you gave the cops," I said. "I heard you had a fight with Robin when she found condoms in your pocket, and as a result you crashed against a parked car. I know you're a lousy driver and that you're not fooling around. Why did you have condoms?"

Tyson said he had been making a commercial earlier in the day and had decided to have a quiet dinner with his wife afterward.

"It's funny," Mike told me, "No one would believe the

story. The truth was that a friend of mine was carrying these condoms and he said to me, 'Hold on to these so he won't get into trouble.' I'm serious. Honest truth. My friend gave me the condoms because he didn't want his wife or his girlfriend, whatever it was, to bust him with the condoms."

"And you put them in your pocket together with your money?"

"That's right," said the champ. They were at dinner. "And my wife went into my pocket to take the money and she found the condoms. You know, there are some situations when the truth just won't work. I had to lie because the truth just didn't sound like the truth." Mike closed his eyes. "I had to lie like *I* was cheating, and it was killing me. It killed me because I'm lying to myself and to her. It hurt. I'm lying to myself! I'm saying to myself, 'I didn't screw anybody. If I'm going to make love, it would be to her.' But then she hit me."

"She what?" I said. "Where?"

"In my face. Can I tell you somethin'? My sweet, loving wife has a revolving streak in her. She doesn't take any shit."

"And what did you do when she slapped you?"

"I can't do anything to my wife," Mike said, sounding like the most civil man in the world. He was laughing. "I didn't do shit . . . couldn't do shit. It's my wife."

"Did you laugh or were you serious?"

"I was serious," he said, "but I wanted to laugh. I think it's cute when she tries to hit me. She hit me and I said, 'Ugh.' That's all . . . 'Ugh.' "

They left the restaurant quietly, but Mike knew she was fuming. He was nervous. "As I was driving," he said, "I saw a cat in the middle of the street and I swerved to the right and bang! I hit a parked car and also two guys who were near the car—"

"Wait a minute, you hit two guys, two human beings?"

"Yes," said Mike, "I hit one guy, he hurt his arm and I gave him five hundred bucks and he ran to the OTB [Off-Track Betting] parlor near there. Then the cops came and I signed them autographs, and they got rid of the other guy I hit, so he won't bother me.

"Then I told the officers, 'Whitey don't think you can own these kind of cars because you're black, right? I want you to keep this one.' I felt like, you know what I mean, I didn't wanna give them a chance to ask for my driver's license. I don't have one. So before I could panic, I said, 'Fuck it. The car is not worth shit.' And I gave it to them.

" 'Take it!' I said. And they took the car. I don't think it's their fault that they took the car. It was *my* fault." Tyson hit the bed with his right hand. "You know," he continued, "as they drove away, I started to think, 'They are two; how in hell are they gonna split the fucking car in half?' "

King tried to reap publicity by purchasing a Rolls for Tyson (it wasn't the first he'd given him), but the promoter didn't get much ink for his effort. Instead, he received a reprimand from Cayton for not properly insuring the automobile.

The two officers meanwhile had returned the Bentley and gotten a reprimand from their own bosses.

After that, the media zeroed in on Tyson, his wife, and his mother-in-law in a take-no-prisoners fashion. Of Robin, who finished high school at age fifteen and enrolled at Sarah Lawrence College, the New York *Daily News* claimed, "her resume reads like it's too good to be true. And it isn't true.

"It says," continued the newspaper, "she was accepted at Harvard Medical School, and Givens has told various interviewers she completed up to three years there. But the registrar's office says she never even applied.

"Her resume also says she 'began studying' at the American Academy in New York at age ten. But Jack Melanos, director of the Academy's Saturday School, says Givens attended only five classes and dropped out.

"The resume also says that she was one of the 'top young models' with the Ford Agency. But Eileen Ford said Givens never worked there."

The same *Daily News* story called Ruth Roper "an ambitious, greedy, and heartless businesswoman who'd stop at nothing to get ahead." Citing court records, the newspaper said that Roper "was hit with a $5,856 judgment for skipping out on a lease for a $750-a-month apartment in Peekskill, New York," and that she was being "sued by Amtec Management Associates, which charges that she owes the company more than $50,000.

"Additionally," the story continued, "Henry Hinden, a former business partner and ex-president of R. L. Roper Associates, has sued her firm for $31,000." The newspaper also reported that New York Yankees slugger Dave Winfield had been encouraged by Roper to invest in her business, and that the two had at one time been romantically involved. It was that relationship, the story said, "that apparently led to the most notorious litigation surrounding Roper—the suit, settled privately, in which she alleged Winfield had given her a sexually transmitted disease."

On May 25, 1988, Tyson finally announced he was ready to train. He and his entourage moved to Tyson's Ocean Club penthouse apartment in Atlantic City to begin preparation for Michael Spinks. But one week later, Tyson's stablemate Edwin Rosario was fighting Ramiro Lozano at the Felt Forum in Madison Square Garden, and the heavyweight champ thought it was only fitting that he travel the 130 miles to urge his friend on to victory. Tyson walked into the Felt Forum quite early and was in the company of a man I'd never seen before. Mike sat in a front-row seat directly across from me—on the other side of the ring, next to the ring's apron where members of the press, commission officials, and the three fight judges sit. Bill Cayton and his wife Doris were sitting nearby, not too far from Tyson. Bill and Mike weren't on speaking terms at the time, and one could almost see the wall rise up between them. Though *New York Newsday*'s Wally Matthews would report the next day that fighter and manager exchanged insults, not even once did I see Bill and Mike look in each other's direction. I walked over to Mike.

"What's happening," I said. Mike smiled, shook my hand, and asked me to sit next to him. He then put his hands over mine and inquired about my family and some mutual friends.

"Everything's cool," he said. Then after watching a fight in the ring for a few minutes, he said, "Let's go see Edwin." Accompanied by Tyson's companion, who I thought was a security person, we went to Rosario's dressing room to wish the fighter good luck. Once in the dressing room, Steve Lott, who was assisting Rosario's trainer, Lalo Medina, made up for Mike's oversight by introducing the man I thought was a security person. He turned out to be Michael Winston, Ruth Roper's lawyer. After a few minutes with Edwin, I left Mike in the dressing room with Winston, Lott, Rosario, and Lalo and went to see some of the preliminary fighters in action.

Forty-five minutes later, Rosario stepped into the ring, but there was no sign of Tyson or Winston. I thought it strange that the champ would leave without seeing Rosario fight. Rosario's trainer had seen Tyson go to the public telephone near the dressing room a couple times. The last time, Tyson had returned to Rosario and said he couldn't stay. "He said he had a very serious emergency," Lalo told me.

Rosario knocked out Lozano in two rounds that night and we all went home happy. Lott took a detour to his apartment to get some stuff before returning to Atlantic City that night. But before leaving he checked his answering machine. To his surprise, there was a message from Robin.

The message said: "Steve, I had a problem. I'm in the hospital. Mike was kind enough to come over. I'm sorry for keeping him overnight. I'll make sure he's in Atlantic City in time for training tomorrow. I just wanted to make sure you knew where he was."

Something about the message didn't jibe, Lott thought to himself.

When Tyson returned the following day, he was downcast. "My wife had a miscarriage," he said to everyone, almost crying. At that point the uneasiness Lott felt ripened into suspicion. Why would a woman who'd just suffered a miscarriage be concerned about upsetting her husband's work schedule? And why would she take it upon herself to make a call her husband could just as easily have made? Had the message simply been an attempt to prove Robin's whereabouts—prove that she *really* was in the hospital that night? Was she feeling so defensive about rumors she really *wasn't* pregnant that she felt the call was necessary? Lott dwelled on the possibilities, but he decided in the end that this was one mystery he wouldn't solve.

A few days later, I went to the Trump Plaza to check on Tyson's training and to conduct interviews for this book. Mike was in the gym, but Rooney had canceled his sparring session because he was too upset. The champ was hitting the heavy bag furiously. When the bell rang for the one-minute rest period, he walked toward me.

"We lost the baby," he said. I put my arm around his sweaty shoulders and told him there was plenty of time for more children. He just shook his head in disgust. I watched the rest of his training, and despite his sadness, or perhaps because of it, he looked fit and vicious.

His ferocious attack on the heavy bag reminded me of a conversation I'd had with him a few weeks before in which we discussed his early brutality:

"Did you ever shoot anybody?"

"I've shot at a lot of people."

"A lot of people? It was like fun for you?"

"Yeah, I like to see them run. I like to see them beg."

"What did they say?"

" 'Please don't shoot me. Don't shoot me. Don't shoot me. I'll do anything you say. Don't shoot me' . . . I'd shoot real close to them, skin them or something . . . make them take off their pants and then go run in the streets. . . . There were times we used to make the other guys scared and make them steal, make them snatch that chain or rob that person."

"And if they didn't do it?"

"We would kick their asses."

When I returned to my room that night I had a message from Roper. I called her back and learned she wanted to talk with me face-to-face. "Can we meet tomorrow for breakfast?" she asked.

It was the first time since the wedding party I'd seen her. She hadn't changed, but she was closer to Mike and had apparently gained his friendship and confidence. We were just making small talk at first, then she asked me about Cus D'Amato. I praised my old manager and told her of the importance of D'Amato, Jacobs, and Cayton to Tyson's career. Then she steered the conversation to Tyson and his behavior. We agreed that he acted much younger than his almost twenty-two years, blaming his immaturity on his background. Then, with the eloquence of a trial lawyer making her summation, she began talking about her son-in-law's sensitivity.

"José, you should've seen him in the hospital," she said, her face turning sad. "You know, my daughter panics when she sees a needle. And last night, Mike was trying to convince her that the injections were for her own good. He said to Robin, 'Do you want the doctor to put the needle in me first just to show you that it's nothing.' He looked so cute and touchy."

Then she planted an important seed. "Did you know," she asked, "that Mike pays for all the expenditures in Camille's house?" I was astonished, to say the least. I'd been with Jacobs the day Cus voiced his concern about Camille's future if he died. Right then and there, after telling Cus that he had many more years on this earth, Jacobs promised eternal care for the woman.

"He even pays for Jay Bright's medical bills," Roper said. I couldn't believe what I was hearing.

"I have the bills," she insisted. "Every penny spent in that house comes from Mike's pocket."

Suddenly I recalled a conversation I'd had with Jacobs a while back concerning these expenditures. He said that since Tyson had bought a Manhattan apartment and was showing a lot of expenses in it, he'd probably have to pay a bundle in city taxes. It was then that his accountant said that for Mike to justify Catskill as his official residence he'd have to spend more money there.

I decided to say nothing of this recollection to Ruth, but that day at the Trump Plaza, she made other points that revealed two things: first, she was well informed, and second, she believed Tyson should break his ties with the old boxing family. The main purpose of our meeting, I soon discovered, was that Roper wanted to arrange a second meeting a day or two later between me and her lawyer, Michael Winston, who I'd heard was now Tyson's lawyer. I told her I had no objection.

As expected, Winston wanted to find out when, where, and what had transpired three months ago—when I was still the chairman of the New York State Athletic Commission and Jacobs was alive—concerning the signing of the additional documents connected to the Tyson-Jacobs boxer-manager contract. I told him that we—Cayton, Jacobs, myself, and Tyson—had met in my office sometime in February, and like a happy family everyone signed the papers prepared by Carl DeSantis, the commission's lawyer.

"Was there anybody else there besides the principals when you people signed those documents?" Winston asked. All of a sudden I got confused. I first said that besides me there was another official from the commission, Peter Della, a former boxer and an outstanding referee, who'd signed the papers as a witness.

"Were Mrs. Cayton or Mrs. Jacobs there?" Winston asked.

"Yes," I said, "I think Jacobs's wife was there, but I don't think Doris [Cayton's wife] was." I thought for a moment and remembered that the documents were signed over a two-day period, first in my office and then at Tyson's wedding party at the Helmsley. I wasn't totally sure and a day later I called my former secretary at the commission's office, Michelle Lavina, who as usual refreshed my memory.

"No, you didn't sign those contracts here," she said. "You went to Jim Jacobs's office first and then you went to the wedding party to sign the rest a couple of days later."

The next day I told Winston about my mistake and apologized for my inaccuracies, blaming my boxing career for dulling my memory a bit. Then I explained in detail what went on that cold day of February 12, 1988.

The signing of the documents had been scheduled to take place at the NYSAC office in downtown Manhattan. Tyson was staying in Catskill, 130 miles away, and when he got up that morning, the town was blanketed in snow. He called Jacobs and said he might not be able to get out of his house. When the news reached Cayton, he came up with the idea of calling the Catskill police. Minutes later, a Catskill cop telephoned Mike and assured him that a car would pick him up in a matter of minutes. The meeting, meantime, was rescheduled for later the same day and switched from the commission office to Jacobs and Cayton's in midtown Manhattan.

When Mike arrived for the meeting he was mumbling something about the way he'd been picked up in Catskill, how it brought back disgusting memories of his childhood. He didn't want to spend a lot of time on the paperwork and asked that we get things over with.

We were waiting for a notary public, and when she arrived, Jacobs began explaining to Tyson the exact contents of the documents. "As you know," Jacobs began, "I'm your manager of record and Bill is the assignee . . ."

Tyson raised his arm and told his manager he didn't have to go through all that. "Come on, man," Tyson said. "I feel funny listening to all that bullshit. You're my manager. I trust you guys a hundred percent. We don't have to go through all that bullshit. Give me the papers," he said, taking a pen from Jacobs's shirt pocket. "Where do I have to sign?"

"Mike, we have a public notary here and she has to know what she came for," Jacobs said, spinning a white lie to get Tyson to listen. "It's a matter of law and proper conduct and not of choice that I have to explain the precise contents of these papers."

"Okay."

"As I started to say, I'm the manager; Bill is the assignee. These papers you're about to sign may sound complicated, but they're not. . . . If anything happens to me after we put our names on these documents," Jacobs continued, "Bill will then become your manager of record, and my wife, Loraine, becomes the assignee; on the other hand, if anything happens to Bill and I'm still alive, then Doris [Bill's wife] becomes the assignee."

I told Mike that his two-thirds share would not be altered. "Your signature only means," I said, "that you accept Bill as the manager of record if anything happens to Jim."

"I thought," Jacobs said, "that since we were all going to be here, we should take the opportunity to sign a new five-year boxer-manager contract, instead of waiting two years to renew the existing one."

"Do you have any objection?" I asked Mike, who started to laugh. "I'm serious," I said. "This is business." He laughed some more, and I struggled to keep from laughing myself. At last all the papers were signed, and Cayton, who had power of attorney for his wife, signed for her.

I telephoned DeSantis to tell him everything was signed and sealed. I also informed him that Cayton had signed for his wife. "But," I assured him, "the champ's assignee is legally authorized to do so."

"I'd prefer that Mrs. Cayton sign the papers herself," DeSantis said.

"Then let's get together at the wedding party on Sunday," Jacobs suggested.

And that's exactly what we did, I told Winston, who thanked me for the information.

18

JUNE 1988 became a month of torment for the heavy-weight champion. His childhood fears were awakened in a series of events that seemed to have no end. By mid-May, Roper and Robin had joined the struggle between King and Cayton, which soon became a public battle. King had seen Tyson getting further from his old boxing family and closer to his new one, so King decided to publicly side with Robin and her mother. This was all going on during the crucial part of Tyson's training for the June 27 fight.

Every newspaper in the country seemed to have something to say about Tyson's private and public life, but interestingly, the press reacted most negatively against King, Roper, and Robin. They were the media bad guys and Tyson was the young, uneducated victim. The ladies were accused of being ''gold diggers'' and ''opportunists,'' while all the old charges against King were trotted out as well. King, however, knew how to deal with it: make your own headlines. At one point, King, indulging in his usual hyperbole, described Cayton as "the most vicious, ruthless, lying individual in boxing history."

Roper and Givens, subjected to consistent public humiliation, fought back.

In his office, Cayton, with Lott joining in, would criticize the two women in Tyson's life, and somehow the exact words would be repeated by either Ruth or Robin to Mike, who'd relay them back to Lott or Rooney. Someone in his office, Cayton assumed, was a spy or at least a professional gossip.

"We'd make comments at the office about the bad things Ruth and Robin were doing to Mike's career," Lott said, "and the next thing we knew, Don, Ruth, and Givens would repeat them verbatim to Mike. . . . The idea was to put a wedge between Bill and Mike so that King could take over Mike's operations."

"These people are putting your wife and mother-in-law down," Robin told Mike, "saying filthy things about us, and you just don't do anything about it. You must stand up for us."

Since the start of training in Atlantic City, Tyson had refused to speak to or look at Lott. The champ was spending more time at his suite at the Trump Plaza than at his penthouse apartment at the Ocean Club. Finally Tyson went to Rooney. "I don't want Steve in camp with us anymore," he said. "He should go home."

"You want Steve to go home," Rooney snapped back, "you tell him to go home."

Despite his retort, Rooney told Lott about the conversation and Lott sat tight and waited. The next day, Tyson had to train at Bally's hotel because the Trump Theater and the Chelsea Room were booked for other activities. As Lott drove the champ to Bally's, Tyson didn't utter a word. In the gym, as Rooney taped his hands, Tyson called Lott over.

"I was standing opposite them," Steve recalled, "when Mike said, 'Steve, come here for a second, please.' I walked over and he said, 'Steve, Kevin and I are going to work together from now on, you can go home. We don't need you anymore.' I said to him, 'Mike, is that what you want?' and he said, 'Yeah.' I said, 'Good luck. I'll see you.' And he said, 'Okay.' "

Minutes later, in a furious exchange of blows in the sparring session with McCall Oliver, Tyson went down and a controversy erupted about what caused his trip to the canvas. Was it a push or a punch?

"To tell you the truth," Cayton told me, "McCall bragged about knocking down Mike, but in reality it was a slip, a push and a slip combined."

A few days later, Cayton and Shelly Finkel started to put pressure on Robin and Roper to talk to Tyson about rehiring Lott. It was for Tyson's sake: Lott understood and handled the champ's prefight emotions better than anyone. Finally the women agreed, and Lott, who still had his doubts, was rehired. The day before his comeback, Tyson's former roommate was walking toward Grand Central Terminal, near the Roper Consultants office at the Lincoln Building, when he and Robin came almost face-to-face in the street. "The woman wouldn't even look at me," Lott said. "She just looked somewhere else and went into the Lincoln Building."

Roper called Cayton the next day to inform him that Tyson had agreed to Lott's rehiring. Lott was with Cayton but wanted to be sure. He took the telephone.

"Ruth, is it possible I can speak to Mike and ask him if it's okay for me to come back?"

"Steve," Roper said, "it's perfectly all right with him, I'm sure it's going to be okay. He said it'll be okay. As a matter of fact, he wants you to be there tomorrow morning for the Pepsi commercial."

The next morning, Lott was at the City Center building on West Thirty-fourth Street when a limousine pulled up next to him. Out jumped Mike and Robin and they both gave him effusive hellos. "It was as if nothing had transpired among us," Lott said.

Roper and Givens wasted no time starting another controversy, this time with the Pepsi-Cola people, demanding more money than had been negotiated. Lott left the premises. "They thought they were in charge," Lott said, "and I didn't want to get involved with that."

That night Lott went to Atlantic City and didn't see Tyson until the following morning at the penthouse. "He arrived in a limousine," Steve told me, "and we hugged just like old times and everything just went back to normal."

In the weeks before the fight, Tyson was appearing on the cover of practically every major magazine in the country, including *Life, Time, People,* and *Sports Illustrated.* Roper had taken charge of scheduling interviews and photo sessions, and Lott, whose instincts told him his days were numbered, tried to follow her instructions to the letter. "We promised *Life* magazine first crack," she told Steve. "I want you to make sure that no one from any other magazine talks to Mike. No one."

"*People* magazine is going to be here this week," Lott said to Ruth, "and *Time* is coming next week. But I'm gonna make sure nobody speaks with Mike until *Life* gets its cover."

"Wonderful," Ruth replied. "Thank you very much."

Two days later a reporter from *People* magazine came to Atlantic City and introduced herself to Lott, asking to talk to the champion.

"You can't speak with him for a few days yet," Lott told her. "But we'll let you know when you'll be able to talk to him."

She asked why not, and Lott told her he couldn't divulge the reasons but would be in touch.

"Can't I stick around and watch him train?" she asked.

"Absolutely, yes, no problem," Lott said. "There'll be a press conference after the workout and you can ask whatever you want. But you can't have an exclusive interview with him just yet."

"Can I speak with Kevin Rooney?"

"Yes, you can speak with him, no problem."

She hung around, asked a few questions, and spoke to Rooney, and everything seemed fine, except that Lott forgot to tell Rooney about his conversation with Roper. After the press conference, Tyson and Rooney stayed behind and Lott went to the Ocean Club. When the reporter from *People* complained to Rooney about not being allowed to talk to Tyson, the trainer telephoned Roper. "I thought it was proper," Rooney told me, "and I did it out of respect, not obligation."

The reporter was present when he called.

"How come *People* magazine can't speak with Mike?" he asked Roper, who started to yell at him. She put Robin on the phone, who proceeded to best her mother in the yelling department. "Obviously," Rooney said, "they didn't want anybody to know they'd put the lid on all the other magazines in favor of *Life* because, unlike the others, it had Mike and Robin on the cover."

After hanging up with Rooney, the women called Lott.

"Ruth spoke first," Lott recalled. " 'Steve,' she said, 'didn't you promise me that *People* magazine wouldn't speak with Mike?' I said, 'They didn't.' She said, 'But didn't you promise that they wouldn't get any interviews, that you wouldn't give them anything?'

" 'I didn't give them anything,' I said. 'I can't bar them from the training. They were here. They wanted to know who the sparring partners were. But I promised you they wouldn't speak with Mike and she didn't speak with Mike.' "

Roper didn't answer. She put Robin on the phone, who, according to Lott, came out swinging harder than her husband. "You motherfucker," Steve said were the first words out of her mouth, "you son of a bitch." She followed, said Lott, with, "Fuck you. Fuck you. You're trying to destroy me. You motherfucker!"

"Wait a second," Lott said to her, "I did nothing wrong and—"

"Fuck you," she said. "I'm gonna make my husband punch you in your fucking face and throw you the fuck out of there. You motherfucker, they said you were a fucking snake, you son of a bitch."

Lott's body began shaking involuntarily. Then he heard Roper's voice again. "Where is Mike?" she asked. "We've got to speak with Mike."

"I knew where he was," Lott told me. "But I didn't want to tell them until I got to him first. So she hung up the phone and I called Rooney at the hotel. As soon as Kevin got on the phone, he was very apologetic."

Rooney told Lott he didn't know what was going on.

"Kevin," Lott said, "you better get Mike in here and have a talk with him to explain exactly what happened so he knows the whole story. Come right now, because I think we can have real big trouble."

"He gets Mike," Lott continued telling me, "and as he told me later, on the way over in the car he started to explain to Mike everything that had happened. As Kevin told me later when he got me alone, he said, 'Mike was embarrassed to see you, Steve, because I told him how she'd insulted you and the language she'd used.'

"So Kevin and Mike came in the door. I said, 'Mike, I wanna explain something to you.' He said, 'Steve, man, it's okay.' I said, 'Mike, please, just let me explain everything that happened.' " Lott explained what had happened.

"Steve, forget about it," Mike responded. Then, Lott recalled, "He went into his room and called Robin at her mother's office. And the next thing I heard was, 'Fuck the cover. I don't want the fucking cover.' And he hung up."

Tyson left the room, came back two minutes later, and asked Lott to go for a walk with him. "I was shaking," Lott told me. "I didn't know what was going to happen." When they reached the boardwalk, they started to walk slowly and Tyson spoke.

"Steve, you probably don't know how they work," Tyson said, referring to the two ladies in his life. "It took *me* a while to get use to them also. The first time they screamed and yelled at me . . . it makes you feel bad, doesn't it? You don't know how to take that, right?''

"Mike, no one ever spoke to me like that."

"You know, when they talked to me like that the first time, I felt just like you're feeling now. You're not used to having people talk to you that way. But they don't understand our business. We're together. We're brothers. They don't understand you and me. They don't understand what's important. They're from a different world. You should forget about it."

Steve was greatly relieved. They walked a couple more blocks, then they came back to the building and Lott drove Tyson to Trump Plaza.

"When we reached the hotel," Steve continued, "he leaned over and kissed me. 'Steve,' he said, 'you and I are brothers, just forget all that bullshit.' "

A couple of days later, on June 14, 1988, Tyson was at the gym, sitting near the ring not saying a word as Rooney bandaged his hands. The champ didn't have a happy face. I walked over to him to ask if he had time to talk that night.

"I don't wanna talk to nobody," he said. "I just don't feel like talking to no fucking one. I know what's going on. I know perfectly well what the fuck is going on. But I'll be all right."

I was surprised, even angry at his answer. There was a long pause and then I punched back.

"I knew you when you were twelve," I said, "I consider our daily interviews for the book brother-to-brother talks. I've treated you with respect ever since you were no more than a punk. I expect the same treatment in return." He knew I was upset.

"Hey, don't take this personally," he said. "What I meant was that I don't feel like talking to anyone. Not only you. No one."

He'd been in a deep depression and was looking awful during the workouts. It was the worst I'd ever seen him. His training was so poor that Rooney was about to explode. Kevin began yelling instructions that showed his irritation. "Punch," he shouted at one point. "Come on, Mike, throw damned punches." Tyson seemed not to hear. By the fourth round of sparring Rooney had seen enough. He called time.

"You're embarrassing me," Tyson told his trainer.

"Bullshit," answered Rooney

"Fuck you," said Tyson, walking away in the ring.

"Fuck *you*," snapped Rooney, his face reddening.

Despite my advice to the contrary, Rooney made Tyson box nine more rounds, in which he intentionally took a few extra punches just to antagonize Rooney. Tyson had told me earlier that Robin had been in camp with him for a while but after a heated quarrel went back to New York.

After the workout, Tyson walked toward Richard Joselit, a businessman and boxing historian, who'd brought Eddie Mustafa, former light-heavyweight champion, to the training session. Mustafa, like Tyson, had been raised in Brownsville and was its first black boxing champion. The three chatted for a while, then Tyson went to his dressing room. Later, Tyson saw the two men leaving and called them over.

"Where're you guys going?"

"Back home," said Mustafa.

"Fuck it, man," Tyson said. "Spend the whole day with me. Come on, I wanna take yous to my new creep in Jersey." He said he wanted to go to Morristown, knowing they'd likely be more familiar with that town than the smaller nearby Bernardsville. He got into Mustafa's car and Joselit followed in his two-passenger Avanti sports car.

An hour after the workout, I got a call at my hotel room from Joselit, who wanted directions to Tyson's Bernardsville home. Tyson had meant "Morristown" in the north central part of the state, not "Moorestown," which was what Joselit and Mustafa thought they'd heard and which was in the other direction. Joselit was calling on his car phone as he followed Mustafa and Tyson, who himself didn't know the correct route. "Make sure he's here tomorrow in time for the press conference," I told Joselit. As soon as I hung up, I called Roper's office.

"Ruth," I said to her, "Mike is not looking good at all in training, and I think it's because he misses his wife immensely."

Roper didn't know what to make of my call and it took her a while to focus in on what I was talking about. "Err . . . I . . . Jesus . . . You think Robin should be there with him?"

"That's right," I said. "As a matter of fact, he's on his way to Bernardsville this minute, and I think you should call your daughter and have her surprise him there. It would be a wonderful psychological lift for him."

Roper called me twice more in the next twenty minutes as she made arrangements for her and her daughter to go to Bernardsville. "You should be there with us," she said, wanting us to arrive as a threesome because of her apprehensiveness about Tyson's mood shifts. "Take a limo, it's not that far."

"He has company," I told her. "He's there with a couple friends of mine."

When Tyson arrived home, it was almost 6 P.M. The two-hour trip had taken them four hours. And to make things worse, Mike discovered he'd left his house keys in Atlantic City. So he went around to the back of the house and kicked open a door.

"He was very proud of the house," Joselit told me later. "And one room simply overwhelmed him. 'You see this room,' he told me very proudly, 'this is for my son.' "

Joselit said Tyson's brown eyes were glassy with emotion. The champ gave them a guided tour and Joselit made a few jokes to keep things light.

"I heard that Dave Winfield is moving in with you guys very soon," Joselit said, alluding to Roper's suit against the New York Yankees star right fielder, who she contended had infected her with a venereal disease.

Tyson didn't know what Joselit was talking about. He

wasn't in the habit of reading newspapers much beyond the sports section. Besides, the front sections of the newspapers, where this story and a growing number of anti-Givens and anti-Roper stories were appearing, were usually tossed into the bottom of the trash can by his wife and mother-in-law.

"Who said that Dave Winfield is moving in?" he asked innocently. Joselit changed the subject.

"I'm hungry," Tyson roared, and suggested a trip to a local restaurant two miles away.

At the restaurant, Mustafa tried to give Tyson a few tips on the boxing business, including some insights into people like Don King. Tyson listened but was having trouble concentrating.

"Every girl he smelled," Joselit said, "over there went his attention." Tyson faced the entrance, and hence had full view of everyone coming into the place.

But Mustafa persisted. He and Tyson had a common bond. Mustafa had been at the top; he knew the game inside and out, and besides, Tyson was his homeboy.

"You have to watch Don," Mustafa told Mike. "Do not get involved with him. He is nothing but a manipulator. Look what he did to Tim Witherspoon; look what he did to Larry Holmes."

After a while, they started to tell jokes and stories about women.

"We were in a very good mood," Mustafa told me later, "talking about sex and having a ball. Mike was kidding and joking and laughing."

All of a sudden, Tyson's expression just changed as if he were in shock. Then he smiled. "And when I turned my back," Joselit said, "there they were: Robin Givens and Ruth Roper. What a coincidence!"

When Tyson's women walked in, he was no longer the same man. "His facial lines were not the same," Joselit said. "From joking and laughing and talking loud, he became very, very serious. He was a different person."

"You mean that now I don't have to drive you all the way to Philadelphia?" Joselit said in jest, a veiled reference to the twenty-four women Tyson claimed he'd had in the City of Brotherly Love.

"Don't you fuck around that way in front of her," Tyson warned Joselit in a harsh whisper. "She doesn't know that you're kidding. Don't fuck around."

The following morning at around nine, I called Robin's number in New York City. I'd hoped she'd accompanied Tyson to Atlantic City and was disappointed to hear her voice.

"You should be here," I told her. "Mike needs you. He's miserable without you. You should be here today, now, next to him." We heard electronic beeps and she put me on hold to check the other line. When she came back, she said, "It's him."

"Okay," I said. "Don't tell him you're talking to me, and please, come down as soon as you can."

Later, at around noon, I went to the gym. Tyson seemed relaxed and ready to train. The past few days in the gym were behind him. "My wife is flying in by helicopter and she should be getting in soon," he said. "And by the way, let's talk tonight some more for the book."

Just before Mike started to hit the heavy bag, Robin made her entrance. Tyson beamed, overflowing with an inner warmth. He thumped the bag with beautiful combinations, his eyes escaping from time to time toward his wife. He appeared to have regained his rhythm, his composure.

Abruptly, Robin got up and walked toward the gym exit with John Horne. The champ spotted her leaving and stopped hitting the bag. "Where the fuck is she going?" he asked of no one in particular. "Go and find out where she's going."

I chased after Robin and Horne. "Your husband wants to know which direction you're taking and why," I said to her.

"I'm going to buy chewing gum," she said, laughing, loving the moment, knowing Tyson was upset because she'd walked out. "Tell him I just went to buy chewing gum." And she laughed again.

*   *   *

On Wednesday, June 15, King and his black limousine were waiting for me in front of the Trump Plaza. It was my first time in the customized Cadillac. We went to a restaurant owned by a large woman who serves soul food. I hadn't spoken to King since warning Tyson not to sign an exclusive contract with anyone, promoter or otherwise. King, whom I'd defended more than I should have in boxing circles, was angry with me.

"We lost the chance of our lives," he grumbled as soon as we sat down at the restaurant. "I wanna know why you told Mike not to sign the contract with me."

Of course, when I was chairman of the New York State Athletic Commission, I couldn't advise Tyson on such matters. It would have been a conflict of interest. But once I'd relinquished that position, how could I tell a friend of mine who happened to be the world heavyweight champion to sign an exclusive contract?

"You'd be giving ammunition to Cayton by signing that exclusive contract," I told King.

"Legal matters? I handle that. That's *my* business," he said, shaking his head in disgust. "We had Tyson and because of you we lost him."

"You mean, *you* lost him," I clarified. "But maybe now that I'm not a commissioner [I'd resigned several weeks earlier], I can get him to reconsider."

King was too smart to believe me. I showed him an article I was just finishing that touched on racism and the prospects for minority political candidates in this country.

"Man," he said, "you really understand the situation between blacks and whites in this country, but you surely don't apply [it with respect to yourself]." He looked around the restaurant. "You know very well, José," he said, "that the Jews want to control Tyson . . . the Jacobses, the Caytons, the Finkels. You know it."

The next morning, I visited Tyson at his penthouse with my tape recorder. It was around 10 A.M. and he was in the kitchen, sitting at a small table, leafing through the morning newspapers. Rooney was next to him; Lott was in the living room.

"How do you feel?" I asked Tyson, who moved his head from side to side. I put two eggs in boiling water and started to walk out of the kitchen with Kevin following me. I then backtracked and sat down next to the fighter. "Anything wrong?" I asked. "I didn't like that wordless answer."

"I feel like killing someone," he snapped, his face contorted with anger.

"That's good," I said. "That's the way you should feel two weeks before an important fight."

"I don't mean it that way. I mean, I'm going to kill someone, maybe today. Please visit me in jail."

Bewildered, I got up and walked to the living room.

"He's in a bad mood," I said to Lott.

"Have you seen the newspapers?" Lott asked. I went back to the kitchen and looked at the papers spread out over the table. One headline announced that Cayton had hired Thomas Puccio, a prominent Manhattan attorney and former Assistant U.S. Attorney, to represent him. Another story mentioned legal problems on the horizon involving the members of Tyson's new family—Robin, Roper, and Winston. There was also a report that the World Boxing Council (WBC) was threatening not to sanction the fight unless it went fifteen rounds.

"Most of those stories are bullshit," I said. "Maybe Butch Lewis is behind them, trying to upset you."

"Not all," responded Tyson. "Some of that shit I know is true. If you are truly my friend, tell both King and Cayton to stop all that bullshit." In front of Mike was a story saying that his personal troubles had helped lower the odds on his winning the fight against Spinks.

ON the night of Friday, June 17, 1988, I was in my hotel room writing a section about Jesse Jackson for my article on minority political candidates when the phone rang. It was Wally Matthews of *New York Newsday*. Matthews was a handsome, ambitious young writer who'd antagonized the entire Tyson entourage but wanted access to them nevertheless. Twice he'd written entire columns about me without ever even interviewing me. The people around Tyson felt he was "insensitive" and "unprofessional."

Now he was on the phone telling me he had to talk to Tyson. He said he was in possession of sensitive information that was both exclusive and explosive. "I can't tell you what it is, José," he said, "but it's serious stuff."

I took down Matthews's numbers and phoned Tyson. He wasn't home but Rooney was. I told him to make sure Tyson talked to Matthews. Half an hour later, Tyson called. "Should I call this guy?" he asked. "You know how he is and—"

"I think you should at once," I interrupted. "Do that for me, please. I think he has important news for you."

On Sunday, June 19, 1988, eight days before the Tyson-Spinks bout, *New York Newsday* ran a devastating article that depicted the young champion as an insensitive and dangerous man. Stephanie Givens, Robin's twenty-one-year-old sister, had called Matthews from Madeira, Portugal, where she was playing in a tennis tournament, and told him she was afraid for her sister. Among other things, she told Matthews:

"I've stayed completely out of this so far, but it's just gotten to be too much. I was kind of reluctant to come forward with this. . . . The whole thing is—the thing I hate is—I've known about Mike from the first day Robin met him. I've felt it's all been a big mistake from the beginning. Michael's supposed to be the good guy and everybody else is supposed to be abusing him. Nobody knows how abusive Mike is. Robin has definitely been harmed emotionally. Not as much physically. But you never know what he is going to do."

She went into the details of some personal experiences with Tyson that made it sound as if the champ should be in a psychiatric ward instead of a boxing ring.

Tyson's sister-in-law told Matthews that Tyson drank heavily every day and that one day he showed up drunk on the set where Robin was videotaping an installment of *Head of the Class*. Stephanie said that Tyson caused "a terrible scene. He started breaking the lights, using foul language, throwing things. They had to stop filming. Robin had to leave the set to calm him down."

She said that on another night Tyson went berserk and couldn't be calmed down. "They had a fight, and he hit Robin in the head, with a closed fist," she said. "He knows how to hit her, and where to hit her, without causing any real damage. We had adjoining rooms and I was scared, so I made Robin come into my room and closed both doors. I put the latch on, and the deadbolt. He just kicked the two doors in. I knew he was strong, but I was like amazed.

"You can be so sweet to him, and you'll never know what will set him off. He's the type of person who feels, he's Mike Tyson, he can do whatever he wants. He loves to damage things in the house, just for no reason. If he feels like kicking in the TV set, he'll do it. If he feels like punching a hole in the wall, he does it. If he feels like hitting you, he does it.

"You wake up in the morning, and you wonder, how is Michael going to be today? Things would be all right for a little while, and then . . . Even if people are around, he'll act up. When you are around him, you do live in fear," she told Wally. "He can just explode. [Robin's] never been alone with him. There is always someone with her, because we are afraid for her.

"It's amazing. He changes his voice, that baby-talk act, and people think he's so sweet. He's the sweetest person to people who don't care about him."

The story was believable. I knew that he'd smacked Robin before they were married. I'd witnessed a few heated arguments and had heard him shouting at her and her mother on the telephone. Stephanie's story also jibed with what I knew about Tyson's childhood and his dark prefight moods. Maybe there were really *two* Tysons. One who laughed, hugged, and kissed and was sensitive and compassionate; and one who enjoyed the sight of pain and hurt in others.

When questioned by the media about Stephanie Givens's story, Cayton, who'd been accused by Ruth and Robin of trying to break up the champ's marriage, was careful with his answer: "I'm an enemy of neither Ruth Roper nor Robin Givens." He also told the press that he was always careful not to offend Tyson's new family.

The day after Stephanie Givens's broadside, Tyson told members of the press that "I'm married to Robin. Fuck everybody else. Bill will be dead and gone in ten years, but I'll still be with my wife."

Forced into the background was the upcoming Tyson-Spinks fight. The controversy hadn't hurt ticket sales, how-

ever, and by the time June 27, 1988, rolled around, the fight
had a place in history. Spinks and Tyson would each make
more money in one fight than any athlete ever. Tyson would
receive more than $21 million; Spinks in excess of $13 million.

Before the opening bell, other games were played. Publi-
cists and press agents from the Trump Plaza, and Donald
Trump himself, didn't sit still for one minute. They set out
to make the bout a truly huge event. The nominal promoter
of the boxing program was King, who would make $3 million
without doing much to earn it.

According to Cayton, in the dealings involving Trump
and King—which also included the Tyson-Biggs and the
Tyson-Holmes fights—King made it very difficult for the
Trump organization to function properly.

"They really didn't want King around in any way, shape,
or form at any time—for any fight," Lott told me. "Of course,
the Tyson-Spinks fight was made, and it had to have a promoter on record, so we selected Don. But for the first time in
his promotional life King was not in full charge of the monies
coming in."

Lott said that King had made such a mess of his last two
promotions at the Trump Plaza that this time the Trump staff
was responsible for accommodating the VIPs and the press.
And at most press conferences, King, the usual master of ceremonies, was replaced by a member of the Trump staff.

Lott said he didn't know what King did to earn his money.
"I can't think of anything, outside of putting on the undercard
(preliminary bouts). He supplied the Trevor Berbick–Carl Williams semifinal and paid for it. But besides doing that and
getting paid for it, there was not one single press conference
he organized, not one newspaper man he sent in, not one news
release he sent out. There was nothing that came out of the
Don King organization to promote that fight—not one single
telephone call . . . nothing."

Lott thought that King's minor role was attributable to
three factors: "Number one," he said, "the Trump organiza-

tion did a marvelous job promoting the live event like never before; two, Shelly Finkel did a magnificent job coordinating the close-circuit and pay-for-view showings and sending news and videotape releases; and three, King was hoping and praying that the promotion would fall flat on its face, enabling him to blame Bill Cayton. Any effort made by King to help the event would only have supported Bill's claim that he was capable of putting on an event of that magnitude successfully—without Don King."

Finally, after all the ballyhoo, all the gossip, all the tension, June 27 mercifully arrived. A mixed crowd—show business personalities, high rollers, and hustlers—overwhelmed the front seats with only a scattering of boxing people among them. One was Bill Cayton, whom I noticed having a quiet conversation with a reporter. As I glanced at the two, a stranger came over and handed Cayton some papers. The documents, I learned later, were a court summons and notice of claim (i.e., notice that a lawsuit was to be filed) from Tyson, who wanted to end his business relationship with his manager.

I visited the dressing room and was impressed by Tyson's obvious self-confidence. He seemed perfectly at ease—almost too at ease.

When word came down for the boxers to get ready to be gloved, Nelson Lewis, Butch's brother, who'd left without saying a word after watching Tyson's hands being wrapped, returned. His face was not the same. He checked Tyson from head to toe, and when both gloves were secured, Lewis objected to a little lump on top of the right glove near the wrist; too much tape, perhaps.

"Change that," Nelson demanded in a loud voice.

"That doesn't violate any rule," Rooney objected. "But I'll put more tape around it if you want."

"That won't be enough," said Nelson. "I'm not satisfied with just putting tape over it."

"It's fine with me," said Larry Lee, a commission boxing inspector.

The argument grew louder. Tyson turned around, throwing a couple of jabs at an invisible opponent, then hitting the wall with a jab-right-cross combination. It was so hard and noisy that Lewis lowered his voice. He left the room and returned with his brother, Butch. Rooney, after consulting with Lee, refused to let Butch Lewis into the dressing room. A fuming Butch Lewis returned with Larry Hazzard, head commissioner and Lewis's longtime friend, who overruled Lee. Lewis and Lee started arguing loudly and making obscene threats.

"I'm not afraid of you," Lee told Lewis. "You bleed just like anybody else."

I told Hazzard that the commotion was not healthy for the champion. "Fighters come here to rest," I said, "to relax and to meditate."

"I'll take care of this," said Hazzard, who eventually convinced Lewis to leave the room after Eddie Futch, Spinks's trainer, came in and said the lump on the glove was harmless. Tyson had thrown a few more punches to the wall but had eventually sat down, allowing his sweat to dry, a boxing no-no. Fifteen minutes later, Spinks was finally waiting in the ring. Tyson looked at me, winked, and began the long walk toward the ring, surrounded by security people.

During the introduction of the referee, Tyson looked at Spinks's eyes. He saw panic in them. The last few seconds before the bell were probably more of a hardship for Tyson than the fight itself. I studied both fighters as objectively as I could and decided the match would be no contest. Getting to my seat, I bumped into Michael Winston.

"What do you think is going to happen?" he asked.

"No contest," I said.

When the bell rang, Tyson, as usual, came out to fight, pursuing Spinks and forcing the issue. Spinks tried to move but Tyson wouldn't let him. Spinks jabbed once, twice, three times. Each punch failed to make contact. Then, Tyson let go a straight right lead that landed high on Spinks's forehead. He was stunned for a second, but the stroke had not hit the right spot. Unable to escape the relentlessness of a charging, stronger opponent, Spinks looked for refuge inside, in Tyson's territory. Tyson exacted more pain with a left half-uppercut-half-hook that landed almost on the mandible, but not quite. This was followed by a left hook to Spinks's hanging right ribs, which cut the air supply to the lungs. Spinks's body wanted to drop, but his pride and ego fought the urge. So he remained on his feet and waited to be put out of his misery. Spinks, always an intelligent fighter, knew that he was about to become one more hopeless victim of Tyson's boxing ingenuity. A short right hook half a second after the body shot sent him to the canvas, his right elbow pressing hard over his right ribs. And when referee Frank Cappuccino started the mandatory eight count, I watched Butch Lewis, his arms resting over the ring's apron, trying to determine the extent of damage to his fighter.

As Cappuccino wiped Spinks's gloves, Lewis started to come into the ring, presumably to stop the one-sided match. But Tyson got to Spinks first. Expecting a left hook, Spinks turned his face to his left to ease the impact. Tyson let go a *right* hook, which, weirdly, smacked Spinks on the right jaw. Just ninety-one seconds after the first bell, Tyson had earned approximately $221,000 per second; the loser $145,000 per second. All for the biggest mismatch I'd ever seen in a heavyweight championship fight.

A few days later I was watching television and heard comedian Jackie Gayle describe what he considered the most intriguing aspect of the fight. "I loved it," he said. "Don King and Donald Trump shook hands on the fight. It will take five years to find out who's the screwer, and who's the screwee."

JUNE 30, 1988, was a good day for Mike Tyson. It was his twenty-second birthday and the town of Bernardsville was throwing the young millionaire a big party.

The event had a late start. Mike had spent the day with Camille in Catskill and was expected to arrive in New Jersey by late afternoon. The mayor of Bernardsville went to the nearby Morristown airport in a limousine and discovered that the champ had missed his flight. So everything started about ninety minutes later than planned.

The festivities began in front of the firehouse with Tyson on top of a fire truck. Some of the townspeople formed up behind the truck. They were followed by a small band. Next came a few limousines. I was in one with Michael Winston, Richard Joselit, and a stranger who turned out to be a lawyer associated with Winston. The little caravan took about forty minutes to make the complete trip through the little, affluent town.

Back at the firehouse waiting patiently was Don King. No one took credit for inviting him, and it was obvious that Robin, who didn't want him anywhere near Tyson, was not happy to see him. When the ceremonies ended, she ignored King's invitation to take her and her husband home in his empty limousine. She told Tyson in no uncertain terms to ride in the one I was traveling in, which was already occupied by four people.

Back at the house King closeted himself in a room with Tyson for about fifteen minutes and came out with a wide grin. A few minutes later, he was in the kitchen being hand-fed Chinese food by Roper.

"I think there is something going on between those two," said Joselit.

"There *is* something going on in this place," I told my friend. "But it has nothing to do with flesh." Money, not romance, was the name of the game being played in this twenty-eight-room mansion, though Tyson wasn't aware of it, nor were guests like Oprah Winfrey, who sat quietly in the trophy room talking to her boyfriend, Stedman Graham.

Winston and his lawyer-friend spoke to me about the Jacobs-Cayton-Tyson contract, and I repeated my conviction that Tyson was being managed by good, decent people. But they continued to press, so I started to leave. It was then that King came in.

"You're a good man," King said to me. "You're an honest and decent human being." Then he turned toward Winston and Roper. "We don't have to worry about him," Don assured them, referring to me. "He's with us . . . with Mike."

A few weeks after his birthday, Tyson called a press conference at the Plaza Hotel in Manhattan to announce his intentions of dumping Bill Cayton. The conference lasted thirteen minutes. Tyson, flanked by Robin, Roper, and his new advisor, Donald Trump, ripped Cayton apart.

"I'm calling the shots," Tyson said. "I will manage my

own self from now on. Anyone who goes against me can no longer be associated with me. . . . He [Cayton] wants to control everything and everybody. . . . I did the sweating inside the ring, not Bill Cayton. . . . Without me Cayton wouldn't have had a chance of even putting his foot in the door at HBO."

There were many inaccuracies and overstatements. The HBO comment was one of the most glaring. Cayton's association with HBO had begun in 1975, when he and Jacobs supplied features, boxing, and Olympic specials as well as films from their huge library to the cable network. "When we were feeding and clothing Mike Tyson [in the early 1980s], we were already doing substantial business with HBO," Cayton said later.

Later that day, Roper had called my home looking for me. I drove to her Upper West Side apartment around 7 P.M. accompanied by John Parsons, Steve Dunleavy, and a television crew. They were filming an episode of "The Reporters" for Fox Television that would be devoted exclusively to Mike Tyson. The doorman, an old boxing fan from my hometown in Puerto Rico, told me, "Roper is not here, but Robin is, with her hairdresser."

I called upstairs. Robin told me over the house phone that her mother would be there soon, but she didn't invite me upstairs. With the camera crew waiting out of sight, I decided to walk around the block, but when I went outside, I ran into Tyson and his mother-in-law stepping out of a limousine. We took the elevator upstairs. Inside the apartment, Tyson tried to go into the bedroom where his wife was having her hair done and wasn't allowed. "I don't want anybody here," she said.

I asked Mike if he'd give an interview to Parsons and Dunleavy, waiting downstairs. "They're good friends," I told him, "and I can promise they'll be fair."

"I'm too tired," he said, taking his jacket off. It was hot

inside and Tyson had started to sweat. He dropped down on a sofa, his forehead, arms, and back soaking wet, and instantly fell asleep.

"I'm going to order Chinese food," Roper said. "What do you want to eat?"

"I'm not hungry," I said.

"Come on, José," she said, smiling, "have something."

"Okay, get me shrimp fried rice and an egg roll." She made a joke about my taste, picked up the phone, and placed the order.

"I want you to know," she said, "that Mike really likes you. He respects you. I assume that you like him."

"Of course," I said, knowing this was the setup.

"I know that you are aware of what's going on, and as Winston told you, you're going to be subpoenaed for the case. . . . You know that this case is very important to your friend."

"He may encounter some problems," I said. "The truth may hurt him. But then again, it may not." Her face dropped, becoming more stern. The pleasantness was gone.

"If Mike is your friend," she said firmly, "then you should be expected to help him." I looked down at Tyson's wet face. He was out cold and snoring loudly.

"Ruth, I can't lie. I just hope that my truth doesn't hurt him, I swear."

"I'm sure that if your positions were reversed, *he'd* help you."

"But I'm not saying I'm not going to help him. What I'm saying is that I will not lie."

At that moment the doorbell rang. I thought I'd been saved by the Chinese food. But it was Winston, who was dressed in white shorts and a T-shirt. He was not there by accident.

"Tell this woman," I yelled at Winston somewhat in jest, "that she can demand no more and no less than the truth from me."

"That's right, Mrs. Roper," said Winston. The sarcasm in

his voice seemed unmistakable. "You should ask Mr. Torres here for no more and no less than the truth." As he said this, I knew his wheels were spinning. Roper had gone into the kitchen, which was separated from the living room by a counter and three tall chairs. Winston cleared his throat.

"Was Tyson represented by a lawyer when he signed the extension of the contracts?"

I shook my head.

"Did you ask him if he'd consulted with his wife about such things?"

I gave him the same answer.

"If you had to do it all over again, would you change anything?"

"If I had to do it all over again," I said slowly and deliberately, "I'd do it exactly the same way and—"

He didn't wait for my full explanation but turned toward Roper. "You see, Ruth," he said. "That's the truth José is talking about."

I was annoyed. "No fighter ever comes to my office with a lawyer," I said. "None [I should have said "few"] of the fighters signing contracts have the resources to afford counsel. That's why the commission is there, to protect them from unscrupulous bastards. If they bring a lawyer to help them, fine. But they never do. I was a fighter myself, a champion. I know who's who in this business. And Mike Tyson has been one of the few lucky ones to have the best managers in the game.

"Regarding the second question," I continued, "I'd never ask a fighter if he'd consulted with his wife about his boxing business. I could get hit by an unexpected left hook."

The food came and we ate—except Tyson, who was still snoring. In the middle of the meal, Winston left the apartment as suddenly as he'd shown up. Roper walked him to the door and whispered something to him. When she returned, she was like Tyson in the ring, not beating around the bush. She went straight for the jugular.

"I think that when you signed those contracts, you were

protecting the rights of Jacobs and Cayton," she declared. "You're not really a friend of Mike's, you're a friend of Cayton's. . . . You're all still taking advantage of Mike."

I didn't want to lose control so I didn't answer.

My silence encouraged her to continue. "If I were to give you advice, it would be to cease your friendship with Mike temporarily, until things quiet down."

"You're entitled to your opinion," I said coolly. "However, your idea about cutting my friendship with Mike temporarily is not a good one. . . . I think that if the only way I can keep my friendship with Mike is to lie in court, I'd rather cease my friendship *permanently.*"

"But before I leave," I said with conviction, "I must tell you something very important. This boy"—I pointed to Tyson, who was shifting positions fitfully and still snoring— "has an attention span of maybe three minutes. Once Thomas Puccio [Cayton's lawyer] gets him on the witness stand for two to three days—poor you, poor your daughter, poor Mike Tyson. Mike is going to tell the truth."

Ruth stood up; her skin turned pale. She was massaging her face involuntarily with both hands. She was trying to say something but could not utter a word. On that note, I left.

At home, I related the evening's events to my wife, Ramona.

"I bet Robin never came out to say hello," Ramona said. I'd never thought of that, but she was right. "And another bet," she said. "With that kind of response from Ruth, I don't think this case is going to go to trial."

Two days later, Roper was looking for me again.

"We've got something very good for you, José," she said over the telephone. "You'll love it. Hold on a second, I'm going to call Winston on the other line."

After a short while she was back on the line with me. "Tomorrow at 10 A.M.," she said, "go to Winston's office." Winston, she said, would tell me all about it.

Winston's law office was big, impressive, and ominous.

After some small talk, he got down to business. "An idea has been developed," he said, "to form an advisory board to help Mike. Because of your link to Cus D'Amato, and because of Mike's respect for you, we feel you should be included. Donald Trump will be in charge, and we're now trying to figure out who should be included."

"What do you want from me?" I asked.

"We'd like you to consider becoming part of it."

I didn't like the idea of Trump's making decisions about Mike's future and I told him. "He's an expert in business, not in boxing," I said. "But I'm ready to listen."

He then suggested I see Peter Parcher and Steven Hayes, litigation attorneys who were representing Tyson in his case against Cayton. Their offices were not too far from his, so I walked there. I knew that their firm also represented Trump. As soon as they opened their mouths, I liked them. Their approach was totally different from Winston's. They were interested in knowing all the facts concerning the signing of Mike's boxer-manager contracts, which I related. I even volunteered information they were not seeking but which I thought was relevant to the case.

"As an ex-commissioner I can guarantee you that there have been very few managerial teams like D'Amato, Jacobs, and Cayton," I told them. "Jacobs and Cayton invested lots of money in Tyson and many other kids for many years. They risked lots of money with Mike and the rest of them out of love for Cus, who always lived with the dream of building one more champion."

I also told them that I thought the legal action Tyson had taken at the behest of Robin and her mother against Cayton was totally unfair and unjust.

A week later, I had what I thought was an off-the-record conversation with Mike Katz of the New York *Daily News*, some of which he reported. I told him that Tyson's mother-in-law had implied I should change my expected court testimony; that she never told me to lie, but that she asked me to "stand by Tyson," and she had offered me a job as one of Tyson's advisors. In the article that resulted from the conversation, Winston was quoted as saying, "I've never approached him (Torres) concerning a position with Mike Tyson Enterprises. Period." And when Katz asked him if *Roper* had made any offer to me, Winston responded, "I don't believe she did it."

Shortly after Winston's denial was printed in the *Daily News*, my publisher, Warner Books, received a letter from Winston indicating that Tyson no longer wanted me to write his biography. The letter was, needless to say, personally upsetting. But since I'd already conducted most of my interviews with Mike, I resolved to go forward.

On July 17, 1988, I accompanied "The Reporters" film crew to Atlantic City to interview Don King. By now, the flamboyant promoter was ready to make his move. Now that Tyson had told the world he wanted Cayton out of his boxing life, King would pitch in to help the champ get rid of his manager.

"I said publicly," King told us, "that Bill Cayton was a liar, a hypocrite in the worst form, Satan in disguise, an egregious, self-centered, egotistical maniac who felt he had control of the universe. He reneged on deals and many other things. These are very strong statements that I'm making, so I must be able to substantiate them. It is no problem, because I feel I'm just like an open book."

King talked about how Cayton failed to show the books to Tyson's lawyer, family, accountant, and Tyson himself.

"This whole thing could have been diffused," he said, "this whole situation could have been avoided totally. All he [Cayton] had to do was let the man know what he had, where he had it and how he got it and how it came about. In other words, how much is he [Cayton] taking out of it in his contracts. Those are the issues. The rest of this is smoke screen.

"The only issue here is how much we were supposed to get, and how much is Bill Cayton taking out of his paycheck. . . . I happen to know for a fact Cayton is taking twenty percent off the top of the gross and taking a third of the net."

Months before, King had told me that Cayton was making deductions from Tyson's revenues that were "not kosher at all." It was, King told me, "an old business trick." What the promoter was referring to specifically was the manner in which Cayton divvied up foreign rights monies.

"When I found out how much King [who promoted virtually all of Mike's important fights] was getting for foreign rights, I thought it was ridiculous," Cayton told me during the writing of this book. "I knew from experience that I could get much more." So after a conversation with King, Cayton took charge of the foreign rights negotiations, and according to him, "I was able to get five to six times over the amount King was able to get."

Cayton figured he was justified in taking as much as twenty percent of the foreign rights revenues, both because outside agents often claimed a larger piece of the pie and because the total volume of rights sales multiplied enormously under his stewardship. Cayton then went on, however, to take one-third, as is the manager's right, out of the net that remained after he deducted his agent's fee, laying himself open to King's charge that he was "double dipping." Cayton still claims that he was legally and morally right, pointing out that the arrangement meant more money, ultimately, for Mike.

Having accomplished the first part of his agenda, King used the remainder of the interview to accomplish the second:

"I support Ruth Roper when she says that her daughter is being mistreated and that she fears for her life because she spoke out and committed the unpardonable sin of asking where the money is, and I support Robin Givens, who is a lovely young lady, the best thing that's ever happened to Mike Tyson, and I feel that this man should be left alone, as would any other human being, to be able to be with the woman of his choice and to be able to love her and to understand her and take care of her as he should."

King took a deep breath and laughed loudly.

"I don't see anything wrong with that, and I would be remiss as a black man if I didn't speak up in these women's behalf because someone has to speak up and support them. They certainly cannot be guilty of action and deed because they've only been there four and a half or five months."

Eventually, the case between Tyson and Cayton was settled out of court with Cayton retaining control until 1992 but having his manager's share lowered from 33⅓ to 20 percent. Tyson seemed bored by the whole thing, but his wife and mother-in-law celebrated.

21

WHILE the featured players in this epic drama butted heads, Howard Rubinstein, Tyson's new publicist and incidentally Trump's, was hard at work to improve the champ's deteriorating image. On August 22, 1988, I learned that Tyson, with the blessing of Schools Chancellor Richard Green, would make a series of visits to schools in bad neighborhoods, starting with the schools in Brownsville and Bedford-Stuyvesant where he was reared. Capital Cities–ABC was going to prepare a special videotape of some of Robin's *Head of the Class* programs to be shown at the schools. It was the first positive news about Tyson—besides his ring victories—that New Yorkers had read in a long time. The champ, who'd been a dropout, was joining a drive to eliminate illiteracy. "I want to give back some of what this country has done for me," Tyson told the press. "I love helping kids who are up against it and are coming up the hard way."

Twenty-four hours after announcing his fabulous school

tour, Tyson was picking up a leather jacket at the Dapper Club Boutique, one of those stores that never close in Harlem. By chance—or maybe not by chance—former ring rival Mitch Green came into the store. Green, once a top contender, had lately been getting more attention from the media for his wild street behavior than for his fighting skills. Within minutes Tyson threw a right cross at Green that closed his left eye and caused a hairline fracture in the third metacarpal of Tyson's lower right hand.

The well-laid plans of Rubinstein and his minions were fast going up in smoke. Green sued Tyson but was persuaded to drop the charges when Cayton promised Green a title shot. "I just told him, through his lawyer, Richard Emery," Cayton said, "to have Green fight any of the top ten contenders, beat him, and he could then have a real money fight with Mike. All parties agreed."

A few weeks after my relationship with Tyson had turned sour, I was having lunch in a midtown restaurant. I'd been seated next to a window looking out onto the street. Tyson was driving his Bentley and stopped his car right by the window. We looked up at the same time and stared at each other. At the same moment our hands came up and we exchanged silent hellos. He showed me his bandaged hand, communicating that he was on his way to see the doctor.

Two days later, Shelly Finkel called me to say that he'd had a conversation with Tyson and that the champ had told him he'd been happy to see me.

"Did you say hello to him," Shelly had asked Mike.

"Yes," said Tyson, "from the car."

"Did you talk to him?"

"No. I stayed in the car."

"Why?"

"I was too embarrassed."

I was not impressed. That had been his line for some time.

Two weeks after the fight with Green, Tyson crashed a new silver BMW he'd bought for Roper against a tree in Camille Ewald's backyard. The media reported that he'd been unconscious for several minutes. A few days later, a New York *Daily News* columnist claimed that the accident had been an attempted suicide. It seemed strange to me that a heavyweight champion and young millionaire would choose to kill himself by running a car—especially a car equipped with airbags—into a tree. There was only one witness to the accident: Camille.

The night before, it had been pouring in Catskill. In addition to Mike and Jay Bright, Camille was playing host to her sister, Nellie, her brother-in-law, John, and their son, and because of the weather they'd decided to eat in. Tyson extended a generous invitation: "Tomorrow," he said, "I want you all to have dinner with me at a fancy Albany Chinese restaurant I know."

"But there are too many of us . . . six," Camille told him.

"That's okay," Mike said. "I'm rich."

"After dinner," Camille recalled, "he went out and came back between twelve-thirty and one in the morning. He went straight to bed." He got up around eight the next morning and she heard him on the phone, "probably with Robin, because he was screaming," she said. "We had breakfast at ten o'clock. He drank his usual quart of orange juice, and I had my coffee with toast."

It was still drizzling when Tyson, who'd parked the car on the grass near the horse-chestnut tree ("A tree that has been hit by a hundred cars," said Camille), decided to go out at around 10:45 A.M. He was dressed in shorts and a short kimono. As he left the house, the telephone rang. It was Finkel. Camille rushed outside to see if she could get Tyson. As she called to him, she saw the car skidding and Tyson struggling to get it off the wet grass.

"I was in the driveway screaming at him that Finkel was on the phone, and I thought he could hear me," she told me. "But I guess he couldn't." She saw the car slide, then take off and hit the tree.

"The first thing I did," Camille told me, "was rush to the car and turn the key off." When she looked at Tyson, he was lying back against the seat, his eyes closed. "I started to holler and to hit his face, but he wouldn't respond. So I told my sister to get Ivonne, a neighbor who is a nurse."

Then she called an ambulance, which came in less than ten minutes. As he was driven to Greene County Hospital in Catskill, with Camille next to him, Tyson, at first, was not moving or talking. But by the time he arrived at the hospital, he was alert. He was given preliminary medical tests, and so that doctors could take a CAT scan, he was transferred an hour later to Hudson Memorial Hospital, a few miles northeast. At around five in the afternoon, Tyson was hungry and demanded Chinese food. Jay Bright and Rory Holloway went for it, and the champ smiled for the first time in hours. At about six, Robin and Roper arrived, and Tyson's eighty-three-year-old surrogate mother went home. "Now that Robin and Ruth are here," Camille told Mike, "I'm gonna go to the house."

Robin decided to transfer Tyson by ambulance to New York City's Columbia-Presbyterian Medical Center in upper Manhattan. She and her mother also arranged for a psychiatrist who specialized in athletes to see him.

The women made a list of people who'd be allowed to visit Tyson. It didn't include Bill Cayton, Steve Lott, Kevin Rooney, Jay Bright, José Torres, Doris Cayton, Loraine Jacobs, Dr. Gene Brody, Dr. Bruce Handelman—none of the people from Tyson's past, none of the pre-Robin people. When actor Danny Aiello and photographer Brian Hamill paid a visit, they were turned away by Robin and her mother. Donald and Ivana Trump didn't have to worry, they were on the list.

In our later conversation I told Camille that I couldn't believe Tyson was unconscious for such a long time. "It's hard for anyone to be out for so long," I told her, "and not have a serious concussion."

"I don't know," she said. "But if he was playing possum,

he did a pretty good job at it. It was the best performance of his life."

Speculation about what really happened ran rampant after the dramatic front-page headlines in the *Daily News* that depicted the accident as an attempted suicide. What no one could figure out was where Mike McAlary, the columnist who'd written the story, had obtained his information. Who was it who'd told him that, just before Tyson walked out of the house, he told his wife over the telephone, "I'm going to go out and kill myself. I'm going to crash my car"? Who told the reporter that the champ had bought two shotguns just before the accident, and that when the guns arrived, he said to his wife, "I'll kill you and then me"? Who told him that the first words uttered by Tyson when he saw his wife at the Hudson Hospital were, "I told you I'd do it. And as soon as I get out of here, I'll do it again"?

Most eyes turned toward Robin and Roper as the two people most likely to benefit from the story, which also went into detail about their arguments and battles with Tyson. Were they afraid of being hurt by the champ? Perhaps.

Yet, two weeks after the accident, Tyson accompanied Givens and Roper to Moscow, where *Head of the Class* was taping two or three episodes. According to divorce papers filed by Robin in Los Angeles on October 6, 1988, barely two weeks after they returned from Moscow, "Mike began to lose control over his emotions [in Moscow]. On one occasion, he started throwing champagne bottles around our room. At the peak of his manic state, Michael went down to the bar and started drinking vodka, glass after glass like it was water. He then returned to our room, grabbed a handful of lithium, and locked himself in the bathroom, saying he was going to kill himself."

And according to news reports about the Moscow trip, Tyson threatened a Russian cop, kicked Roper's secretary,and chased Robin through the hotel for about ten minutes, threatening to kill her.

The New York *Daily News* quoted Robin as saying that

"on the plane [back from Russia] Michael swore at me, called me a 'whore' and a 'slut' and said he was going to kill me and said, 'The world will forgive me because I have succeeded in making everyone think you are the bad one.' "

When Tyson, Robin, and Roper arrived at the mansion in Bernardsville, two private detectives, hired by Roper as body-guards, were waiting for them.

"Get rid of them," Mike told his wife.

Around midnight, Tyson went out with Rory Holloway and called Camille in Catskill and told her to leave the door open. He slept there and was back at the mansion the next day. He tried to do some roadwork but ran into a WNBC-TV camera crew.

"Get the fuck out," he screamed at them, hurling his Walkman and grabbing a camera from the shoulders of Craig Sandbourne and slamming it to the ground. Later that day, he drove to Roper's New York City apartment and posed calmly for photographers with his wife.

A few days later Tyson told the *New York Post* that he was a manic-depressive and was taking steps to do something about it.

"I was born with this disease," he said. "I can't help it. Maybe that's why I'm successful at what I do.

"It's not scary—it's just that I'm very abnormally high-strung. There is another, I forget the scientific name . . . there's a mania, a manic depression, and it's a form of something you're born with."

Robin told the same newspaper: "He's been manic-depressive for many years and they [his old boxing family] have been ignoring it. Michael takes a great deal of protect-ing . . . you can't put a Band-Aid on it. Who cares if he fights again. This guy's got to live the rest of his life."

Accordingly, she and her mother made sure Tyson saw Dr. Henry L. McCurtis, a black psychiatrist based at Harlem Hospital. As they spread the word of Tyson's supposed mental illness, other stories began to appear. McAlary of the *Daily News* interviewed Maury Diaz and his wife Lilly, who'd worked at the mansion. He was a chauffeur and butler; she a maid. "Mike started liking us," Diaz told McAlary. "Ruth Roper gets scared when Mike Tyson starts liking people." Diaz recalled that one morning after a fiery argument between Robin and Mike, Robin came into the kitchen and asked Lilly for an ice pack.

"Her face," Maury told McAlary, "I thought looked not so good."

The two domestics mentioned the time Tyson bought a bull mastiff for $1,200 in Connecticut and how he insisted on having the dog inside the house. Roper, according to Maury, "would have none of it," and when Tyson was not around, the women called the dog by his name: "Here, Mike Tyson."

On September 30, 1988, Tyson and his women were at the mansion. The champ had awakened in an unusually happy mood. The first thing he did was summon to the house furrier Stuart Cohen from Jack/Paul Waltzer, Inc., so that he could look at a selection of their fur coats.

"Me and my brother-in-law, Paul Waltzer," Cohen told me, "put a couple of coats in a car and we went out to the house and we showed them to him. After checking them over, the champ made the selection: a golden sable coat worth eighty-five thousand dollars, plus tax.

"It all came out to $92,012.50," said Cohen.

Tyson handed him a credit card, but neither Cohen nor Waltzer had the credit card machine with them.

Cohen told them, however, that he had to take the coat back to New York City anyway to "line it" and to put Roper's name in it. By then, he said, they could arrange payment for it. Roper didn't like that idea; she, according to the furrier, wanted the coat "right now," because she was going to wear it that Friday night and throughout "the whole weekend." The furriers were happy to comply. "Tyson agreed to send us the check by mail," said Cohen. "And that was the last time

I heard from him." (As of this writing, five months later, the coat has still not been paid for.)

Later that night, Robin and her mother took one of the biggest risks of their lives. Decked out for ABC's "20/20" television program, they told the country how Tyson was a sick, sick man and that life with him was hell.

Robin, an actress by profession, used a combination of eloquence and assertiveness to introduce a new Tyson to the world. In the eyes of his wife, Mike was a "scary and frightening person." She told interviewer Barbara Walters that her marriage had been "pure hell." Tyson was seated next to her for the on-camera interview. His glassy eyes moved slowly from side to side. He looked like a boxer who'd been stunned by a powerful combination and was trying to put his senses together. At the same time, he gently stroked his wife's small neck with his left hand as if encouraging her to go on.

Watching the program from Catskill, Camille Ewald and Jay Bright were in pain. "I'm not a violent man," Jay told me over the phone the following morning, "but I was yelling at the TV set, 'Hit her, Mike. Punch the shit out of her.' "

Camille, too, was outraged by the shameless way in which Tyson was treated, but her response was more subdued. "You can't watch the abuse and emasculation of a boy you love like a son and not get mad," she told me. "So I was sick watching the program. But I knew Mike was not going to take this lightly. Their [Roper and Robin's] contempt for Mike was too obvious. Anybody could see through it, even a boy madly in love."

The new tenant at Tyson's old East Side apartment, his sister, Denise, watched "20/20" with a friend from Brownsville.

"We were hollering at the set as if they could hear us," Denise said, "and at one point I felt like going to the house in Bernardsville and beating the shit out of both Ruth and Robin. What they did was unforgivable."

22

FOR days after the Barbara Walters interview people talked of little else. And forty-eight hours after the show was aired, Tyson apparently woke up from his state of lethargy and went into a rage.

Bernardsville patrolman Kevin Valentine put it this way in his official report, dated October 2, 1988:

"At 1014 hours the Somerset County radio Dispatcher #4 received a telephone call from a woman who identified herself as Auga [Olga]. She indicated that a signal 9 [domestic dispute] was taking place at the Tyson residence. Both Sergeant Howell and myself responded to that location.

"Upon my arrival, I spoke with Sergeant Howell, who related he spoke to victim Mrs. Given, and Mrs. Ruth Givens [sic]. They requested we speak to Mr. Tyson to see that he was okay, and try to calm him down. Myself and Sergeant Howell met with him at the front door. He seemed calm and was very soft-spoken. He indicated that everything was fine, and that he just wanted to be alone. Sergeant Howell only spoke with him for about thirty seconds, and Mr. Tyson had no more to say.

"We returned to victim and several other residential staff people who were present. There seemed to be some confusion over what had just occurred and what course of action should be taken. I spoke with victim, who went on to relate that she was afraid of Mr. Tyson and that he caused damage to the kitchen. She then offered to show us the kitchen. Sergeant Howell accompanied victim into kitchen. I went to the front door again to speak to Mr. Tyson. The reason for this was to talk to him so as to keep him away from victim. By keeping them separated we were hoping to avoid any further confrontations. As I talked to Mr. Tyson, Sergeant Howell and victim entered kitchen through a side door.

"In speaking to Mr. Tyson I went on to explain we just wanted to check on his welfare and wanted to make sure this was resolved before we left. He asked what I wanted him to do, and I explained he could take several options to resolve this situation. I was leading to a peaceful solution when he said there was no problem and asked why police were there. I explained that his wife was concerned about him because of the damage to the kitchen. With that he became angry and indicated he could do whatever he wanted to in his own property. I remained calm and tried to reason with him and tried to explain the Domestic Violence Law as it applied to this situation. He became more agitated and began to yell, saying that he owned the house and everything in it. He said if he wanted to break something no one could stop him. With that he then picked up a large brass fireplace ornament and threw it through a glass window next to the front door. He then walked away into an adjoining room. At that time I was advised that his doctor was on the phone. I asked him if he wanted to talk to his doctor, and told him he was on the phone. Mr. Tyson continued to walk away.

"At that time I decided the best action was to leave him

and let him calm down. At the same time I could speak to the doctor and seek advice on how to best deal with Mr. Tyson. Mr. Tyson did not appear to be an immediate threat to himself or to anyone else in the house.

"I then spoke to Dr. Henry McCurtis on the telephone. He indicated that it would be best to separate him from the victim and allow her and her family to leave the house. He also indicated that the victim should apply for an Emergency Domestic Violence hearing and seek an Emergency Psychiatric examination. He also suggested someone should stay with him so he would not be alone.

"I continued my conversation with the victim in the kitchen. Mr. Tyson was in another part of the house. I observed broken plates and glasses throughout the kitchen and pantry. Victim explained that Mr. Tyson had thrown the objects around. I explained to her what Dr. McCurtis had recommended, and I explained her alternatives and the resources that were available to her. After discussions with her mother, victim was unsure of what to do. I recommended we all go to police headquarters and talk this over, leaving Mr. Tyson at the house. We moved into the side driveway to go to the car. As we were talking, Mr. Tyson came back out of the house and confronted all of us. He became angry and said he was leaving.

"Mr. Tyson told the police to leave his private property. He began yelling, 'Fuck you all. Fuck you cops. You are all fucked, even you cops.' He then called myself and Sergeant Howell 'Scum,' told us to 'Get off my property and fuck off.' He got in his car and drove off. During the time in the driveway, we stayed close to victim and Mrs. Givens. Mr. Tyson was standing about twenty yards away in the driveway. At no time did this officer observe Mr. Tyson strike or threaten anyone. The dispute was a verbal one.

"After Mr. Tyson left, victim decided she didn't want to pursue any criminal complaints or sign any papers requesting emergency relief. At 1104 hours victim signed Domestic Violence notification form indicating she did not want any further assistance. She related they will be going to Finley Manor to call Dr. McCurtis. Sergeant Howell escorted them to town. They then advised that they were going directly to New York City.

"As we exited the driveway, Mr. Tyson returned. He would be alone and was no threat to other household members. We then left the premises as Mr. Tyson obviously did not want police presence. Our presence only seemed to excite him and make him angry.

"Sergeant Howell then notified Chief Sciaretta of the incident. I remained in the area for approximately ten minutes and then returned to headquarters for reports.

"I advised Sergeant Howell of the situation and we also notified Chief Sciaretta, who authorized us to respond and provide assistance until Mr. Tyson was confirmed okay. We requested Bedminster Police Department and Peapack Police Department patrol assist at the scene.

"Upon arrival we rang the doorbell with no response. We observed the Mercedes-Benz (black) with New York plates was no longer in the driveway. That was the same car that Mr. Tyson used when he left the first time.

"We observed the side pantry door of the house was open. I also observed that the lock on the door was broken. As we were about to enter the house, Mr. Rory Holloway arrived without any knowledge of what was going on. I advised him of the situation and he assisted us in checking the house, barns, and grounds.

"I spoke with Mr. Holloway. He related Mr. Tyson was most likely driving to Camille Ewald's house in Catskill, New York. At 1538 hours, Officer Jacobs, Catskill Police Department, was advised of the incident for their information only. Mr. Holloway related he has been staying at the house and took responsibility for the door being left unsecured. . . ."

By the time news of the incident hit the papers, Robin and Roper were already on their way to Hollywood, and Tyson was looking for someone to lean on. He called his old friend, 1984 Olympic gold medalist and former world welterweight champ Mark Breland, who was in training for a fight three days away.

Tyson's choice of companionship brought to mind the day Breland had fought Marlon Starling to a dreadful draw in Columbia, South Carolina. As the decision was announced, Breland had looked down to see Tyson in the audience, weeping.

"It moved me," Breland said. "It really threw me off."

Thus, now, when Tyson was calling Breland for help, the tall twenty-five-year-old didn't care about his upcoming fight. He was there for his friend.

"He was somewhere on Columbus Avenue and the seventies when I went to pick him up," Breland told me. They spoke for a while and then Breland warned him about King.

"I don't know Bill Cayton that well," Breland said he told Mike, "but I know about Don King. Look at your financial situation now, and look at the financial condition of all the heavyweights that were controlled by King during the last several years. The difference is day and night between King and Cayton." Breland said Tyson listened intently and nodded his head in agreement. "He understood everything I said," continued Breland, who was born and reared in the same slums as Tyson.

Breland then suggested they visit Cayton.

"I'm embarrassed. I've said too many bad things about him."

"Just forget about the past and look into the future."

"Okay, let's go."

Breland called Cayton and told him Tyson wanted to see him. "I'm bringing him over," Breland said, "but he says that he feels a little embarrassed."

"Tell Mike to forget about that," Cayton told Mark. "I'll be delighted to see him. Nothing would please me more than to see Mike coming back."

The two champions got into Breland's 1984 Golden Mercedes 380 and drove to East Fortieth Street in Manhattan.

At just about 11 A.M. on October 3, 1988, they reached Cayton's seventeenth-floor office.

"He came upstairs where I waited," Cayton recalled, "and we embraced warmly."

"I'm glad to be back," Tyson said. "Sorry about the things I've said. I wanna work with you."

"Nothing would please me more than working with you," Cayton replied. "Don't be concerned, we're ready to work together. In fact, the first thing we have to do is to get rid of that manic-depressive stigma that's been put on you."

Cayton, like many others who knew Tyson, was convinced that the champ was not suffering from manic depression as claimed by his wife and mother-in-law. He told Tyson to come back the following day. "By then," he said, "I hope to get the most credible psychiatrist available to examine you."

Tyson showed up at 1 P.M., and Dr. Abraham Halpern, a renowned psychiatrist of the United Hospital Medical Center in Portchester, New York, was waiting for him. The doctor had already telephoned some of the people close to Tyson: his sister, Denise; his brother, Rodney; Camille Ewald, Jay Bright, and me. When Tyson arrived, Halpern took him to an empty room. After an hour, they walked into Cayton's office and the doctor announced, "Mike Tyson is definitely not manic-depressive."

"Let's call the press and make an announcement," was Cayton's reaction.

"No," said Halpern. "I first have to call Henry McCurtis, the psychiatrist who supposedly made the initial diagnosis." After a long telephone discussion with McCurtis, Halpern made an important discovery.

"McCurtis said he has never diagnosed Mr. Tyson as a manic-depressive," Halpern told Cayton.

McCurtis may have denied diagnosing Tyson a manic-depressive to Halpern, but that's not the impression he left with Camille on numerous occasions.

Camille told me, "Doctor McCurtis called me up to make

sure Mike was taking lithium." When the doctor told her that Mike was manic-depressive, she replied, "That boy has been with me since he was thirteen years old and I have never felt he was manic-depressive."

When I called Dr. Halpern, he told me Dr. McCurtis had said that, rather than manic depression, Mike was suffering from an ailment called "atypical pugilistic disorder" and that he had "mood regulatory problems." Dr. Halpern had never heard of this disorder.

Since the use of lithium is not limited to people suffering from manic depression, it's possible McCurtis legitimately felt lithium was the drug of choice to combat Tyson's "atypical pugilistic disorder." But why did Camille Ewald have such a vivid recollection of McCurtis calling Mike a "manic depressive" if, in fact, that wasn't the operative diagnosis at the time? I attempted to contact McCurtis to ask him that question, but he did not return my call.

Back in Cayton's office, Halpern was telling Tyson that the most important thing for him to do was to get back into the discipline of training and boxing, an idea that fit into a five-bout-plan Cayton was working on at the moment. It included, said Cayton, Frank Bruno in London; followed by Addison Rodriguez as part of the Mardi Gras celebration in Brazil; then Carl "the Truth" Williams for the mandatory IBF championship; followed by a big close-circuit and pay-per-view event against Evander Holyfield (assuming Holyfield defeated Michael Dokes first) in June 1989. Finally, he was to fight Francisco Damiani in Italy.

Cayton estimated that this schedule would earn Tyson additional gross income of more than $50 million. "When I told Mike," Cayton said, "he seemed enthusiastic and very receptive."

When Breland and Tyson left Cayton's office, they were greeted in the street by the media and a huge crowd yelling their support. Tyson told the crowd that he wasn't anxious to see his wife. "Love is a feeling," he said, "but I'm not going to give up my life for it. I have to do what's right for me." He said he was still in love and that he was not taking any pills.

"If you change a person," Tyson said, "you can destroy the person that is Mike Tyson. But I'm not a loser. I'm coming back. I'm happy when I'm in the gym. I'm going back to the way I was before, but better."

A few days later, Robin, tears rolling down her cheeks, told Barbara Walters on a follow-up "20/20" segment that calling Tyson a manic-depressive, and saying he was a dangerous man and that living with him was "hell," wasn't meant as an insult. "If I offended anyone," she said, "I apologize."

Cayton was in heaven, but not for long.

The next thing he would hear from his boxer was a volley of epithets. Tyson had spoken to Don King, who'd engaged in a desperate search for "the lost soul," finally locating the champ at a rock concert. The first thing King did was inspect with Tyson all joint bank accounts he had with his wife. And when King stopped payment on a check that had been written by an assistant in Ruth Roper's office, involving a transfer of $581,000 from Tyson's account to Robin Givens Productions, Tyson felt the promoter was the master of the right tricks. In less than a week's time, Mike's head had masterfully been rearranged by the master of the right tricks. Cayton had no chance, and Tyson's old boxing family became devils once again as far as Tyson was concerned. Camille would receive telephone calls—some collect—during those turbulent days when King's was the last face Tyson would see before bedtime, and the first one when he got up in the morning.

"I'm homesick. I'm homesick. I miss you and I miss being there," Tyson would tell his surrogate mother. And the old, bright woman who loved and cared for him like her own son would tell him to relax and take care of himself.

"It's a stage Mike is going through," she told me. "I'm absolutely sure that he'll come out of it someday."

Holloway and Horne, whose financial compensation had

wisely been arranged by King, were the only others who had access to Tyson.

"In a struggle for the control of Tyson involving the old family, Don King, and the new family, it would be no contest," said former heavyweight champion Larry Holmes. "I'll put all my money on Don, by a long shot."

Holmes, for years, has claimed he was used by the controversial promoter. "He treated me like a sucker," Holmes said in a New York *Daily News* article, "but I respect him for getting away with it. You know he's the best. He sells black. Don King is the black KKK, a black supremacist."

Michael Dokes, managed by King's son Carl, was a King fighter who realized the hard way that his relationship with the colorful promoter was over. The epiphany came in a boxing ring on September 23, 1983, in Richfield, Ohio, not too far from Akron, Dokes's hometown. The fighter entered the ring as the WBA heavyweight champion defending his title against South African Gerrie Coetzee. In the tenth round Coetzee got hold of one of his roundabout left hooks, which he was able to combine with a right cross, and suddenly as the referee finished the ten-count, Dokes no longer had the crown.

"The only thing I remember about that night," Dokes told syndicated sports columnist Jerry Izenberg later, "was being half-conscious on the floor, looking up and seeing Don King step over me to get to Gerrie Coetzee."

On October 7, 1988, Marvin Mitchelson, who made "palimony" a household word, announced in Los Angeles that Robin Givens was divorcing her husband of eight months due to "irreconcilable differences." The action was filed in Los Angeles County Superior Court in California, where the divorce law—unlike in New York and New Jersey, Tyson's official residences—provides for a fifty-fifty split of assets gathered from the moment of marriage until the point of separation.

"My husband has been violent and physically abusive and prone to unprovoked rages of violence and destruction," Robin said in a written declaration filed with her divorce petition. The documents included allegations of beatings and threats by Tyson to kill his wife, his mother-in-law, his sister-in-law, and Roper's secretary, Olga Rosario. It also mentioned his rages in Russia and the latest one at Bernardsville.

"I was awakened by Michael's hitting about my body and my head with his closed fist and open hand," Robin alleged in her divorce petition. "Michael appeared, by his actions and by his breath, to be intoxicated, and I discovered that he had been drinking champagne early in the morning. I was frightened for my life and terrorized."

Mitchelson spoke about his client's right to sue for a financial settlement. "Should someone be treated differently because they were married a short period of time?" he said at a press conference. "If there were two dollars in this case, they'd each be entitled to a dollar."

Mitchelson got a temporary protective order that would keep Tyson one thousand yards from his wife and mother-in-law. Soon afterward, Robin, the catalyst for the rupture between Tyson and his old boxing family, called Cayton.

"She called to apologize," Cayton told me, "for being wrong in her judgment about me, and for believing all the lies fed to them by Don King. In fact, she called me twice. Both times to admit they had done wrong by us."

The calls led many to believe that the divorce petition was just a smoke screen to force Tyson to leave King and go back to Cayton, Rooney, and Lott; that Robin and her mother figured out that King and his band were too dangerous, too slick, too savvy for them.

Still, Cayton was moved by Robin's apologies and told me that if he had to select between Robin and her mother and Don King, he would go for the ladies.

I wasn't so sure. "A champion hurt by hunger and poverty and deception can still function at his best in the ring," I said. "But a champ with a broken heart can hardly think or raise his arms. . . . With the girls and their problems Tyson may last only months. But with King, we may get five or six more years of exciting performances."

That Tyson might eventually end up broke, working as King's chauffeur and making three or four hundred dollars a week, well, that was another story.

Two days after the divorce announcement, Robin dropped Mitchelson in favor of New York's matrimonial specialist Raoul Felder. But the more publicity the case received, the more public support the champ amassed. Talk-show hosts had a lot of fun with the Tyson-Givens "soap opera," and surveys and polls all favored Tyson. He was the hero; Robin the villain.

"I was not surprised at all," Camille told me after hearing of the divorce action. "From the very beginning I knew it would not work. Robin was ashamed of him. She didn't like the way he walked, the way he ate, the way he cut the meat, or even the way he expressed himself. And . . . that's not love."

Jay Bright was more candid. "If you were getting a divorce from Robin Givens, wouldn't you be happy?" he asked. "Actually Mike is getting divorced from the two of them."

Now openly portrayed as gold diggers, Robin and Roper launched a vigorous—but ultimately assailable?—defense. In Los Angeles, Robin said, according to friends, that "she never claimed she was pregnant before the marriage. She said she became pregnant after they married and that she was a victim of a miscarriage shortly before Tyson knocked out Spinks in June."

She also told friends that she had sonograms proving she was pregnant in early spring, and that Tyson accompanied her to the Park Avenue offices of Dr. Sheldon Cherry where the obstetrician advised them the unborn child was in danger, that Michael was right there when Dr. Cherry showed them the pictures.

ON Thursday, October 20, 1988, I was on the Isle of Margarita in Venezuela, attending the convention of the World Boxing Association. The election of a WBA president was the most important item on the agenda. I'd gone there to help campaign against the incumbent, Gilberto Mendoza, who was a Don King crony and could be counted on, I felt, to help the promoter continue his stranglehold on the sport. To add to his aura among the representatives from more than seventy member nations, King had brought along his most illustrious fighter, Mike Gerard Tyson.

Mike, Don, and their hangers-on were picked up at the airport by none other than Gilberto Mendoza, Jr., the WBA president's son. It was late in the morning when they arrived at the ballroom of the Concorde Hotel in Porlamar. King's voice could be heard booming throughout the chamber, proclaiming the presence of the "number uno" fighter in the world. His theatrics caused business at the meeting to be suspended while King and Tyson announced their endorsement of Mendoza. I heard King, but I was unable to actually see either him or Tyson.

The next day, however, Tyson, King, Horne, and Holloway were shopping in a clothing store in front of the hotel I was staying at with my wife—the Margarita Plaza. It was the first time I'd seen Tyson in the flesh in months. A cast was still on his right hand as the result of a reinjury.

"What's up?" he said.

"Not much," I said, shaking his wounded hand. "How are you feeling?"

"I feel fine."

"How's the hand?"

"It's getting there. It'll be fine in just a few days."

Then I shook hands with King and walked out of the store. My wife was coming in. "Mike is there," I said to her as I pointed toward him.

"*Ramona!*" he said loudly as he rushed toward us. He put his arms around my wife and walked to the back of the store with her, away from both King and I. And as I left the store, he kissed and hugged her with what seemed to be sincere joy.

Later, my wife, who's got real intuition, was pensive.

"That poor boy is torn," she said. "He's lost within himself. His eyes were watery. He even made me cry. He does not trust anybody but Camille. . . . He asked about the kids and said not to worry, that everything was going to be all right."

The last thing he'd told Ramona was that he'd call me as soon as we got back home. "It was obvious," my wife said, "that he was afraid to talk to you in front of King."

Almost at the same time in New York, Raoul Felder was reading from a prepared statement made by the twenty-three-year-old Robin Givens. It said: "I unequivocally and irrevocably state as follows: (1) Michael can have his divorce. (2) I will not seek nor accept any money for myself." The young actress, who was known only to sitcom fans when she met Mike, had become one of the world's most unpopular women.

A life where the sky had been the limit had now become a nightmare.

"I never married Michael for money," she stated. "Therefore, this represents no loss for me other than the loss of losing my husband and the effect this whole situation has had on both our lives. . . . I wish him well."

On the Isle of Margarita, Mendoza was reelected and Tyson was joining in the celebration by drinking beer and champagne. I don't know if he was aware then of his wife's latest move. But we all came back to North America and he never did call me.

Instead I got a call from Don King just as Tyson was beginning preparations to defend his title against Great Britain's Frank Bruno in Las Vegas. "I've been trying to get you for a while," the promoter claimed from Vegas. "But I wanted to invite you to come and see Chavez fight here." The Mexican lightweight marvel was scheduled to fight his countryman José Luis Ramirez on October 29, 1988.

"As a matter of fact," I said to him, "I'll be there a couple of days before fight time."

"Why not today . . . tomorrow," he said.

"I can't," I told him. "I have to finish a book."

It so happened that Bill Cayton was about to meet with King and his lawyers to discuss the promoter-boxer contract that King had been able to persuade Tyson to sign, the one I told Tyson months before to ignore. And soon after I hung up, I called a friend in Las Vegas who told me that Tyson and King had been arguing and shouting at each other. Four days later I was in Las Vegas.

The first call I received was from Cayton. "Today is my meeting with King and company," he told me. "And I have to decide what to do with the promoter-boxer contract he's offering."

"If you want to be known as the worst manager in the history of boxing, then you sign the contract," I told him.

"Otherwise, you'd better reject it. You must show you're acting in the best interest of your fighter."

At the meeting, Loraine Jacobs opened by saying, "Before we start, I'd like to say hello to Mike." She looked at the man her dead husband helped transform from a vicious hooligan into the richest athlete in the world. "Hello, Mike."

The champ's head was down. It remained that way. Not a word came out of his mouth. I knew what he was thinking: "I'm too embarrassed to speak to her."

By the meeting's end nothing had been decided. King and his people had come to an agreement with Cayton and his, but Tyson vetoed their agreement.

"No," the champion said. He wanted no compromises of any kind. He wanted Don King to get his way or there would be *no* deal.

That night Gene Kilroy of the Golden Nugget got a call from Tyson informing him that he'd be stopping by the hotel. "I'm going to see you with a couple of girls," the champ said. Surprisingly, there would be no Rory Holloway and no John Horne. Almost simultaneously, Steve Wynn, chairman of the Golden Nugget, got a call from King.

"My man," the promoter yelled into the phone, "I just sent you Mike Tyson there. Take good care of him."

Later I learned that Tyson had gotten bored at the Hilton Hotel and had talked two women into accompanying him to the Golden Nugget. He'd turned to Horne and Holloway and said, "I'm going to the Nugget to see Gene—by myself." And then he left. Horne and Holloway duly rushed to report all this to their boss, Don King, who called Wynn, suggesting he'd sent Tyson.

At the Golden Nugget, I saw Tyson and the two women walk with Kilroy toward a table in the back. Then Wynn and his wife, Elaine, joined them. Aware of all the pressure Tyson was under, Wynn decided to offer some consolation:

"When my father died and I found out in the hospital, I

thought my world had come to an end," he told Mike. "I thought I had no one to turn to. He left me all by myself. My father and I were buddies. He believed in me and I believed in him. But I also knew that my dad would want me to go on and face life. Every day I look at my dad's picture and I say to him, 'What do you think, Mike?' My father's name was the same as yours."

Tyson looked down and his mind traveled to who knows where. He just nodded.

"Mike," Wynn said, "you must go on. You must be strong. You're only twenty-two and you'll be making some mistakes. But you must trust yourself with the right people."

Immediately after the breakup Tyson wouldn't criticize Robin and her mother publicly. But after a few months with King he did it with relish.

"Robin and Ruth," he announced on November 7, 1988, "are the slime of the slime, and anyone associated with them is a slime. The nature of those two women is to be mean and vindictive."

Robin answered the charges with a $125-million libel and slander suit. She also accused Tyson of forcing her to change her home telephone number because of his constant calls. The talk around town was that the champ was still in love and that his tough public attitude toward his wife was King's doing. The rumors made sense. If you understood the way King operated, you could imagine how the promoter, after convincing Tyson he was his best friend and only ally, had to keep maneuvering to keep him under control, trying everything he could think of to instill in the champ a "them versus us" sensibility.

King had mentioned to Cleveland City Council President George Forbes that Tyson wanted to be baptized. Forbes got in touch with the Reverend Henry Payden of the Holy Trinity Baptist Church and arrangements were made to have Tyson baptized on Sunday, November 27, 1988. Payden would be assisted by the Reverend Jesse Jackson. King, one of seven hundred people at the ceremony, watched as Tyson, dressed in a white robe, immersed himself in a pool of water and stepped out a Christian.

However, just days after being introduced to God, when Tyson watched Kevin Rooney on television insinuate that Robin was better to deal with than King, the champion fired his longtime trainer.

"He called me early in December and asked me why I had said on television that the women were nice," Rooney told me. According to the trainer, the dialogue went like this:

Tyson: "Why you said the women are nice?"

Rooney: "I didn't say they were nice."

Tyson: "Yes, you did. Yes, you did. I heard you."

Rooney: "What did I say? I said you may date your wife. . . . I said I wouldn't be surprised if you dated your wife again."

Tyson: "All right, Kev, all right . . . all right."

Tyson hung up the phone. The following day, newspaper accounts said that Tyson had dismissed the last real link to Cus D'Amato remaining in his boxing camp. Following D'Amato's school of thought, which was brutally unbusinesslike, Rooney never had a signed contract with Tyson.

"I have not spoken to Tyson ever since that morning's conversation," Kevin told me. "And I've tried to contact him a few times. But he never returns my calls. I know the decision to fire me was made by Don King, not by Mike. I know Mike. He's *my* true friend."

Ironically, one year to the day Ruth Roper staged her Helmsley Palace soirée—Valentine's Day, 1988—the Tysons were officially divorced in the Dominican Republic. Details of the divorce settlement were not made public. But it had cost Tyson money, millions, and whatever happens, his world is changed forever.

EPILOGUE

One of the last times I saw Mike Gerard Tyson, he was next to the Caesars Palace Sports Complex boxing ring in Las Vegas. He was laughing and gesturing wildly, rooting for Mark Breland, who was about to step into the ring to face South Korea's welterweight champion Seung-Soon Lee.

"What's up?" he asked. He was the first to talk. He looked fit and his pronounced cheekbones reminded me of the time a few years back when training was his religion. When his face is drawn and tight, it's a sign that his condition has reached its peak.

"Did you see that?" Tyson asked, pointing to boxing promoter Bob Arum. "King and Arum had a fight. They were insulting each other. I thought they were going to have a fistfight." The argument over, King walked over to the entrance of the technical zone—which separates the media from the ringside seats—and held court with a few boxing people. Arum was back in the first row of the ringside seats, closer to Tyson, who was standing near the apron of the ring. I turned toward Arum.

"What are you guys fighting about?" I asked. "Mike said you had a fight with Don and—"

"It's time for someone to stand up to that bastard," Arum said. He was grinning. "This man really thinks he's God."

Tyson thought the whole scene was funny. "Oh, shit," Tyson said, still chuckling. "They almost had a fistfight."

"Well," I told him, "you look happy and in a good mood. And you look in fantastic shape." His eyes were searching all around, as is his habit when holding conversations in public.

"Move to this side a little bit," he said, pushing me lightly to his right. "I wanna check on that girl." I looked back, and in the distance there was a shapely young woman with a light-brown dress that seemed pasted to her body. She did a good job getting the champ's attention. As she disappeared from view, Mike turned toward me.

"I'd love to talk to you," I said.

"Why not?" he said.

"At the gym?"

"Uh-huh."

As I moved to my seat, I stumbled into King. I told him how good Tyson looked. "He looks spirited," I said. "He's relaxed . . . at ease."

"That's nothing, José," King said. "His mental attitude is terrific . . . like never before. He has matured. I know you don't think so, but that man Cayton was ruining this kid's career. He had him in a frame of mind that was destroying the kid as a fighter and as a man." King always likes what comes from his mouth, no matter how ridiculous it sounds.

"You're an honest man and you're loyal to Cayton and his people. But, José, let me tell you something, they were no good for Mike. He's in heaven now. The boy is fine. He's finally pulled together. His mind is at its best." Then King inadvertently exposed himself—his true role.

"Do you think that a Bill Cayton could baby-sit this kid like I do?"

"*I* wouldn't do that myself," I answered. "Too much trouble." King smiled and I went to my seat at the opposite end of the ring. I sat down, watching Tyson and trying *not* to figure him out. He was sitting near Breland's corner and spoke sporadically with the few well-wishers who entered the technical zone. No matter who spoke to him, his eyes wandered, examining the crowd. When the opening bell rang, Tyson switched his attention to the fight.

In the ring, Breland moved forward and dominated the action from the very first second. Fifty-four seconds later a devastating left hook, a right cross, and a combination of punches ended the match, the second-fastest welterweight (147 pounds) championship knockout in history. Tyson jumped into the ring to contgratulate his buddy.

The next morning I walked into the Golden Nugget's coffee shop and the hostess rushed toward me. "Are you part of the Tyson entourage?" she asked. "Mr. Tyson called Mr. Kilroy a few minutes ago and said he was on his way here." At that moment, Mike came in—by himself—and an instant later Gene Kilroy showed up.

Tyson, wearing a light-blue jogging suit with white stripes and white running shoes, didn't notice me until I walked to his table. He seemed disappointed to see me.

"I'm on my way to California," I said, trying for a friendly, nonthreatening tone. "Could I see you for ten or fifteen minutes *now*."

"No," he said, "I can't now because I have things to do. But why don't you come to the gym tomorrow?"

"I'd love to take a walk with you after the workout," I said, "the way we used to do, to talk about old times . . . about girls . . ."

"Girls ain't shit," he snapped. Kilroy gave me a look.

"Good," I said, "we can talk about that," and I went back

to my table. Later, I walked back to Tyson to find out when he was training.

"You know," he said, "I just remembered that tomorrow I'm going to be doing some television and radio shows for the fight. You'd better come on Tuesday."

"I was planning to go back to New York tomorrow, but for this I'll stay an extra day."

With that, he stood up, greeted a few strangers who'd called out his name, signed a few autographs, and posed for some photographs.

"Can we take a picture together?" I asked. He walked toward me and put his heavy left arm around my shoulder as Kilroy snapped the picture. "I'll see you on Tuesday," I said before I left.

King had some security men—reporters referred to them as "goons"—at the gymnasium to keep "undesirables" away. One day, at Tyson's invitation, Bruce Handelman, the physician whose house was Tyson's residence whenever the champ fought in Las Vegas, brought some children to the gym. The "goons" decided Handelman was an "undesirable" and prevented him and the children from watching the show. Handelman asked for Tyson, but no one relayed the message.

On Tuesday I arrived with Gene Kilroy at Johnny Tocco's Ringside Gym at 12:30 P.M., thirty minutes before training was supposed to begin. A few young boxers were there training, hurrying to finish before Tyson and his entourage arrived.

We came in by the parking lot entrance in the back and walked by two small dressing rooms where the fighters changed. The smell of sweat and grease mixed with alcohol and liniment lives in these places. A few steps later we came upon the large ring, which occupied most of the space in the room. I thought of the many dreams and fantasies rings like this represented to the young. Beside it were two chairs and a couple of benches and a public telephone. The *rat-tat-tat-*

tat of the speed bag and *thump-thump-thump* of the heavy bag came from the adjacent room.

I sat on a wooden bench near the ring and a large man named Dale Edwards came to me. "Mr. Torres," he said gently, "today's workout is private and I've been told that no one will be allowed in."

"I was invited here by Tyson himself," I told him.

"Well,," he said, "I've got my orders and—"

"I'm not getting out," I said firmly. "I was invited by the champ himself and only *he* has the right to ask me out." The big man stepped away to make two calls on his portable telephone and then returned.

"José," he said humbly, "if you remain here, I'm going to be in trouble. I know who you are and I have great respect for you and for what you represent. But I just work—"

He was violently interrupted by a rather tall man named Lenny Worthington. Worthington had the truculent expression of a boy who always wanted to be a cop so he could be a bully.

"You! Out!" Worthington shouted, a finger pointing at me menacingly. As soon as he said that, the brave man did a quick about-face and walked away. Edwards, somewhat embarrassed, apologized. And for Edwards's sake Kilroy and I decided to wait outside.

As we walked out, Tyson came in, his head down. He was mumbling, "Motherfucker. Shit. Fuck that shit."

"Hey, Mike," I yelled. The champ raised his head and gave me the thumbs-up.

"Hi," he responded as he walked inside the gym and out of sight. I saw Rory Holloway talking to Kilroy beside Tyson's Lincoln Continental in the parking lot. Holloway had Tyson's boxing gear with him.

"I'm here," I told Rory, "because Mike himself invited me. Otherwise I'd be home with my kids in New York."

Rory shook his head. "Mike said specifically: 'No José and no Kilroy.' "

* * *

Every now and then, pictures of Tyson and his life run uncontrollably through my head. The savage childhood, the perverse boyhood, the spoiled adolescence, the crazy adulthood. The deaths of his mother, his mentor, his manager, and his marriage. He didn't have a fighting chance.

When Cus D'Amato first saw Tyson in action, his heart pounded with euphoria. He saw the raw anger, the determination to inflict pain, the will to win, the lack of grace and tolerance, the meanness and the so-called killer instinct. No true boxing man could've asked for more. Cus took this kid's ghetto instincts and honed them. He didn't take Tyson away from his blood family; he took him away from the street, reform school, and a possible premature death.

But when Cus and Jimmy Jacobs died, Tyson became an orphan. His civilizing influences were no longer around. People trying to survive in the street often say they have no friends, just acquaintances. If Tyson was not the undisputed heavyweight champion of the world, worth untold millions of dollars, would 1989 have found Don King constantly at his side?

In Tyson's last fight as of this writing, a scheduled twelve-rounder against Great Britain's Frank Bruno on February 25, 1989, the champion had Aaron Snowell as his trainer, Jay Bright as his second, and an anonymous cut man picked off a list. In the first round, Bruno attempted to make a fight of it, even though he went down in the first half-minute of boxing. He hit Tyson with two left hooks that Tyson later admitted were the hardest he'd taken in the ring. I was broadcasting the fight for HBO's Spanish language feed. I saw Tyson wobble, and I was worried. But then in the second round, although Tyson was missing with wild, badly timed strokes, strangely, I noticed Bruno's discouragement and knew it was a matter of time. Between rounds, Snowell and Bright shouted instructions at Tyson, which the champion brilliantly ignored. It was as if *no one* was in his corner. Matt Baransky was in Albany,

Kevin Rooney was in an HBO studio in Schenectady, Steve Lott (who bet Tyson before four—and of course lost) rooted for Mike from the *fiftieth* row.

In the fifth round, Tyson put Bruno away with a barrage of unsynchronized punches. Jim Jacobs's widow, Loraine, watched from the fourth ringside row as Tyson's natural power and speed concealed his inadequacies. That night Mike was a great puncher, but not the great fighter he could be. Not even close. The complex championship skills Cus D'Amato had drilled into him, the timing, the patience, the lightning combination punches, the side-to-side moves, and even the basic left jab, were missing—and so were Tyson's *real* cornermen, Mike's last link to the old man of boxing.

A man from Queens recently told me to leave Mike Tyson alone, to forget him. "I was in the concentration camp and I know what it is to survive," the man told me. "You should only know what I did in order to pull through. I cheated and I lied and I robbed; I became a master of deception and I wounded and killed people. I had six nice, nonviolent, decent brothers and sisters, and they all went straight to the ovens. I was the only one to survive. But I have never recovered." The man had Tyson figured out, he said. Bedford-Stuyvesant and Brownsville were Tyson's concentration camps, he insisted. "Only a very few ever recover, and Tyson is not one of them."

The realist in me suspects the man may be right. But the young, starry-eyed fighter from a Puerto Rican ghetto who still has a place in my being—that part of me that still yearns for those "special moments" in the ring—says it cannot be. Fight fans have waited too long, Mike Tyson has struggled too hard, for him not to get up off the canvas.